PERSEPOLIS

By the same author

Embroideries

PERSEPOLIS

MARJANE SATRAPI

JONATHAN CAPE
LONDON

Published by Jonathan Cape 2006

13

Persepolis: The Story of a Childhood was originally published in France in two volumes as *Persepolis 1* and *Persepolis 2* by L'Association, 16 rue de la Pierre Levée, 75011 Paris, in 2000 and 2001, respectively. First published in English by Pantheon Books, a division of Random House, Inc. and by Jonathan Cape in 2003.

Translation copyright © 2003 by L'Association, Paris, France

Persepolis: The Story of a Return was originally published in France in two volumes as *Persepolis 3* and *Persepolis 4* by L'Association, in 2002 and 2003 respectively. *Persepolis 3* copyright © L'Association, Paris, France 2002. *Persepolis 4* copyright © L'Association, Paris, France 2003. First published in English by Pantheon Books and Jonathan Cape in 2004.

Translation copyright © 2004 by Anjali Singh

First published in Great Britain in 2006 by
Jonathan Cape
Random House, 20 Vauxhall Bridge Road, London SW1V 2SA

Random House Australia (Pty) Limited
20 Alfred Street, Milsons Point, Sydney,
New South Wales 2061, Australia

Random House New Zealand Limited
18 Poland Road, Glenfield,
Auckland 10, New Zealand

Random House (Pty) Limited
Isle of Houghton, Corner of Boundary Road & Carse O'Gowrie,
Houghton 2198, South Africa

The Random House Group Limited Reg. No. 954009
www.randomhouse.co.uk

A CIP catalogue record for this book is available from the British Library

ISBN 9780224080392 (from Jan 2007)
ISBN 0224080393

Papers used by Random House are natural,
recyclable products made from wood grown in sustainable forests;
the manufacturing processes conform to the environmental
regulations of the country of origin

Printed and bound by CPI Group
(UK) Ltd, Croydon, CR0 4YY

PERSEPOLIS

INTRODUCTION

In the second millennium B.C., while the Elam nation was developing a civilization alongside Babylon, Indo-European invaders gave their name to the immense Iranian plateau where they settled. The word "Iran" was derived from "Ayryana Vaejo," which means "the origin of the Aryans." These people were semi-nomads whose descendants were the Medes and the Persians. The Medes founded the first Iranian nation in the seventh century B.C.; it was later destroyed by Cyrus the Great. He established what became one of the largest empires of the ancient world, the Persian Empire, in the sixth century B.C. Iran was referred to as Persia — its Greek name — until 1935 when Reza Shah, the father of the last Shah of Iran, asked everyone to call the country Iran.

Iran was rich. Because of its wealth and its geographic location, it invited attacks: From Alexander the Great, from its Arab neighbors to the west, from Turkish and Mongolian conquerors, Iran was often subject to foreign domination. Yet the Persian language and culture withstood these invasions. The invaders assimilated into this strong culture, and in some ways they became Iranians themselves.

In the twentieth century, Iran entered a new phase. Reza Shah decided to modernize and westernize the country, but meanwhile a fresh source of wealth was discovered: oil. And with the oil came another invasion. The West, particularly Great Britain, wielded a strong influence on the Iranian economy. During the Second World War, the British, Soviets, and Americans asked Reza Shah to ally himself with them against Germany. But Reza Shah, who sympathized with the Germans, declared Iran a neutral zone. So the Allies invaded and occupied Iran. Reza Shah was sent into exile and was succeeded by his son, Mohammad Reza Pahlavi, who was known simply as the Shah.

In 1951, Mohammed Mossadeq, then prime minister of Iran, nationalized the oil industry. In retaliation, Great Britain organized an embargo on all exports of oil from Iran. In 1953, the CIA, with the help of British intelligence, organized a coup against him. Mossadeq was overthrown and the Shah, who had earlier escaped from the country, returned to power. The Shah stayed on the throne until 1979, when he fled Iran to escape the Islamic revolution.

Since then, this old and great civilization has been discussed mostly in connection with fundamentalism, fanaticism, and terrorism. As an Iranian who has lived more than half of my life in Iran, I know that this image is far from the truth. This is why writing *Persepolis* was so important to me. I believe that an entire nation should not be judged by the wrongdoings of a few extremists. I also don't want those Iranians who lost their lives in prisons defending freedom, who died in the war against Iraq, who suffered under various repressive regimes, or who were forced to leave their families and flee their homeland to be forgotten.

One can forgive but one should never forget.

Marjane Satrapi
Paris, September 2002

PERSEPOLIS

The Story of a Childhood

THE VEIL

THIS IS ME WHEN I WAS 10 YEARS OLD. THIS WAS IN 1980.

AND THIS IS A CLASS PHOTO. I'M SITTING ON THE FAR LEFT SO YOU DON'T SEE ME. FROM LEFT TO RIGHT: GOLNAZ, MAHSHID, NARINE, MINNA.

IN 1979 A REVOLUTION TOOK PLACE. IT WAS LATER CALLED "THE ISLAMIC REVOLUTION".

THEN CAME 1980: THE YEAR IT BECAME OBLIGATORY TO WEAR THE VEIL AT SCHOOL.

WEAR THIS!

WE DIDN'T REALLY LIKE TO WEAR THE VEIL, ESPECIALLY SINCE WE DIDN'T UNDERSTAND WHY WE HAD TO.

IT'S TOO HOT OUT!

EXECUTION IN THE NAME OF FREEDOM.

OOH! I'M THE MONSTER OF DARKNESS.

GIVE ME MY VEIL BACK!

YOU'LL HAVE TO LICK MY FEET!

GIDDYAP!

AND ALSO BECAUSE THE YEAR BEFORE, IN 1979, WE WERE IN A FRENCH NON-RELIGIOUS SCHOOL.

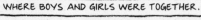

WHERE BOYS AND GIRLS WERE TOGETHER.

AND THEN SUDDENLY IN 1980...

ALL BILINGUAL SCHOOLS MUST BE CLOSED DOWN.

THEY ARE SYMBOLS OF CAPITALISM.

BRAVO!

WHAT WISDOM!

OF DECADENCE.

THIS IS CALLED A "CULTURAL REVOLUTION."

WE FOUND OURSELVES VEILED AND SEPARATED FROM OUR FRIENDS.

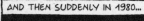

AND THAT WAS THAT...

EVERYWHERE IN THE STREETS THERE WERE DEMONSTRATIONS FOR AND AGAINST THE VEIL.

AT ONE OF THE DEMONSTRATIONS, A GERMAN JOURNALIST TOOK A PHOTO OF MY MOTHER.

I WAS REALLY PROUD OF HER. HER PHOTO WAS PUBLISHED IN ALL THE EUROPEAN NEWSPAPERS.

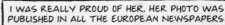

AND EVEN IN ONE MAGAZINE IN IRAN. MY MOTHER WAS REALLY SCARED.

HAVE YOU SEEN THIS?

DON'T WORRY, DARLING.

SHE DYED HER HAIR,

AND WORE DARK GLASSES FOR A LONG TIME.

5

I REALLY DIDN'T KNOW WHAT TO THINK ABOUT THE VEIL. DEEP DOWN I WAS VERY RELIGIOUS BUT AS A FAMILY WE WERE VERY MODERN AND AVANT-GARDE.

I WAS BORN WITH RELIGION.

AT THE AGE OF SIX I WAS ALREADY SURE I WAS THE LAST PROPHET. THIS WAS A FEW YEARS BEFORE THE REVOLUTION.

O' Celestial light!

BEFORE ME THERE HAD BEEN A FEW OTHERS.

A WOMAN?

I AM THE LAST PROPHET.

I WANTED TO BE A PROPHET...

BECAUSE OUR MAID DID NOT EAT WITH US.

BECAUSE MY FATHER HAD A CADILLAC.

AND, ABOVE ALL, BECAUSE MY GRANDMOTHER'S KNEES ALWAYS ACHED.

COME HERE MARJI! HELP ME TO STAND UP.

DON'T WORRY, SOON YOU WON'T HAVE ANY MORE PAIN. YOU'LL SEE.

6

LIKE ALL MY PREDECESSORS I HAD MY HOLY BOOK.

THE FIRST THREE RULES CAME FROM ZARATHUSTRA. HE WAS THE FIRST PROPHET IN MY COUNTRY BEFORE THE ARAB INVASION.

YOU MUST BASE EVERYTHING ON THESE THREE RULES: BEHAVE WELL, SPEAK WELL, ACT WELL.

I ALSO WANTED US TO CELEBRATE THE TRADITIONAL ZARATHUSTRIAN HOLIDAYS. LIKE THE FIRE CEREMONY,

BEFORE THE PERSIAN NEW YEAR, NOROUZ, ON MARCH 21ST, THE FIRST DAY OF SPRING.

ONLY MY GRANDMOTHER KNEW ABOUT MY BOOK.

RULE NUMBER SIX: EVERY-BODY SHOULD HAVE A CAR.

RULE NUMBER SEVEN: ALL MAIDS SHOULD EAT AT THE TABLE WITH THE OTHERS.

RULE NUMBER EIGHT: NO OLD PER-SON SHOULD HAVE TO SUFFER.

IN THAT CASE, I'LL BE YOUR FIRST DISCIPLE.

REALLY?

BUT TELL ME HOW YOU'LL ARRANGE FOR OLD PEOPLE NOT TO SUFFER?

IT WILL SIMPLY BE FORBIDDEN.

EVERY NIGHT I HAD A BIG DISCUSSION WITH GOD.

GOD, GIVE ME SOME MORE TIME. I AM NOT QUITE READY YET.

YES YOU ARE, CELESTIAL LIGHT, YOU ARE MY CHOICE, MY LAST AND MY BEST CHOICE.

EXCEPT FOR MY GRANDMOTHER I WAS OBVIOUSLY THE ONLY ONE WHO BELIEVED IN MYSELF.

WHAT DO YOU WANT TO BE WHEN YOU GROW UP?

I'LL BE A PROPHET.

HAHA! HAHA! HAHA!

SHE'S CRAZY.

MY PARENTS WERE CALLED IN BY THE TEACHER.

YOUR CHILD IS DISTURBED. SHE WANTS TO BECOME A PROPHET.

WHAT ABOUT IT?

DOESN'T THIS WORRY YOU?

NO! NOT AT ALL!

NONETHELESS, MY PARENTS WERE PUZZLED.

SO TELL ME, MY CHILD, WHAT DO YOU WANT TO BE WHEN YOU GROW UP?

A PROPHET.

I WANT TO BE A DOCTOR.

THAT'S FINE MY LOVE. THAT'S FINE.

I FELT GUILTY TOWARDS GOD.

YOU WANT TO BE A DOCTOR? I THOUGHT THAT...

NO, NO, I WILL BE A PROPHET BUT THEY MUSTN'T KNOW.

I WANTED TO BE JUSTICE, LOVE AND THE WRATH OF GOD ALL IN ONE.

9

THE BICYCLE

MY FAITH WAS NOT UNSHAKABLE.

THE YEAR OF THE REVOLUTION I HAD TO TAKE ACTION. SO I PUT MY PROPHETIC DESTINY ASIDE FOR A WHILE.

TODAY MY NAME IS CHE GUEVARA.

I AM FIDEL.

AND I WANT TO BE TROTSKY.

WE DEMONSTRATED IN THE GARDEN OF OUR HOUSE.

DOWN WITH THE KING!

DOWN WITH THE KING!

THE REVOLUTION IS LIKE A BICYCLE. WHEN THE WHEELS DON'T TURN, IT FALLS.

WELL SPOKEN!

AND SO WENT THE REVOLUTION IN MY COUNTRY.

"AFTER A LONG SLEEP OF 2500 YEARS, THE REVOLUTION HAS FINALLY AWAKENED THE PEOPLE."

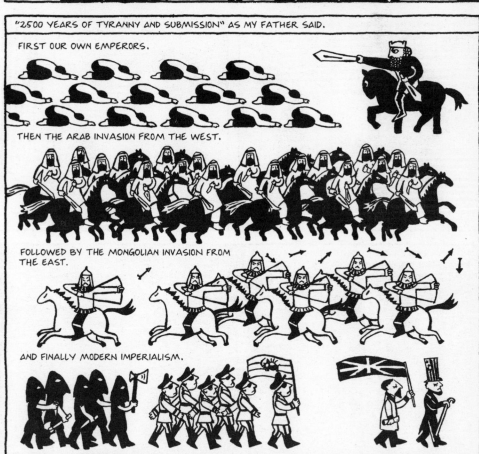

"2500 YEARS OF TYRANNY AND SUBMISSION" AS MY FATHER SAID.

FIRST OUR OWN EMPERORS.

THEN THE ARAB INVASION FROM THE WEST.

FOLLOWED BY THE MONGOLIAN INVASION FROM THE EAST.

AND FINALLY MODERN IMPERIALISM.

TO ENLIGHTEN ME THEY BOUGHT BOOKS.

I KNEW EVERYTHING ABOUT THE CHILDREN OF PALESTINE.

ABOUT FIDEL CASTRO.

ABOUT THE YOUNG VIETNAMESE KILLED BY THE AMERICANS.

ABOUT THE REVOLUTIONARIES OF MY COUNTRY...

F. REZAÏ 1942-72

Dr. FATEMI 1928-58

H. ASHRAF 1938-72

BUT MY FAVORITE WAS A COMIC BOOK ENTITLED "DIALECTIC MATERIALISM."

IN MY BOOK YOU COULD SEE MARX AND DESCARTES.

THE MATERIAL WORLD DOESN'T EXIST, IT'S ONLY A REFLECTION OF OUR OWN IMAGINATION.

SAYS YOU!

YOU MEAN THAT EVEN THOUGH YOU SEE THIS STONE IN MY HAND IT DOESN'T EXIST SINCE IT'S ONLY IN YOUR IMAGINATION?

EXACTLY.

OUCH! WHAT ARE YOU DOING, KARL, YOU BROKE MY SKULL!

HA! HA! HA! HA! HA! HA!

IT WAS FUNNY TO SEE HOW MUCH MARX AND GOD LOOKED LIKE EACH OTHER. THOUGH MARX'S HAIR WAS A BIT CURLIER.

DESPITE EVERYTHING, GOD CAME TO SEE ME FROM TIME TO TIME.

SO YOU DON'T WANT TO BE A PROPHET ANYMORE?

LET'S TALK ABOUT SOMETHING ELSE.

YOU THINK I LOOK LIKE MARX?

I TOLD YOU TO TALK ABOUT SOMETHING ELSE.

TOMORROW THE WEATHER IS GOING TO BE NICE.

?

IT WILL BE 75°F IN THE SHADE.

SHHH! WAIT A SECOND!

THEY BURNED DOWN THE REX CINEMA TONIGHT.

OH MY GOD.

THE DOORS HAD BEEN LOCKED FROM THE OUTSIDE A FEW MINUTES BEFORE THE FIRE.

MGM

MA REX

THE POLICE WERE THERE.

THEY FORBADE PEOPLE TO RESCUE THOSE LOCKED INSIDE.

THEN THEY ATTACKED THEM.

THE FIREMEN DIDN'T ARRIVE UNTIL FORTY MINUTES LATER.

THE BBC SAID THERE WERE 400 VICTIMS. THE SHAH SAID THAT A GROUP OF RELIGIOUS FANATICS PERPETRATED THE MASSACRE. BUT THE PEOPLE KNEW THAT IT WAS THE SHAH'S FAULT !!!

TOMORROW THERE WILL BE ANOTHER DEMONSTRATION.

OBVIOUSLY! WE CAN'T LET THINGS LIKE THAT HAPPEN.

I WANT TO GO TOO.

DON'T YOU THINK I LOOK LIKE CHE GUEVARA?

MAYBE I'LL BE EVEN BETTER AS FIDEL CASTRO!

WHERE ARE YOU?

ARE YOU THERE?

KNOCK!
KNOCK! KNOCK! KNOCK!

I WANT TO COME WITH YOU TOMORROW!

16

WHERE?

TO DEMONSTRATE ON THE STREET! I AM SICK AND TIRED OF DOING IT IN THE GARDEN.

IT IS VERY DANGEROUS. THEY SHOOT PEOPLE!

FOR A REVOLUTION TO SUCCEED, THE ENTIRE POPULATION MUST SUPPORT IT.

YOU CAN PARTICIPATE LATER ON.

SURE, SURE! WHEN IT'S ALL OVER.

MOM, PLEASE.

OH NO!

COME ON, YOU'RE GOING TO BED NOW.

PLEASE, PLEASE, PLEASE, PL...

GOD, WHERE ARE YOU?

THAT NIGHT HE DIDN'T COME.

17

MY PARENTS DEMONSTRATED EVERY DAY.

DOWN WITH THE KING!

THINGS STARTED TO DEGENERATE. THE ARMY SHOT AT THEM.

AND THEY THREW STONES AT THE ARMY.

AFTER MARCHING AND THROWING STONES ALL DAY, BY EVENING THEY HAD ACHES ALL OVER, EVEN IN THEIR HEADS.

HEY MOM, DAD, LET'S PLAY MONOPOLY.

DARLING, WE ARE TIRED.

NOW IS NOT THE RIGHT TIME.

MONOPOLY! I CAN'T BELIEVE IT. HA! HA!

IT IS NEVER THE RIGHT TIME!

AS FOR ME, I LOVE THE KING, HE WAS CHOSEN BY GOD.

WHO TOLD YOU THAT?

MY TEACHER AND GOD HIMSELF.

COME SIT ON MY LAP. I'LL TRY TO EXPLAIN IT TO YOU.

GOOD, EXPLAIN EVERYTHING. I'M GOING TO BED.

GOD DID NOT CHOOSE THE KING.

HE DID SO! IT'S WRITTEN ON THE FIRST PAGE OF OUR SCHOOLBOOK.

THAT'S WHAT THEY SAY.

THE TRUTH IS THAT 50 YEARS AGO THE FATHER OF THE SHAH, WHO WAS A SOLDIER, ORGANIZED A PUTSCH TO OVERTHROW THE EMPEROR AND INSTALL A REPUBLIC.

IF IT IS GOD'S WILL, WE WILL REACH THE CAPITAL IN 19 DAYS.

GOD IS WITH US REZA, GOD IS WITH US.

AND EVEN IF HE ISN'T, WHAT CAN STOP US?

AT THE TIME THE REPUBLICAN IDEAL WAS POPULAR IN THE REGION BUT EVERYBODY INTERPRETED IT IN HIS OWN WAY.

GANDHI IN INDIA

THE HINDUS AND THE MUSLIMS MUST MAKE PEACE TO OVERTHROW THE BRITISH.

ATATURK IN TURKEY

WE, THE TURKS, ARE SECULAR WESTERNERS. FOR PROOF, LOOK AT MY GREEN EYES.

SO THE FATHER OF THE SHAH WANTED TO DO THE SAME.

BUT HE WASN'T EDUCATED LIKE GANDHI, WHO WAS A LAWYER...

...NOR WAS HE A LEADER OF MEN LIKE ATATURK, WHO WAS A GENERAL.

HE WAS AN ILLITERATE LOW-RANKING OFFICER.

A BLESSING FOR THE VERY INFLUENTIAL BRITISH WHO SOON LEARNED OF HIS PROJECTS.

THE COUNTRY IS RICH!

AND THE BOLSHEVIKS ARE NEAR.

WHAT'S THAT SOLDIER'S NAME AGAIN?

REZA! WE SHOULD GO MEET HIM.

IMMEDIATELY! PERSIA IS FULL OF OIL!

WELL REZA, SHINING YOUR BOOTS?

WHEN YOU ARE EMPEROR, YOUR SECRETARY OF STATE WILL SHINE THEM FOR YOU.

EMPEROR, ME?

BUT OF COURSE, MY FRIEND. IT'S MUCH BETTER THAN BEING PRESIDENT.

BUT THERE ALREADY IS AN EMPEROR! I WANT TO CREATE A REPUBLIC.

THE RELIGIOUS LEADERS ARE AGAINST IT AND THEY'RE RIGHT. A VAST COUNTRY LIKE YOURS NEEDS A HOLY SYMBOL.

YOU WILL HAVE EVERYTHING. POWER, SHOE SHINERS...

AND EVEN MORE. ANYTHING YOU WANT IN CASH!

WHAT DO I HAVE TO DO?

NOTHING!

YOU JUST GIVE US THE OIL AND WE'LL TAKE CARE OF THE REST.

AND THAT'S HOW HE BECAME KING AND NATURALLY HIS SON SUCCEEDED HIM. GOD HAS NOTHING WHATSOEVER TO DO WITH THIS STORY.

MAYBE GOD HELPED THEM NEVERTHELESS.

I THINK YOU ARE OLD ENOUGH TO UNDERSTAND CERTAIN THINGS. YOU SHOULD KNOW...

I SHOULD KNOW WHAT?

THE EMPEROR THAT WAS OVERTHROWN WAS GRANDPA'S FATHER.

MY GRAND-PA?

GRANDPA WAS A PRINCE?

YES, AMONG OTHERS. BUT THAT'S NOT THE QUESTION.

WHAT DO YOU MEAN, THAT'S NOT THE QUESTION?

My grandpa was a prince

AT THE TIME, YOUR GRANDPA WAS A YOUNG MAN AND THE FATHER OF THE SHAH CONFISCATED EVERYTHING HE OWNED.

DON'T FORGET THE TILES IN THE BATHROOM.

GO RIGHT AHEAD, DON'T LET ANYTHING STOP YOU.

AND SINCE HIS ENTOURAGE WAS UNEDUCATED, YOUR GRANDPA WAS NAMED PRIME MINISTER.

AS OF TODAY YOU ARE MY PRIME MINISTER.

YOU'RE PLEASED, AREN'T YOU? YOU HAVE DIPLOMAS, THEY HAVE TO BE PUT TO USE.

UHH...THANKS.

HE HAD STUDIED IN EUROPE. HE WAS A VERY CULTIVATED MAN. HE HAD EVEN READ MARX.

THE WORKERS! HOW CAN HE BELIEVE THAT THE RABBLE CAN RULE?

ONCE HE WAS SIDETRACKED FROM HIS PRINCELY DESTINY, HE BEGAN TO MEET INTELLECTUALS.

THE BOLSHEVIKS MAKE MIRACLES.

THE EMPEROR OF PERSIA IS NOT REZA SHAH BUT THE KING OF ENGLAND.

WHEN I WAS PRINCE, ALL OF THIS SEEMED SO DISTANT.

THAT IS REALLY THE PROBLEM OF OUR COUNTRY: ONLY A PRINCE CAN ALLOW HIMSELF TO HAVE A CONSCIENCE.

SO HE BECAME A COMMUNIST.

IT DISGUSTS ME THAT PEOPLE ARE CONDEMNED TO A BLEAK FUTURE BY THEIR SOCIAL CLASS. LONG LIVE LENIN.

SO HE WAS OFTEN SENT TO PRISON.

SOMETIMES THEY PUT HIM IN A CELL FILLED WITH WATER FOR HOURS.

I REMEMBER WHEN I WAS A SMALL GIRL...

...EVERY TIME THERE WAS A KNOCK ON THE DOOR I THOUGHT THEY WERE COMING TO TAKE MY FATHER TO PRISON.

KNOCK! KNOCK! KNOCK!

AND ONE TIME OUT OF TWO IT WAS REALLY TRUE.

HELLO! IS YOUR MOTHER THERE?

IS YOUR FATHER HOME?

N...NO! WHY?

NO!

YOUR GRANDMA AND I WENT TO VISIT HIM.

DADDY, CAN I RIDE ON YOUR BACK?

STOP IT, HE IS TIRED.

OF COURSE YOU CAN.

GIDDYAP! GIDDYAP!

THE POOR MAN!!! PRISON HAD DESTROYED HIS HEALTH. HE HAD RHEUMATISM.

ALL HIS LIFE HE WAS IN PAIN.

COME ON. THAT TIME IS PAST.

DO YOU WANT TO PLAY MONOPOLY?

I WANT TO TAKE A BATH.

WE CAN PLAY AFTER YOUR BATH IF YOU WANT TO.

NO! I WANT TO TAKE A REALLY LONG BATH.

THAT NIGHT I STAYED A VERY LONG TIME IN THE BATH. I WANTED TO KNOW WHAT IT FELT LIKE TO BE IN A CELL FILLED WITH WATER.

WHAT ARE YOU DOING?

MY HANDS WERE WRINKLED WHEN I CAME OUT, LIKE GRANDPA'S.

ONE DAY AFTER SCHOOL...

HI, MOM.

HI. GO AND LOOK IN THE GUEST ROOM. THERE'S A SURPRISE FOR YOU.

GRANDMA!

ARE YOU LEAVING ALREADY?

NO, I'M JUST CHANGING.

MOM TOLD ME THAT GRANDPA HAD BEEN IN PRISON.

HMM, HOW WAS SCHOOL...

IT MUST HAVE BEEN VERY HARD ON YOU.

OH, MY BACK!

CAN I HELP YOU?

NO, I'M OK. AS YOU SAY, IT WAS VERY HARD FOR ME BUT ALSO FOR YOUR MOTHER AND FOR YOUR UNCLES.

THE SHAH'S FATHER TOOK EVERYTHING WE OWNED. I LIVED IN POVERTY.

WHAT? YOU MEAN YOU WERE POOR TOO?

OH, YES. SO POOR THAT WE HAD ONLY BREAD TO EAT. I WAS SO ASHAMED THAT I PRETENDED TO COOK SO THAT THE NEIGHBORS WOULDN'T NOTICE ANYTHING.

MMM! MOM IS COOKING SOMETHING GOOD!

COME ON! SHE IS JUST BOILING WATER AGAIN.

TO SURVIVE I TOOK IN SEWING AND WITH LEFTOVER MATERIAL, I MADE CLOTHES FOR THE WHOLE FAMILY.

LOOK HOW WELL DRESSED WE ALL ARE IN THIS PHOTO.

WHY ISN'T GRANDPA THERE? WAS HE IN PRISON?

YES, THE FATHER OF THE SHAH WAS VERY TOUGH BUT HIS SON WAS TEN TIMES WORSE.

EVEN WORSE!

YOU KNOW, MY CHILD, SINCE THE DAWN OF TIME, DYNASTIES HAVE SUCCEEDED EACH OTHER BUT THE KINGS ALWAYS KEPT THEIR PROMISES. THE SHAH KEPT NONE; I REMEMBER THE DAY HE WAS CROWNED. HE SAID:

I AM THE LIGHT OF THE ARYANS. I WILL MAKE THIS COUNTRY THE MOST MODERN OF ALL TIME. OUR PEOPLE WILL REGAIN **THEIR SPLENDOR.**

HE EVEN WENT TO THE GRAVE OF CYRUS THE GREAT, WHO RULED OVER THE ANCIENT WORLD.

CYRUS, REST IN PEACE, WE ARE LOOKING AFTER PERSIA.

ALL THE COUNTRY'S MONEY WENT INTO RIDICULOUS CELEBRA-TIONS OF THE 2500 YEARS OF DYNASTY AND OTHER FRIVOLITIES... ALL OF THIS TO IMPRESS HEADS OF STATE; THE POPULATION COULDN'T HAVE CARED LESS.

I AM SO HAPPY THAT THERE IS FINALLY A REVOLUTION BECAUSE THE SHAH...

I'M HUNGRY!

I BOUGHT YOU SOME BOOKS. YOU WILL SEE WHY THE PEOPLE ARE REVOLTING.

SHE WON'T TELL ME ABOUT GRANDPA.

YOUR DAUGHTER SAYS SHE IS HUNGRY!

WELL, SHE HAS TO WAIT FOR HER FATHER.

им ип ии ии PHOTO! им им им!

HE'LL BE BACK SOON.

WHO?

MY FATHER HAD GONE TO TAKE SOME PHOTOS OF THE DEMONSTRATION BUT THIS TIME HE WAS VERY LATE.

HE TOOK PHOTOS EVERY DAY. IT WAS STRICTLY FORBIDDEN. HE HAD EVEN BEEN ARRESTED ONCE BUT ESCAPED AT THE LAST MINUTE.

WE WAITED FOR HIM FOR HOURS. THERE WAS THE SAME SILENCE AS BEFORE A STORM.

I THOUGHT THAT MY FATHER WAS DEAD, THAT THEY HAD SHOT HIM.

HELLO, I'M HOME!

EBY!

THANK GOD!

IF YOU ONLY KNEW HOW WORRIED I WAS!

SOMETHING INCRE- DIBLE HAPPENED!

YES, I ALMOST HAD A HEART ATTACK.

DAD!

I WAS SURE YOU WERE DEAD!

TODAY I WENT TO REY HOSPITAL WITH MY CAMERA.

PEOPLE CAME OUT CARRYING THE BODY OF A YOUNG MAN KILLED BY THE ARMY. HE WAS HONORED LIKE A MARTYR. A CROWD GATHERED TO TAKE HIM TO THE BAHESHTE ZAHRA CEMETERY.

THEN THERE WAS ANOTHER CADAVER, AN OLD MAN CARRIED OUT ON A STRETCHER. THOSE WHO DIDN'T FOLLOW THE FIRST ONE WENT OVER TO THE OLD MAN, SHOUTING REVOLUTIONARY SLOGANS AND CALLING HIM A HERO.

HERE IS ANOTHER MARTYR.

WELL, I WAS TAKING MY PHOTOS WHEN I NOTICED AN OLD WOMAN NEXT TO ME. I UNDERSTOOD THAT SHE WAS THE WIDOW OF THE VICTIM. I HAD SEEN HER LEAVE THE HOSPITAL WITH THE BODY.

PLEASE! STOP IT! STOP IT!

WHAT? WHAT IS IT?

STOP IT!

WHO ARE YOU?

HIS WIDOW!

ARE YOU A ROYALIST?

NO, BUT MY HUSBAND DIED OF CANCER...

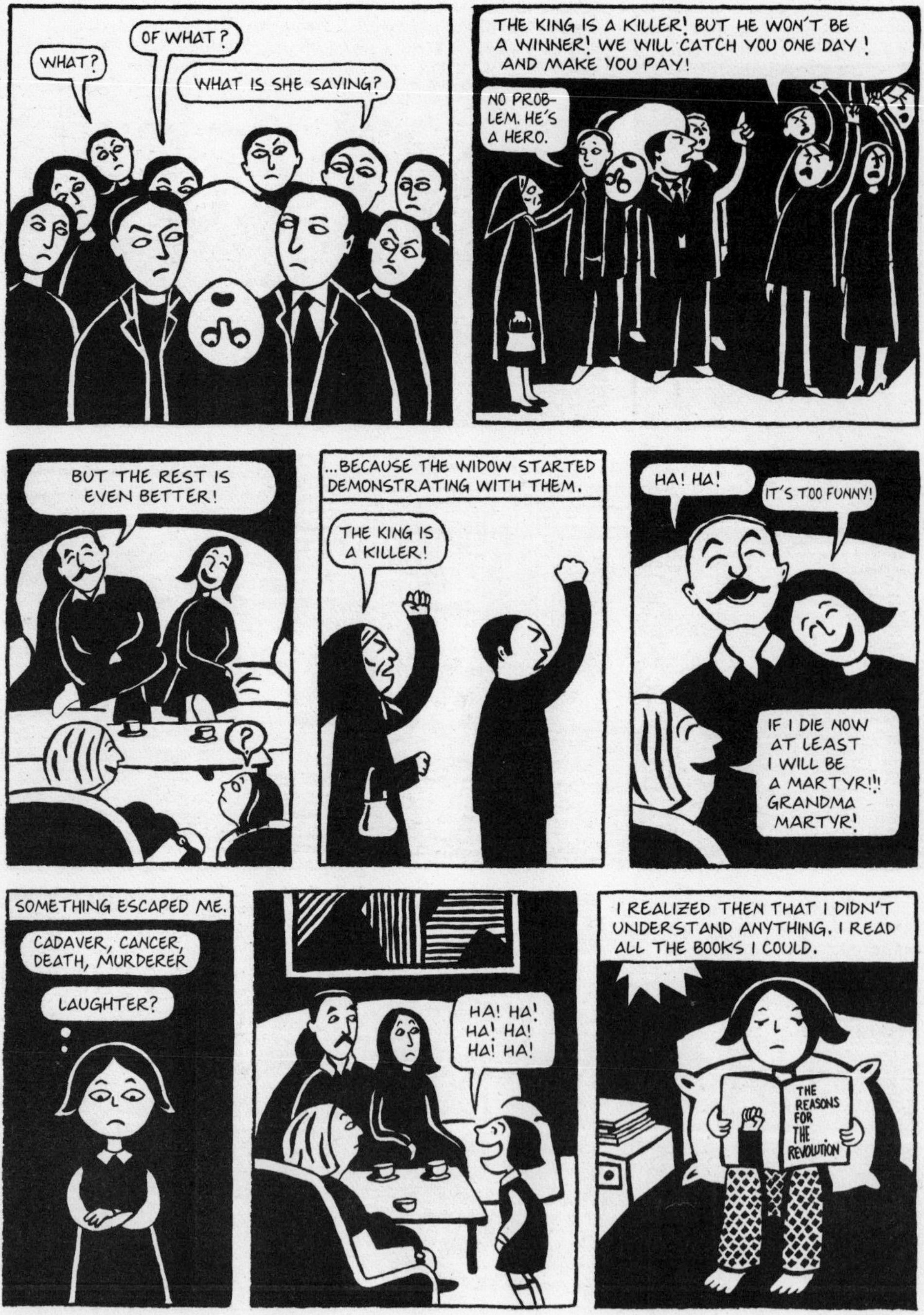
WHAT?
OF WHAT?
WHAT IS SHE SAYING?
THE KING IS A KILLER! BUT HE WON'T BE A WINNER! WE WILL CATCH YOU ONE DAY! AND MAKE YOU PAY!
NO PROBLEM. HE'S A HERO.
BUT THE REST IS EVEN BETTER!
...BECAUSE THE WIDOW STARTED DEMONSTRATING WITH THEM.
THE KING IS A KILLER!
HA! HA!
IT'S TOO FUNNY!
IF I DIE NOW AT LEAST I WILL BE A MARTYR!!! GRANDMA MARTYR!
SOMETHING ESCAPED ME.
CADAVER, CANCER, DEATH, MURDERER
LAUGHTER?
HA! HA! HA! HA! HA! HA!
I REALIZED THEN THAT I DIDN'T UNDERSTAND ANYTHING. I READ ALL THE BOOKS I COULD.
THE REASONS FOR THE REVOLUTION

THE LETTER

I'D NEVER READ AS MUCH AS I DID DURING THAT PERIOD.

MY FAVORITE AUTHOR WAS ALI ASHRAF DARVISHIAN, A KIND OF LOCAL CHARLES DICKENS. I WENT TO HIS CLANDESTINE BOOK-SIGNING WITH MY MOTHER.

FER ME FRIEND KOUROSH.

WHY DOES HE SPEAK LIKE THAT?

IT'S JUST HIS KURDISH ACCENT.

HE TOLD SAD BUT TRUE STORIES: REZA BECAME A PORTER AT THE AGE OF TEN.

LEILA WOVE CARPETS AT AGE FIVE.

HASSAN, THREE YEARS OLD, CLEANED CAR WINDOWS.

GET DOWN FROM THERE, STUPID!

I FINALLY UNDERSTOOD WHY I FELT ASHAMED TO SIT IN MY FATHER'S CADILLAC.

THE REASON FOR MY SHAME AND FOR THE REVOLUTION IS THE SAME: THE DIFFERENCE BETWEEN SOCIAL CLASSES.

BUT NOW THAT I THINK OF IT... WE HAVE A MAID AT HOME !!!

HER →

THIS IS MEHRI.

SHE WAS EIGHT YEARS OLD WHEN SHE HAD TO LEAVE HER PARENTS' HOME TO COME TO WORK FOR US. JUST LIKE REZA, LEILA AND HASSAN.

WE HAVE TOO MANY CHILDREN, 14 OR 15 INCLUDING HER.

SHE WILL EAT WELL AT YOUR HOUSE.

WE WILL TAKE CARE OF HER.

SHE WAS JUST TEN YEARS OLD WHEN I WAS BORN...SHE TOOK CARE OF ME.

SHE PLAYED WITH ME.

AND SHE ALWAYS FINISHED MY FOOD.

SHE ALSO TOLD ME STORIES ABOUT JACKALS THAT SCARED ME.

AND IT CAME CLOSER! AND IT CAME CLOSER!

IN OTHER WORDS, WE GOT ALONG WELL.

AT THE BEGINNING OF THE REVOLUTION, IN 1978, SHE FELL IN LOVE WITH THE NEIGHBOR'S SON. SHE WAS SIXTEEN YEARS OLD.

CAN YOU HELP ME LACE MY SHOES?

la la la la la

EVERY NIGHT THEY LOOKED AT EACH OTHER FROM THE WINDOW OF MY ROOM.

UNTIL THE DAY HE SLIPPED HER A LETTER.

LIKE MOST PEASANTS, SHE DIDN'T KNOW HOW TO READ AND WRITE...

CAN YOU READ ME MY LETTER?

WHAT WILL YOU GIVE ME IN EXCHANGE?

MY MOTHER HAD TRIED TO TEACH HER BUT APPARENTLY SHE WAS NOT VERY TALENTED.

SO LET'S REPEAT. M AS IN...

CARROT!

SO I WROTE THE LETTERS FOR HER. ONE EACH WEEK FOR SIX MONTHS.

MY DEAR HOSSEIN, I MISS YOU A LOT. IT HAS BEEN THREE DAYS SINCE I SAW YOU AT THE WINDOW. I OFTEN TALK ABOUT YOU TO MY SISTER.

WHICH SISTER?

YOU!

I WAS VERY DEVOTED.

MEHRI HAD A REAL SISTER, ONE YEAR YOUNGER, WHO WORKED AT MY UNCLE'S HOUSE.

YOU KNOW, I HAVE A FIANCE.

OH REALLY, WHO?

IT'S HIM! IN FRONT OF THE TV. ISN'T HE HANDSOME?

NOT BAD!

AFTER A FEW VISITS, SHE FELL IN LOVE WITH HIM TOO.

HER JEALOUSY WAS MORE THAN SHE COULD BEAR AND SHE TOLD MEHRI'S STORY TO MY UNCLE, WHO TOLD IT TO MY GRANDMA, WHO TOLD IT TO MY MOM. THAT IS HOW THE STORY REACHED MY FATHER...

...WHO DECIDED TO CLARIFY THE SITUATION.

WHO'S THERE?

I AM YOUR NEIGHBOR. I WOULD LIKE TO HAVE A FEW WORDS WITH YOUR SON.

OK, I'LL GET STRAIGHT TO THE POINT: I KNOW THAT MEHRI PRETENDS SHE IS MY DAUGHTER. IN REALITY SHE IS MY MAID.

REALLY?

BEE GEES

DO YOU WANT TO CONTINUE SEEING HER?

EHH...

BEE GEES

WITHOUT ANY HESITATION, HOSSEIN GAVE ALL THE LETTERS HE HAD RECEIVED TO MY FATHER!

BUT THIS IS MARJI'S HANDWRITING!

TELL ME WHAT THESE ARE!

LETTERS!

WHY DIDN'T YOU TELL US ANYTHING?

YOU MUST UNDERSTAND THAT THEIR LOVE WAS IMPOSSIBLE.

WHY IS THAT?

BECAUSE IN THIS COUNTRY YOU MUST STAY WITHIN YOUR OWN SOCIAL CLASS.

BUT IS IT HER FAULT THAT SHE WAS BORN WHERE SHE WAS BORN???

DAD, ARE YOU FOR OR AGAINST SOCIAL CLASSES?

WHEN I WENT BACK TO HER ROOM SHE WAS CRYING. WE WERE NOT IN THE SAME SOCIAL CLASS BUT AT LEAST WE WERE IN THE SAME BED.

WHEN I FINALLY UNDERSTOOD THE REASONS FOR THE REVOLUTION I MADE MY DECISION.

TOMORROW WE ARE GOING TO DEMONSTRATE.

WE ARE NOT ALLOWED!

DON'T WORRY! WE ARE GOING ANYWAY!

SO THE NEXT DAY...

TAKE CARE!

MEHRI, DON'T FORGET TO COOK HER SOME CHICKEN.

YES, MADAM.

SEE YOU LATER!

FOR ONCE SHE DIDN'T INSIST ON COMING WITH US.

THERE IS THE DEMONSTRATION...

WE SHOUTED FROM MORNING TILL NIGHT.

IT'S LATE. WE HAVE TO GO HOME.

YES.

LONG LIVE THE REPUBLIC!

DOWN WITH THE SHAH!

GOOD LORD! WHERE THE DEVIL WERE YOU?

WE HAD DEMONSTRATED ON THE VERY DAY WE SHOULDN'T HAVE: ON "BLACK FRIDAY." THAT DAY THERE WERE SO MANY KILLED IN ONE OF THE NEIGHBORHOODS THAT A RUMOR SPREAD THAT ISRAELI SOLDIERS WERE RESPONSIBLE FOR THE SLAUGHTER.

BUT IN FACT IT WAS REALLY OUR OWN WHO HAD ATTACKED US.

THE PARTY

AFTER BLACK FRIDAY, THERE WAS ONE MASSACRE AFTER ANOTHER. MANY PEOPLE WERE KILLED.

THE END OF THE SHAH'S REIGN WAS NEAR.

ONE DAY HE MADE A DECLARATION ON TV.

I UNDERSTAND YOUR REVOLT.

TOGETHER WE WILL TRY TO MARCH TOWARDS DEMOCRACY.

AFTER ALL THAT HE HAS DONE!

QUIET!

FOR A FEW MONTHS, HE ACTUALLY DID TRY: HE TESTED A DOZEN PRIME MINISTERS.

A FREEMASON? THAT'S NOT SUITABLE.

YOU REMIND THEM TOO MUCH OF MY FATHER!

TOO THIN!

TOO SHORT!

ONE-EYED!

....

THE MORE HE TRIED DEMOCRACY, THE MORE HIS STATUES WERE TORN DOWN.

PULL A LITTLE MORE TO THE LEFT.

...THEN HIS EFFIGY WAS BURNED.

THE PEOPLE WANTED ONLY ONE THING: HIS DEPARTURE! SO FINALLY...

OUT!

OUT!

OUT!

WE WILL NEVER FOR-GET YOU!

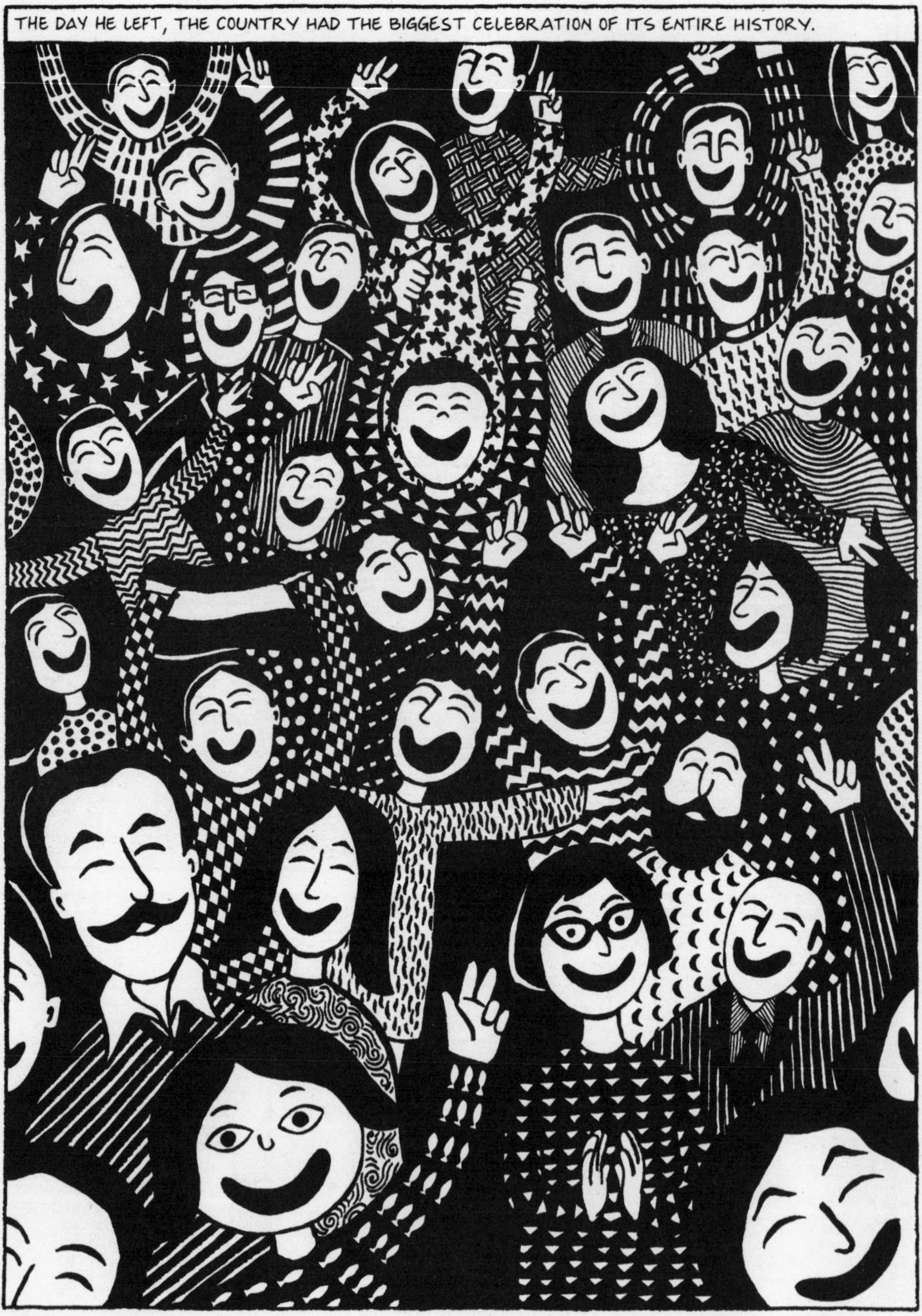
THE DAY HE LEFT, THE COUNTRY HAD THE BIGGEST CELEBRATION OF ITS ENTIRE HISTORY.

JIMMY CARTER, THE PRESIDENT OF THE UNITED STATES, REFUSED TO GIVE REFUGE TO THE EXILED SHAH AND HIS FAMILY.

IT LOOKS LIKE CARTER HAS FORGOTTEN HIS FRIENDS. ALL THAT INTERESTS HIM IS OIL!

IT'S ANWAR AL-SADAT WHO WILL ACCEPT HIM IN HIS COUNTRY.

WHO'S HE?

HE IS THE PRESIDENT OF EGYPT.

AND WHY IS HE TAKING IN THE SHAH?

THEY'VE BEEN FRIENDS FOR A LONG TIME. THEY BOTH BETRAYED THE COUNTRIES OF OUR REGION BY MAKING A PACT WITH ISRAEL.

IN ANY CASE, AS LONG AS THERE IS OIL IN THE MIDDLE EAST WE WILL NEVER HAVE PEACE.

LET'S TALK ABOUT SOMETHING ELSE. LET'S ENJOY OUR NEW FREEDOM!

NOW THAT THE DEVIL HAS LEFT!

MAYBE SADAT WELCOMED THE SHAH BECAUSE HIS FIRST WIFE WAS EGYPTIAN.

SURELY NOT! POLITICS AND SENTIMENT DON'T MIX.

AFTER ALL THIS JOY, A MAJOR MISFORTUNE TOOK PLACE: THE SCHOOLS, CLOSED DURING THIS PERIOD, REOPENED AND...

CHILDREN, TEAR OUT ALL THE PHOTOS OF THE SHAH FROM YOUR BOOKS.

BUT SHE WAS THE ONE WHO TOLD US THAT THE SHAH WAS CHOSEN BY GOD!

TEACHER! SHE SAYS THAT THE SHAH WAS CHOSEN BY GOD!!!

SATRAPI! YOU SHOULDN'T SAY THINGS LIKE THAT. STAND IN THE CORNER!

THESE STRANGE PHENOMENA WERE EVERYWHERE.

HELLO DEAR NEIGHBORS.

HELLO.

HELLO! ALL THOSE DEMON- STRATIONS WERE REALLY TIRING BUT WE FINALLY SUCCEEDED.

LOOK! A BULLET ALMOST HIT MY WIFE'S CHEEK. LIBERTY IS PRICELESS.

OH!

WHAT NERVE! SHE ALWAYS HAD THAT NASTY SPOT. IF WE WEREN'T NEIGHBORS, HE WOULD HAVE SAID SHE'S A MARTYR RAISED FROM THE DEAD.

IT IS NOT IMPORTANT.

THE BATTLE WAS OVER FOR OUR PARENTS BUT NOT FOR US.

MY FATHER SAYS RAMIN'S FATHER WAS IN THE SAVAK*. HE KILLED A MILLION PEOPLE.

A MILLION?

* SECRET POLICE OF THE SHAH'S REGIME.

44

IN THE NAME OF THE DEAD MILLION, WE'LL TEACH RAMIN A GOOD LESSON. I HAVE AN IDEA...

MY IDEA WAS TO PUT NAILS BETWEEN OUR FINGERS LIKE AMERICAN BRASS KNUCKLES AND TO ATTACK RAMIN.

RAMIN! RAMIN! COME OUT OF HIDING! DON'T BE A WIMP!

BUT MY MOTHER ARRIVED IN THE MIDDLE OF OUR EUPHORIA...

SO KIDS, WHAT ARE YOU UP TO?

MARJI FOUND SOME NAILS!!!

WE ARE GOING TO BEAT UP RAMIN!

HIS FATHER HAS KILLED A MILLION PEOPLE!

SO THAT'S WHAT YOU WANT, TO NAIL RAMIN? GET INTO THE CAR, I HAVE A BETTER SOLUTION.

REALLY? WHAT'S THAT?

WHERE DID YOU FIND THE NAILS?

IN DAD'S TOOL BOX!

WHAT WOULD YOU SAY IF I NAILED YOUR EARS TO THE WALL?

WOW! IT WOULD HURT A LOT.

I'LL LET IT GO THIS TIME. BUT DON'T DO IT AGAIN.

BUT MOM, RAMIN'S FATHER KILLED...

I KNOW.

HIS FATHER DID IT. BUT IT'S NOT RAMIN'S FAULT.

ANYWAY IT IS NOT FOR YOU AND ME TO DO JUSTICE. I'D EVEN SAY WE HAVE TO LEARN TO FORGIVE.

YOUR FATHER IS A MURDERER BUT IT'S NOT YOUR FAULT, SO I FORGIVE YOU.

HE IS NOT A MURDERER! HE KILLED COMMUNISTS AND COMMUNISTS ARE EVIL.

MOM, I SPOKE TO RAMIN. HE SAYS HIS FATHER DID THE RIGHT THING IN KILLING COMMUNISTS.

MY GOD! HE REPEATS WHAT THEY TELL HIM. HE WILL UNDERSTAND LATER...

YOU HAVE TO FORGIVE!

YOU HAVE TO FORGIVE!

I HAD THE FEELING OF BEING SOMEONE REALLY, REALLY GOOD.

THE HEROES

THE POLITICAL PRISONERS WERE LIBERATED A FEW DAYS LATER. THERE WERE 3000 OF THEM.

WE KNEW TWO OF THEM.

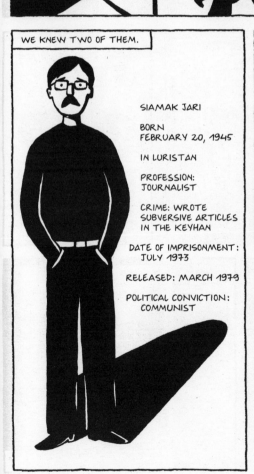

SIAMAK JARI

BORN
FEBRUARY 20, 1945

IN LURISTAN

PROFESSION:
JOURNALIST

CRIME: WROTE
SUBVERSIVE ARTICLES
IN THE KEYHAN

DATE OF IMPRISONMENT:
JULY 1973

RELEASED: MARCH 1979

POLITICAL CONVICTION:
COMMUNIST

MOHSEN SHAKIBA

BORN
NOVEMBER 22, 1947

IN RACHT

PROFESSION:
REVOLUTIONARY

CRIME:
REVOLUTIONARY

DATE OF IMPRISONMENT:
APRIL 1971

RELEASED: MARCH 1979

POLITICAL CONVICTION:
COMMUNIST

I HAD HEARD ABOUT SIAMAK EVEN BEFORE THE REVOLUTION. HE WAS THE HUSBAND OF MY MOTHER'S BEST FRIEND.

HOW LONG SINCE YOU HAD ANY NEWS ABOUT HIM?

TEN MONTHS??

BRING LALY WITH YOU AND COME BY TODAY. WE'LL TALK ABOUT IT.

LALY WAS SIAMAK'S DAUGHTER.

WHERE IS YOUR FATHER?

ON A TRIP.

DON'T YOU KNOW THAT WHEN THEY KEEP SAYING SOMEONE IS ON A TRIP IT REALLY MEANS HE IS DEAD?

AT LEAST THAT WAS THE CASE WITH MY GRANDPA.

BOO...HOO!

THE TRUTH IS SOMETIMES HARD TO ACCEPT.

BOO...HOO! MARJI SAYS... THAT DADDY... IS DEAD!

NO, NO... OF COURSE HE'S NOT.

GO TO YOUR ROOM AND STAY THERE!

NOBODY WILL ACCEPT THE TRUTH.

48

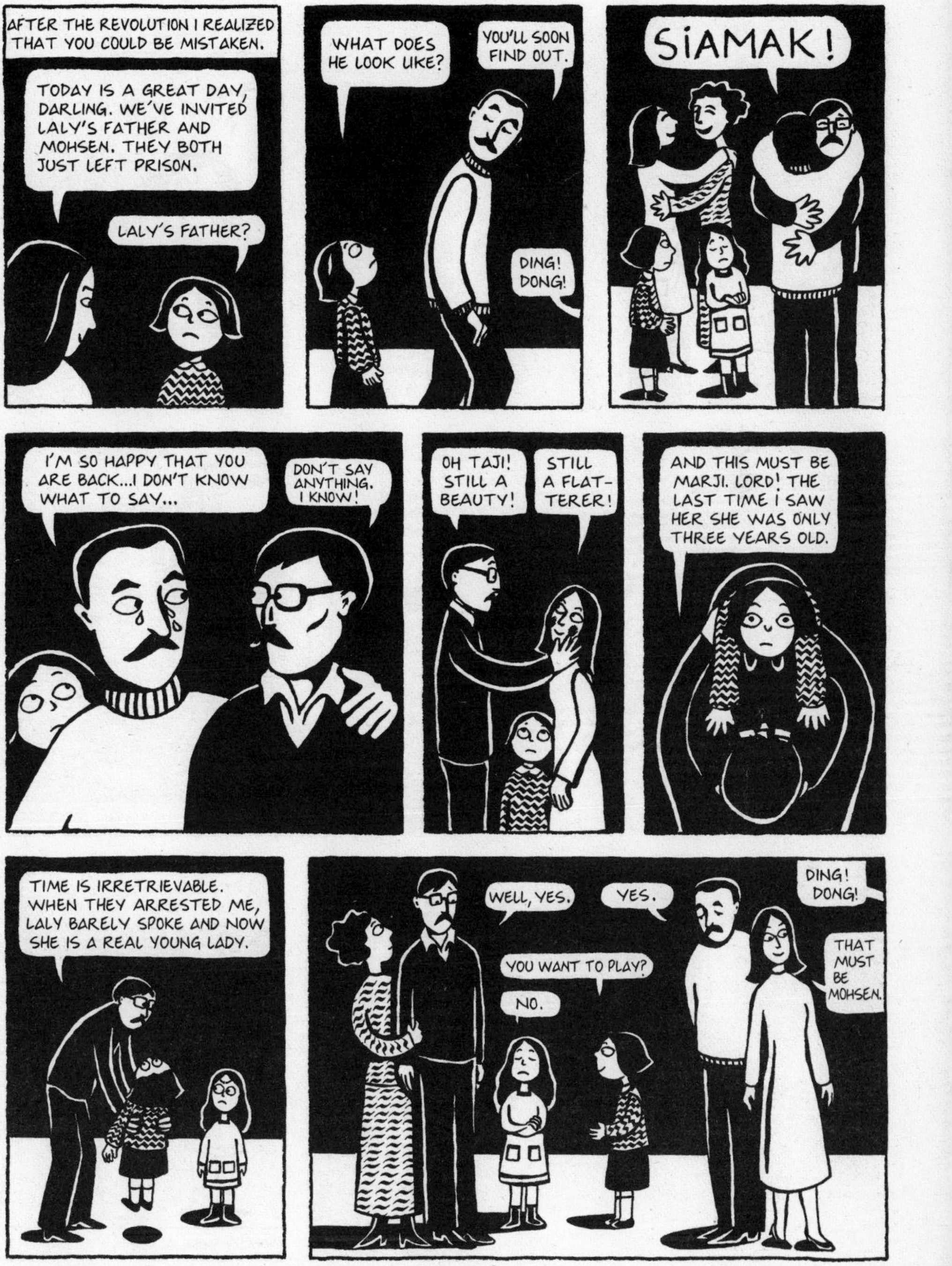
AFTER THE REVOLUTION I REALIZED THAT YOU COULD BE MISTAKEN.
TODAY IS A GREAT DAY, DARLING. WE'VE INVITED LALY'S FATHER AND MOHSEN. THEY BOTH JUST LEFT PRISON.
LALY'S FATHER?
WHAT DOES HE LOOK LIKE?
YOU'LL SOON FIND OUT.
DING! DONG!
SIAMAK!
I'M SO HAPPY THAT YOU ARE BACK...I DON'T KNOW WHAT TO SAY...
DON'T SAY ANYTHING. I KNOW!
OH TAJI! STILL A BEAUTY!
STILL A FLAT-TERER!
AND THIS MUST BE MARJI. LORD! THE LAST TIME I SAW HER SHE WAS ONLY THREE YEARS OLD.
TIME IS IRRETRIEVABLE. WHEN THEY ARRESTED ME, LALY BARELY SPOKE AND NOW SHE IS A REAL YOUNG LADY.
WELL, YES.
YES.
YOU WANT TO PLAY?
NO.
DING! DONG!
THAT MUST BE MOHSEN.

MOHSEN! FOR GOD'S SAKE! I THOUGHT YOU WERE DEAD.

ME DEAD? WHAT A JOKE! IN PRISON THEY CALLED ME THE MAN WITH SEVEN LIVES.

?!

YOU KNOW EACH OTHER?

IN PRISON, WE ALL KNEW EACH OTHER.

YOU REMEMBER THE DAY THEY PULLED OUT MY NAILS? THEY HAVE GROWN BACK SINCE. NOT IN A NORMAL WAY... BUT AT LEAST I HAVE THEM.

OUR TORTURERS RECEIVED SPECIAL TRAINING FROM THE C.I.A.

REAL SCIENTISTS!!! THEY KNEW EACH PART OF THE BODY. THEY KNEW WHERE TO HIT!

LOOK! ON YOUR SOLES THERE ARE NERVES THAT LEAD DIRECTLY TO THE BRAIN.

THEY WHIPPED ME WITH THICK ELEC-TRIC CABLES SO MUCH THAT THIS LOOKS LIKE ANYTHING BUT A FOOT.

NOT TO MENTION PUTTING OUT THEIR CI-GARETTES ON OUR BACKS AND THIGHS...

MY PARENTS WERE SO SHOCKED...

THAT THEY FORGOT TO SPARE ME THIS EXPERIENCE...

ANY NEWS OF AHMADI?

AHMADI... AHMADI WAS ASSASSINATED. AS A MEMBER OF THE GUERILLAS, HE SUFFERED HELL. HE ALWAYS HAD CYANIDE ON HIM IN CASE HE WAS ARRESTED, BUT HE WAS TAKEN BY SURPRISE AND UNFORTUNATELY HE NEVER HAD A CHANCE TO USE IT... SO HE SUFFERED THE WORST TORTURE...

HOW DO YOU LIKE THIS?

CONFESS! WHERE ARE THE OTHERS!

THEY BURNED HIM WITH AN IRON.

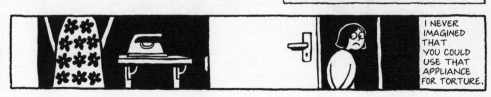

I NEVER IMAGINED THAT YOU COULD USE THAT APPLIANCE FOR TORTURE.

IN THE END HE WAS CUT TO PIECES.

HE WAS IN MY CLASS AT THE UNIVERSITY.

IT'S A GOOD THING THEY DIDN'T KILL YOUR FATHER IN PRISON.

BUT YOU HAVE TO ADMIT I WASN'T COMPLETELY WRONG WHEN I SAID HE WAS NOT ON A TRIP.

MAYBE, BUT MY FATHER IS A HERO!

ALL TORTURERS SHOULD BE MASSACRED!

MY FATHER WAS NOT A HERO, MY MOTHER WANTED TO KILL PEOPLE...SO I WENT OUT TO PLAY IN THE STREET.

THOSE STORIES HAD GIVEN ME NEW IDEAS FOR GAMES.

THE ONE WHO LOSES WILL BE TORTURED.

YEAH!

WHAT KIND OF TORTURE?

I HAVE IMAGINATION TOO... THE MUSTACHE-ON-FIRE TORTURE CONSISTS OF PULLING ON THE TWO SIDES OF THE UPPER LIP.

THE TWISTED ARM.

THE MOUTH FILLED WITH GARBAGE.

BACK AT HOME THAT EVENING, I HAD THE DIABOLICAL FEELING OF POWER...

BUT IT DIDN'T LAST. I WAS OVERWHELMED.

DON'T CRY DARLING. THEY WILL PAY FOR WHAT THEY HAVE DONE.

BUT I THOUGHT ONE SHOULD FORGIVE.

BAD PEOPLE ARE DANGEROUS BUT FORGIVING THEM IS TOO. DON'T WORRY, THERE IS JUSTICE ON EARTH.

I DIDN'T KNOW WHAT JUSTICE WAS. NOW THAT THE REVOLUTION WAS FINALLY OVER ONCE AND FOR ALL, I ABANDONED THE DIALECTIC MATERIALISM OF MY COMIC STRIPS. THE ONLY PLACE I FELT SAFE WAS IN THE ARMS OF MY FRIEND.

MOSCOW

SO MY FATHER WAS NOT A HERO.

IS EVERYTHING ALL RIGHT, MARJI?

YEAH, SURE...

IF ONLY HE HAD BEEN IN PRISON.

THEY CUT MY DAD'S LEG OFF, BUT HE STILL DIDN'T CONFESS!... SO THEY CUT OFF AN ARM AS WELL.

TOO MUCH!

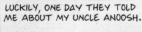

LUCKILY, ONE DAY THEY TOLD ME ABOUT MY UNCLE ANOOSH.

THE ONLY ONE OF MY FATHER'S BROTHERS I HAD NEVER MET, BECAUSE HE HAD BEEN IN PRISON. AND NOW, FOR THE FIRST TIME IN 30 YEARS, MY GRANDMA WAS REUNITED WITH HER SIX CHILDREN.

AND I HAD A HERO IN MY FAMILY... NATURALLY I LOVED HIM IMMEDIATELY.

WHY DON'T YOU COME AND LIVE WITH US?

SUCH A SWEET CHILD! I'LL SLEEP HERE TONIGHT AND TELL YOU STORIES.

ARE YOU MARRIED? DO YOU HAVE CHILDREN? HOW OLD ARE YOU?

LATER MARJI, LATER.

DON'T BOTHER HIM TOO MUCH, HE'S TIRED.

GOOD NIGHT.

DON'T WORRY, WE'RE FINE.

OK, HERE GOES: I WAS 18 YEARS OLD WHEN MY UNCLE FEREYDOON AND HIS FRIENDS PROCLAIMED THE INDEPENDENCE OF THE IRANIAN PROVINCE OF AZERBAIJAN...

WOW!

FEREYDOON ELECTED HIMSELF MINISTER OF JUSTICE OF THIS NEW LITTLE REPUBLIC.

GENTLEMEN, JUSTICE IS THE BASIS OF DEMOCRACY. ALL MEN SHOULD BE EQUAL IN THE EYES OF THE LAW.

MY IDEAS WERE THE SAME AS HIS BUT YOUR GRANDFATHER REMAINED FAITHFUL TO THE SHAH.

MY SON, A TRAITOR! GO AWAY AND JOIN UP WITH MY IDIOTIC BROTHER!

YOU'LL BOTH END UP BEING EXECUTED! DO YOU HEAR ME? EXECUTED!

I BECAME FEREYDOON'S SECRETARY. IT WAS A TIME OF DREAMS AND ENTHUSIASM.

AZERBAIJAN IS ONLY THE BEGINNING. WE ARE GOING TO FREE IRAN PROVINCE BY PROVINCE!!!

I'M CERTAIN YOU'RE RIGHT, UNCLE.

ONE NIGHT I HAD A TERRIBLE NIGHTMARE: DEAD PEOPLE, BLOOD...

THE NEXT MORNING, I WAS SO TORMENTED. I HAD TO SEE FEREYDOON.

SHIT! THE SHAH'S SOLDIERS!

GOOD GOD! FEREYDOON!

I WANTED TO DO SOMETHING... BUT THERE WAS NOTHING I COULD DO...THEY ARRESTED HIM AND I RAN AWAY.

WHAT A STORY!

FOR DAYS AND DAYS I WALKED THROUGH THE FALLING SNOW. I CROSSED THE ALBORZ MOUNTAINS TO FIND REFUGE AT MY PARENTS' HOUSE IN ASTARA.

I WAS HUNGRY, I WAS COLD, BUT I CONTINUED.

I WAS NEARLY DEAD WHEN I ARRIVED.

BANG! BANG! BANG!

MY GOD! ANOOSH!!!

WHAT'S GOING ON? WHO'S BOTHERING US AT THIS HOUR?

COME QUICKLY! IT'S OUR SON ANOOSH! HE HAS FAINTED!

WHAT IS HE DOING HERE? WHY DIDN'T HE STAY WITH HIS NICE UNCLE?

YOU ALWAYS SAY THE RIGHT THING AT THE RIGHT TIME! HELP ME NOW!

OK, OK, CALM DOWN!

OH MY GOD... MY SON, MY DEAR SON...

IT'S A BIT LATE TO SHOW YOUR AFFECTION!!!

BUT THE SHAH'S POLICE WERE LOOKING FOR ME. I WAS NOT SAFE WITH MY PARENTS. SO I DECIDED TO GO INTO EXILE.

I SWAM ACROSS THE ARAS RIVER AND ARRIVED IN THE U.S.S.R.

HOLY SMOKE! LALY'S DAD HASN'T EVEN BEEN TO THE U.S.S.R.

WHAT HAPPENED TO YOUR UNCLE FEREYDOON?

HE MET HIS DESTINY...

I LEARNED THAT HE KNEW THE SHAH'S ARMY WAS COMING TO ARREST HIM. HE COULD HAVE RUN AWAY LIKE MOST OF HIS FRIENDS DID. BUT HE DECIDED TO STAY.

ALL IS LOST. I AM AT YOUR MERCY, GENTLEMEN.

AT THE TIME HE HAD A GIRLFRIEND WHO WAS INVOLVED IN HIS POLITICAL MOVEMENT. A GIRL FROM A GOOD FAMILY.

FEREYDOON, YOU HAVE A VISITOR.

MY LOVE...

MY DARLING, YOU SHOULDN'T HAVE COME, YOU ARE MAKING IT WORSE FOR YOURSELF.

LET'S MAKE A CHILD.

?

HERE? RIGHT NOW?

YES, I PAID THE GUARD. HE WON'T BOTHER US.

I AM GOING TO BE EXECUTED TOMORROW.

I KNOW, I WANT A LIVING MEMORY OF YOU.

YOU KNOW WHAT IT IS LIKE TO BE AN UNMARRIED MOTHER IN THIS COUNTRY. YOU WILL BE SHUNNED. LIFE WILL BE HELL.

I DON'T CARE. LET'S MAKE A CHILD.

SHE BECAME PREGNANT THAT VERY NIGHT AND LEFT FOR SWITZERLAND SOON AFTER. I KNOW THAT SHE HAD A SON. I HEARD HE LOOKS A LOT LIKE HIS FATHER.

ARE YOU ALRIGHT?

EHH...DO YOU HAVE OTHER STORIES LIKE THAT?

...? YES.

I'LL MAKE YOU A HOT CHOCOLATE.

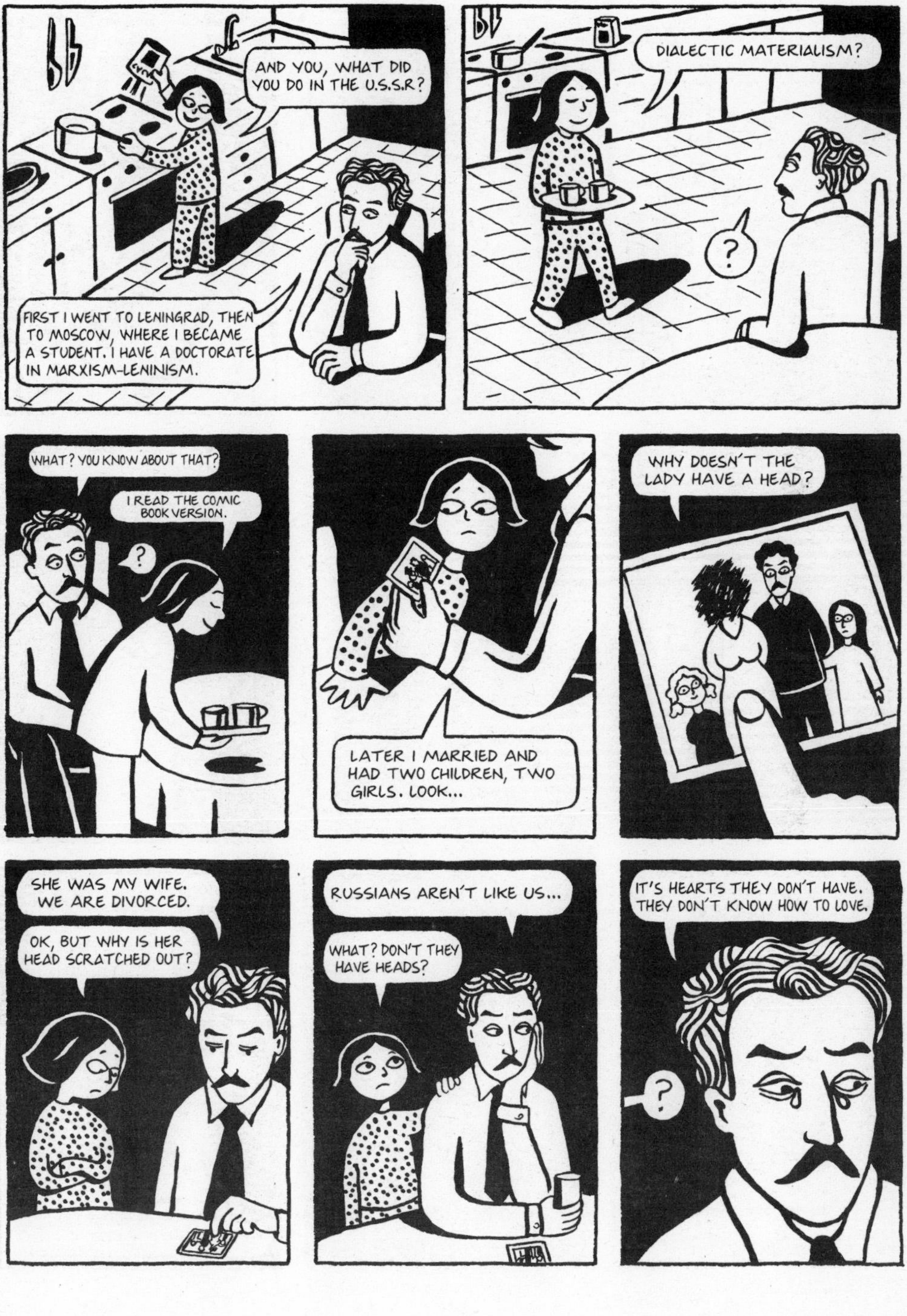
AND YOU, WHAT DID YOU DO IN THE U.S.S.R?
FIRST I WENT TO LENINGRAD, THEN TO MOSCOW, WHERE I BECAME A STUDENT. I HAVE A DOCTORATE IN MARXISM-LENINISM.
DIALECTIC MATERIALISM?
?
WHAT? YOU KNOW ABOUT THAT?
I READ THE COMIC BOOK VERSION.
?
LATER I MARRIED AND HAD TWO CHILDREN, TWO GIRLS. LOOK...
WHY DOESN'T THE LADY HAVE A HEAD?
SHE WAS MY WIFE. WE ARE DIVORCED.
OK, BUT WHY IS HER HEAD SCRATCHED OUT?
RUSSIANS AREN'T LIKE US...
WHAT? DON'T THEY HAVE HEADS?
IT'S HEARTS THEY DON'T HAVE. THEY DON'T KNOW HOW TO LOVE.
?

AFTER THE SEPARATION, I FELT VERY LONELY. I MISSED MY COUNTRY, MY PARENTS, MY BROTHERS. I DREAMT ABOUT THEM OFTEN.

I DECIDED TO GO HOME. I GOT A FALSE PASSPORT AND DISGUISED MYSELF.

I GUESS I WASN'T VERY CONVINCING. THEY SOON RECOGNIZED ME.

HEY! YOU WITH THE BEARD AND SUNGLASSES!

HALT!

THEY PUT ME IN PRISON FOR NINE YEARS.

NINE YEARS!

BETTER THAN LALY'S FATHER!

THEY SAY YOU WERE TORTURED TERRIBLY, LIKE SIAMAK, LALY'S FATHER.

YOUR FATHER TOLD YOU THAT?

NO, HE TOLD IT TO MOM AND I HEARD HIM.

WHAT MY WIFE MADE ME SUFFER WAS MUCH WORSE.

I TELL YOU ALL THIS BECAUSE IT'S IMPORTANT THAT YOU KNOW. OUR FAMILY MEMORY MUST NOT BE LOST. EVEN IF IT'S NOT EASY FOR YOU, EVEN IF YOU DON'T UNDERSTAND IT ALL.

DON'T WORRY, I'LL NEVER FORGET.

AND NOW IT'S TIME FOR BED!

WHAT? THE STORY'S FINISHED?

HERE, TAKE THIS SWAN I MADE IN PRISON. OUT OF BREAD.

IN PRISON?

PLEASANT DREAMS.

THERE ARE LOTS OF HEROES IN MY FAMILY. MY GRANDPA WAS IN PRISON, MY UNCLE ANOOSH TOO: FOR NINE YEARS! HE WAS EVEN IN THE U.S.S.R. MY GREAT-UNCLE FEREYDOON PROCLAIMED A DEMOCRATIC STATE AND HE WAS...

TOO MUCH!

DURING THE TIME ANOOSH STAYED WITH US I HEARD POLITICAL DISCUSSIONS OF THE HIGHEST ORDER.

IT'S INCREDIBLE. THE REVOLUTION IS A LEFTIST REVOLUTION AND THE REPUBLIC WANTS TO BE CALLED ISLAMIC.

IT'S NOT IMPORTANT. EVERYTHING WILL TURN OUT FINE. IN A COUNTRY WHERE HALF THE POPULATION IS ILLITERATE YOU CANNOT UNITE THE PEOPLE AROUND MARX. THE ONLY THING THAT CAN REALLY UNITE THEM IS NATIONALISM OR A RELIGIOUS ETHIC...

BUT THE RELIGIOUS LEADERS DON'T KNOW HOW TO GOVERN. THEY WILL RETURN TO THEIR MOSQUES. THE PROLETARIAT SHALL RULE! IT'S INEVITABLE!!! THAT'S JUST WHAT LENIN EXPLAINED IN "THE STATE AND THE REVOLUTION."

SOMETIMES I EVEN TOLD THEM MY OPINION...

ON TV THEY SAY THAT 99.99% OF THE POPULATION VOTED FOR THE ISLAMIC REPUBLIC.

DID YOU HEAR THAT, ANOOSH? DO YOU REALIZE HOW IGNORANT OUR PEOPLE ARE? THE ELECTIONS WERE FAKED AND THEY BELIEVE THE RESULTS: 99.99%!! AS FOR ME, I DON'T KNOW A SINGLE PERSON WHO VOTED FOR THE ISLAMIC REPUBLIC. WHERE DID THAT FIGURE COME FROM? FROM THEIR ASSES, THAT'S WHERE!

CALM DOWN EBY, SHE'S JUST A CHILD WHO REPEATS WHAT SHE HEARS!

BUT IT'S NOT MY FAULT! IT'S THE TV!! BOO HOO!!!

HEY, WANT TO PLAY?

HE'S GOING TO THE UNITED STATES !

TO THE UNITED STATES? WHY?

MY PARENTS SAY IT'S IMPOSSIBLE TO LIVE UNDER AN ISLAMIC REGIME, IT'S BETTER TO LEAVE.

BUT THE RELIGIOUS LEADERS ARE VERY STUPID, THEY WON'T LAST.

YEAH!

MY DAD SAYS NOBODY REALIZES THE DANGER.

SO WHEN ARE YOU LEAVING?

IN ABOUT A MONTH.

OH.

I THINK I REALLY LIKED THIS BOY...

BUT THE UNITED STATES IS TERRIFIC! YOU'LL FINALLY SEE BRUCE LEE IN PERSON!

YEAH...THAT WOULD BE NICE.

BRUCE LEE IS DEAD...

ACTUALLY I LIKED HIM VERY, VERY MUCH.

IT WAS THE END OF THE WORLD !...

AFTER MY FRIEND'S DEPARTURE, A GOOD PART OF MY FAMILY ALSO LEFT THE COUNTRY.

NOW BOARDING FLIGHT 6702 TO LOS ANGELES GATE 26. NOW BOARDING FLIGHT 6702 TO LOS ANGELES GATE 26.

MAYBE WE SHOULD LEAVE TOO...

SO THAT I CAN BECOME A TAXI DRIVER AND YOU A CLEANING LADY?

MY FRIEND KAVEH LEFT FOR THE UNITED STATES TOO.

DON'T WORRY. EVERYONE WHO LEFT WILL COME BACK. THEY'RE JUST AFRAID OF CHANGE.

LET'S HOPE SO!

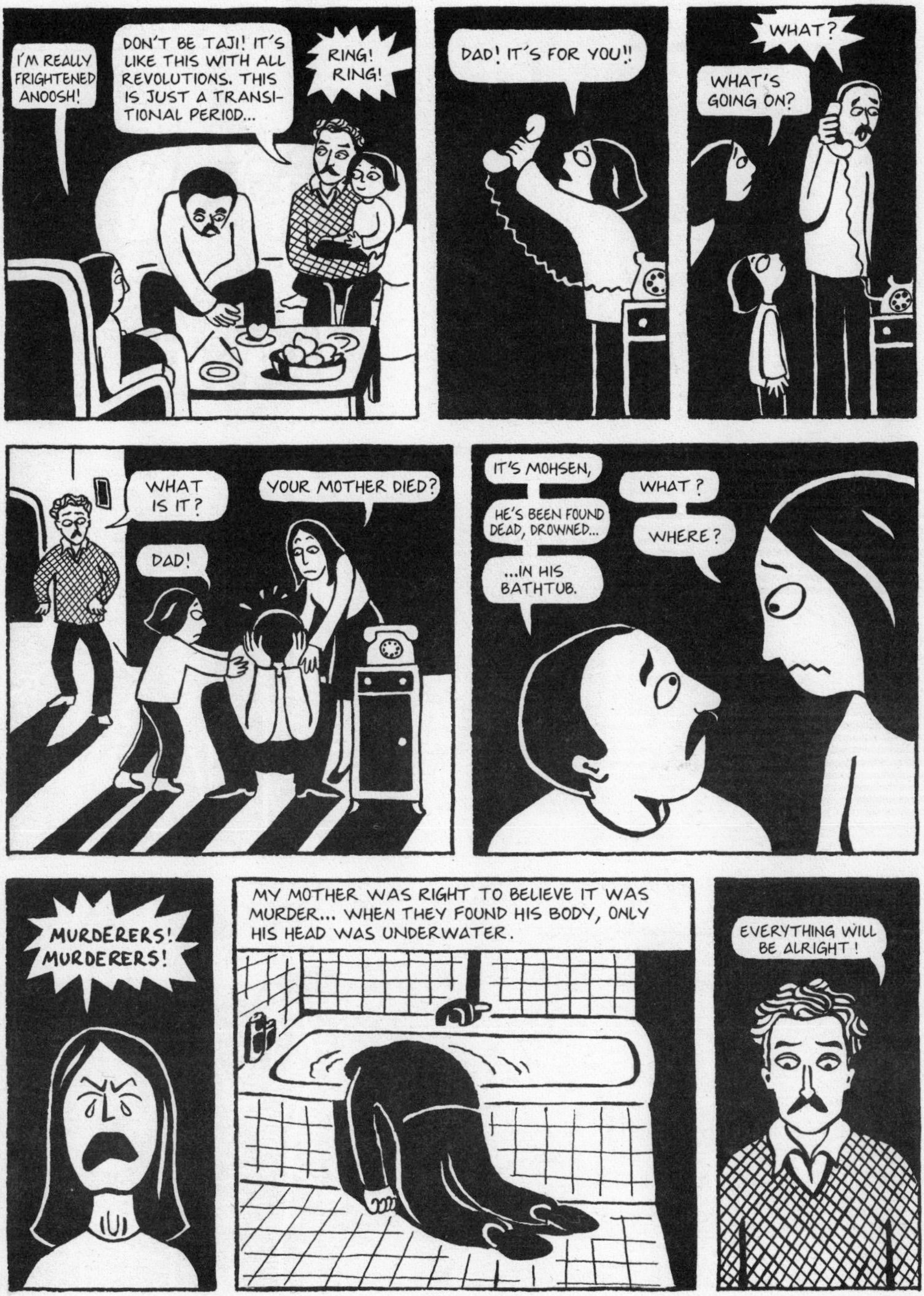
I'M REALLY FRIGHTENED ANOOSH!
DON'T BE TAJI! IT'S LIKE THIS WITH ALL REVOLUTIONS. THIS IS JUST A TRANSITIONAL PERIOD...
RING! RING!
DAD! IT'S FOR YOU!!
WHAT?
WHAT'S GOING ON?
WHAT IS IT?
YOUR MOTHER DIED?
DAD!
IT'S MOHSEN,
HE'S BEEN FOUND DEAD, DROWNED...
...IN HIS BATHTUB.
WHAT?
WHERE?
MURDERERS! MURDERERS!
MY MOTHER WAS RIGHT TO BELIEVE IT WAS MURDER... WHEN THEY FOUND HIS BODY, ONLY HIS HEAD WAS UNDERWATER.
EVERYTHING WILL BE ALRIGHT!

AFTER MOHSEN, IT WAS SIAMAK'S TURN.

IS THIS SIAMAK JARI'S HOUSE?

YES!

WE ARE THE DELIVERERS OF DIVINE JUSTICE!

HIS SISTER WAS EXECUTED IN HIS PLACE.

DO YOU KNOW WHERE SIAMAK AND HIS FAMILY ARE NOW?

NO MORE THAN YOU DO, BUT THEY MUST SURELY HAVE HIDDEN SOMEWHERE.

AND LALY?

LATER ON WE LEARNED THEY CROSSED THE BORDER HIDDEN AMONG A FLOCK OF SHEEP.

EVERYTHING WILL BE ALRIGHT...

66

AND THAT IS HOW ALL THE FORMER REVOLUTIONARIES BECAME THE SWORN ENEMIES OF THE REPUBLIC.

WASN'T ANOOSH GOING TO PICK ME UP?

...

WHAT? WASN'T HE SUPPOSED TO COME?

WELL...

YES?

HE WENT BACK TO MOSCOW.

WHAT?

OH NO! THAT OLD TALE ABOUT BEING ON A TRIP HAD COME BACK...

HE HAD TO LEAVE QUICK-LY... HIS WIFE CALLED HIM. HE ASKED ME TO TELL YOU GOODBYE...

HE DOESN'T EVEN TALK TO HIS WIFE.

DARLING! DID YOU HAVE A GOOD DAY AT SCHOOL?

YOU MUST BE HUNGRY.

WHERE IS ANOOSH?

DON'T YOU WANT TO EAT A LITTLE?

I'M NOT HUNGRY.

WHY DIDN'T HE STAY TO SAY GOODBYE TO ME?

HE WAS IN A HURRY, A BIG HURRY.

I THINK WE NEED TO TALK.

GOD, DON'T LET HIM BE DEAD.

THE TRUTH IS, THEY HAVE ARRESTED ANOOSH.

I KNOW...

DADDY.

YES, MY BABY.

DO YOU WANT TO DO SOMETHING FOR HIM?

YES!

ANOOSH HAS THE RIGHT TO ONLY ONE VISITOR AND IT'S YOU HE WANTS TO SEE.

DO YOU THINK I'M DRESSED NICELY ENOUGH?

OF COURSE.

WE'RE ALMOST THERE.

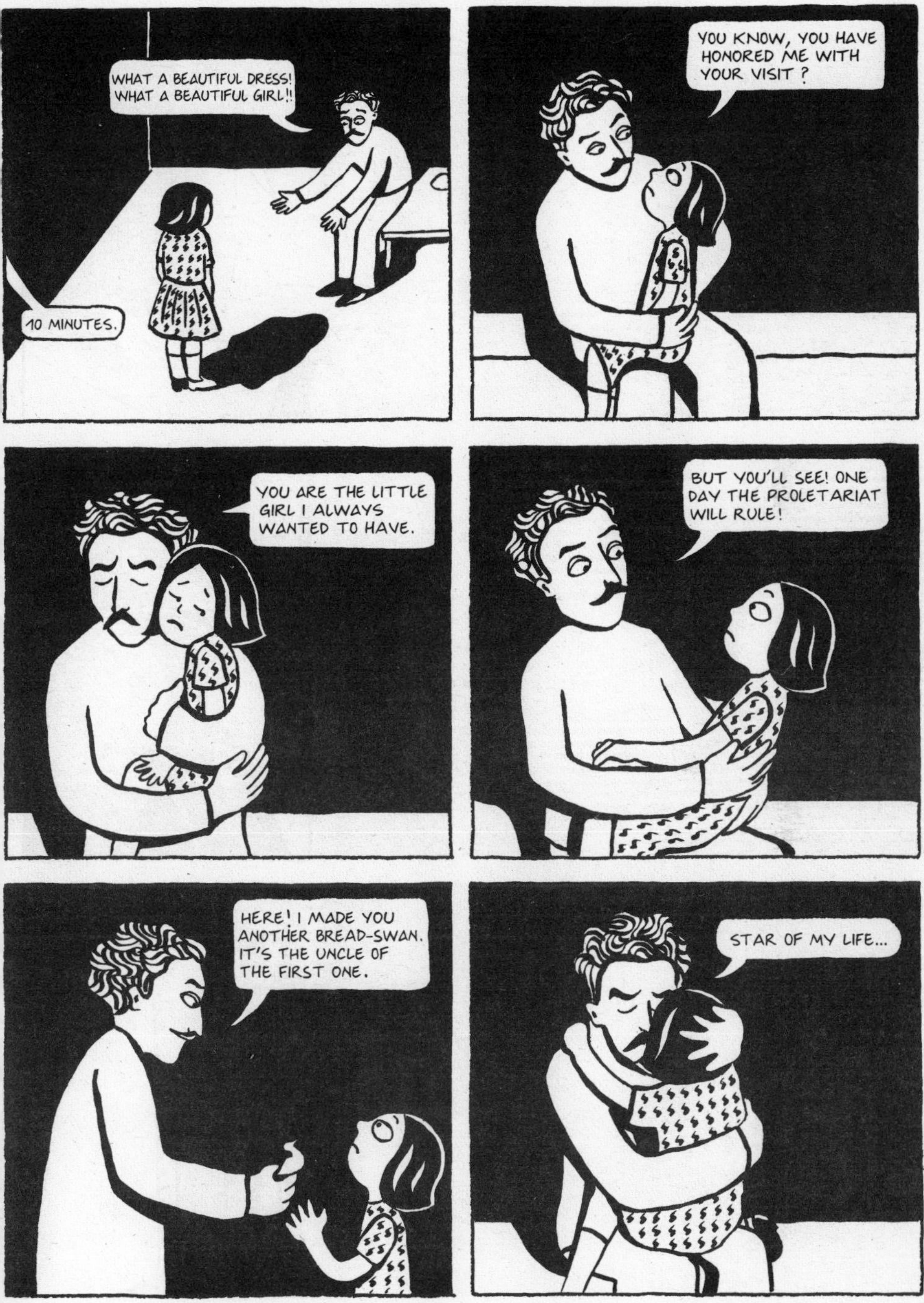
WHAT A BEAUTIFUL DRESS! WHAT A BEAUTIFUL GIRL!!
10 MINUTES.
YOU KNOW, YOU HAVE HONORED ME WITH YOUR VISIT ?
YOU ARE THE LITTLE GIRL I ALWAYS WANTED TO HAVE.
BUT YOU'LL SEE! ONE DAY THE PROLETARIAT WILL RULE!
HERE! I MADE YOU ANOTHER BREAD-SWAN. IT'S THE UNCLE OF THE FIRST ONE.
STAR OF MY LIFE...

THAT WAS MY LAST MEETING WITH MY BELOVED ANOOSH...

AND SO I WAS LOST, WITHOUT ANY BEARINGS... WHAT COULD BE WORSE THAN THAT?
MARJI, RUN TO THE BASEMENT! WE'RE BEING BOMBED!
IT WAS THE BEGINNING OF THE WAR.

THE TRIP

OH SHIT!

They've occupied the U.S. embassy!!

Who's "they"?

Who do you think? The fundamentalist students have taken the Americans hostage!!

Really?

They call it "a nest of spies." Ha ha! You'd think it was a James Bond movie.

You're not interested?

I couldn't care less.

Anyway, the Americans are dummies.

Maybe, but now no one can go to the United States.

Why's that??

Think about it. No embassy, no visa!

So, my great dream went up in smoke. I wouldn't be able to go to the United States.

Kaveh, they closed the U.S. embassy today. I won't be able to come and see you...

The dream wasn't the USA. It was seeing my friend Kaveh, who had left to go live in the States a year earlier.

AND THEN SOME DAYS LATER...

THE MINISTERY OF EDUCATION HAS DECREED THAT UNIVERSITIES WILL CLOSE AT THE END OF THE MONTH.

OH NO!

THE EDUCATIONAL SYSTEM AND WHAT IS WRITTEN IN SCHOOL BOOKS, AT ALL LEVELS, ARE DECADENT. EVERYTHING NEEDS TO BE REVISED TO ENSURE THAT OUR CHILDREN ARE NOT LED ASTRAY FROM THE TRUE PATH OF ISLAM.

OF COURSE, OF COURSE!

THAT'S WHY WE'RE CLOSING ALL THE UNIVERSITIES FOR A WHILE. BETTER TO HAVE NO STUDENTS AT ALL THAN TO EDUCATE FUTURE IMPERIALISTS.

THUS, THE UNIVERSITIES WERE CLOSED FOR TWO YEARS.

YOU'LL SEE. SOON THEY'RE ACTUALLY GOING TO FORCE US TO WEAR THE VEIL AND YOU, YOU'LL HAVE TO TRADE YOUR CAR FOR A CAMEL. GOD, WHAT A BACKWARD POLICY!

A CAMEL?

NO MORE UNIVERSITY. AND I WANTED TO STUDY CHEMISTRY. I WANTED TO BE LIKE MARIE CURIE.

I WANTED TO BE AN EDUCATED, LIBERATED WOMAN. AND IF THE PURSUIT OF KNOWLEDGE MEANT GETTING CANCER, SO BE IT.

IT'S I WHO DISCOVERED THE NEWEST RADIOACTIVE ELEMENT.

AND SO ANOTHER DREAM WENT UP IN SMOKE.

MISERY! AT THE AGE THAT MARIE CURIE FIRST WENT TO FRANCE TO STUDY, I'LL PROBABLY HAVE TEN CHILDREN...

73

ONE NIGHT...

YOUR MOTHER'S CAR BROKE DOWN, WE HAVE TO PICK HER UP.

EBi!

MOM!

TWO GUYS...TWO BEARDED GUYS!... TWO FUNDAMENTALIST BASTARDS... THE BASTARDS...THE BASTARDS...THEY...

CALM DOWN DARLING, CALM DOWN, WHAT DID THEY DO?

MOM!

THEY INSULTED ME. THEY SAID THAT WOMEN LIKE ME SHOULD BE PUSHED UP AGAINST A WALL AND FUCKED. AND THEN THROWN IN THE GARBAGE.

...AND THAT IF I DIDN'T WANT THAT TO HAPPEN, I SHOULD WEAR THE VEIL...

FORGET ABOUT THOSE MORONS!! LET'S GO HOME...

THAT INCIDENT MADE MY MOTHER SICK FOR SEVERAL DAYS.

ANYTHING I CAN GET YOU, MOM?

...

AND SO TO PROTECT WOMEN FROM ALL THE POTENTIAL RAPISTS, THEY DECREED THAT WEARING THE VEIL WAS OBLIGATORY.

WOMEN'S HAIR EMANATES RAYS THAT EXCITE MEN. THAT'S WHY WOMEN SHOULD COVER THEIR HAIR! IF IN FACT IT IS REALLY MORE CIVILIZED TO GO WITHOUT THE VEIL, THEN ANIMALS ARE MORE CIVILIZED THAN WE ARE.

INCREDIBLE! THEY THINK ALL MEN ARE PERVERTS!!

OF COURSE, BECAUSE THEY REALLY ARE PERVERTS!

74

IN NO TIME, THE WAY PEOPLE DRESSED BECAME AN IDEOLOGICAL SIGN. THERE WERE TWO KINDS OF WOMEN.

THE FUNDAMENTALIST WOMAN

THE MODERN WOMAN

YOU SHOWED YOUR OPPOSITION TO THE REGIME BY LETTING A FEW STRANDS OF HAIR SHOW.

THERE WERE ALSO TWO SORTS OF MEN.

THE FUNDAMENTALIST MAN

BEARD

SHIRT HANGING OUT

THE PROGRESSIVE MAN

SHAVED, WITH OR WITHOUT MUSTACHE

SHIRT TUCKED IN

ISLAM IS MORE OR LESS AGAINST SHAVING.

BUT LET'S BE FAIR. IF WOMEN FACED PRISON WHEN THEY REFUSED TO WEAR THE VEIL, IT WAS ALSO FORBIDDEN FOR MEN TO WEAR NECKTIES (THAT DREADED SYMBOL OF THE WEST). AND IF WOMEN'S HAIR GOT MEN EXCITED, THE SAME THING COULD BE SAID OF MEN'S BARE ARMS. AND SO, WEARING SHORT-SLEEVED SHIRTS WAS ALSO FORBIDDEN.

THERE WAS A KIND OF JUSTICE, AFTER ALL.

IT WASN'T ONLY THE GOVERNMENT THAT CHANGED. ORDINARY PEOPLE CHANGED TOO.

LOOK AT HER! LAST YEAR SHE WAS WEARING A MINISKIRT, SHOWING OFF HER BEEFY THIGHS TO THE WHOLE NEIGHBORHOOD. AND NOW MADAME IS WEARING A CHADOR. IT SUITS HER BETTER, I GUESS.

AS FOR HER FUNDAMENTALIST HUSBAND WHO DRANK HIMSELF INTO A STUPOR EVERY NIGHT, NOW HE USES MOUTHWASH EVERY TIME HE UTTERS THE WORD "ALCOHOL."

AND THEIR SON SAYS HE PRAYS EVERY DAY!

IF ANYONE EVER ASKS YOU WHAT YOU DO DURING THE DAY, SAY YOU PRAY, YOU UNDERSTAND??

OK...

AT FIRST, IT WAS A LITTLE HARD, BUT I LEARNED TO LIE QUICKLY.

I PRAY FIVE TIMES A DAY.

ME? TEN OR ELEVEN TIMES... SOMETIMES TWELVE.

IN SPITE OF EVERYTHING, THE SPIRIT OF REVOLUTION WAS STILL IN THE AIR. THERE WERE SOME OPPOSITION DEMONSTRATIONS.

TOMORROW THERE'S GOING TO BE A MEETING AGAINST FUNDAMENTALISM.

I'M COMING TOO!

NO! IT'S TOO DANGEROUS.

SHE'S COMING TOO.

SHE SHOULD START LEARNING TO DEFEND HER RIGHTS AS A WOMAN RIGHT NOW!

SINCE THE 1979 REVOLUTION, I'D GROWN OLDER (WELL, A YEAR OLDER) AND MOM HAD CHANGED.

SO I WENT WITH THEM. I PASSED OUT FLYERS...

GUNS MAY SHOOT AND KNIVES MAY CARVE, BUT WE WON'T WEAR YOUR SILLY SCARVES!

...WHEN SUDDENLY THINGS GOT NASTY.

THE SCARF OR A BEATING!

FOR THE FIRST TIME IN MY LIFE, I SAW VIOLENCE WITH MY OWN EYES.

DAD!

THAT WAS OUR LAST DEMONSTRATION.

EVERY MAN FOR HIMSELF!

THINGS GOT WORSE FROM ONE DAY TO THE NEXT. IN SEPTEMBER 1980, MY PARENTS ABRUPTLY PLANNED A VACATION. I THINK THEY REALIZED THAT SOON SUCH THINGS WOULD NO LONGER BE POSSIBLE. AS IT HAPPENED, THEY WERE RIGHT. AND SO WE WENT TO ITALY AND SPAIN FOR THREE WEEKS...

...IT WAS WONDERFUL.

RIGHT BEFORE GOING BACK, IN THE HOTEL ROOM IN MADRID.

LOOK AT THIS.

IRAN

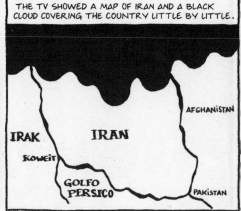

THE TV SHOWED A MAP OF IRAN AND A BLACK CLOUD COVERING THE COUNTRY LITTLE BY LITTLE.

IRAK

KOWEIT

IRAN

GOLFO PERSICO

AFGHANISTAN

PAKISTAN

WHAT IN THE WORLD IS THIS?

TOO BAD WE DON'T KNOW SPANISH.

MAYBE THEY'RE TALKING ABOUT POLLUTION. YOU KNOW, TEHRAN IS THE FOURTH MOST POLLUTED CITY IN THE WORLD.

IT LOOKS LIKE THEY'RE TALKING ABOUT THE WHOLE COUNTRY, NOT JUST THE CAPITAL.

THE NEXT DAY MY GRANDMOTHER CAME TO PICK US UP AT THE AIRPORT.

GRANDMA! I GOT YOU A BLACK DRESS!

SHE LOOKED WORRIED.

EVERYTHING OK, MOM?

YES...

OH! I'M TAKING THIS THING OFF. IT'S TOO HOT.

IT'S GOOD TO BE BACK. THERE'S NO PLACE LIKE HOME.

TRUE. BUT SOON THERE'LL BE NO HOME.

WHY DO YOU SAY THAT?

YOU HAVEN'T HEARD?

HAVEN'T HEARD WHAT?

WE'RE AT WAR!

WHAT!?

...THEY ONLY OFFICIALLY ANNOUNCED IT TWO DAYS AGO, BUT REALLY, IT'S BEEN A MONTH... THE IRANIAN FUNDAMENTALISTS TRIED TO STIR UP THEIR IRAQI SHIITE ALLIES AGAINST SADDAM. HE'S BEEN WAITING FOR THE CHANCE. HE'S ALWAYS WANTED TO INVADE IRAN, AND HERE'S THE PRETEXT. IT'S THE SECOND ARAB INVASION...

THE SECOND INVASION IN 1400 YEARS! MY BLOOD WAS BOILING. I WAS READY TO DEFEND MY COUNTRY AGAINST THESE ARABS WHO KEPT ATTACKING US.

I WANTED TO FIGHT.

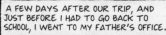

THE F-14s

A FEW DAYS AFTER OUR TRIP, AND JUST BEFORE I HAD TO GO BACK TO SCHOOL, I WENT TO MY FATHER'S OFFICE.

TYPE THIS AND MAKE THREE COPIES.

OK

BOOM

HELP!!

IT WAS THE FIRST TIME I'D SEEN FIGHTER JETS...

TOO MUCH! IT'S OUR ARMY FLYING!

I DON'T THINK SO. THOSE ARE PROBABLY IRAQIS.

WHAT? WHY DO YOU SAY THAT???

BECAUSE THEY DON'T LOOK LIKE OUR F-14S!

IT WAS A TOUGH CALL, BUT DAD WAS AN ENGINEER. HE WAS THE SPECIALIST.

IRANIAN OR IRAQI, THE JETS HUGGED THE GROUND BEFORE SUDDENLY ZOOMING UP INTO THE SKY RIGHT BEFORE THE MOUNTAINS ON THE HORIZON.

QUICK, THE RADIO.

HERE, DAD!

IRAQI MIGS HAVE BOMBED TEHRAN...

NO! THE BASTARDS!

THOSE ASSHOLES!

LET'S GO HOME NOW! YOUR MOTHER MUST BE TERRIFIED.

DAD! DO YOU REMEMBER WHAT YOU LEARNED DURING YOUR MILITARY SERVICE? ARE YOU GOING TO WAR? ARE YOU GOING TO FIGHT? WE HAVE TO TEACH THOSE IRAQIS A LESSON!

WHAT ARE YOU TALKING ABOUT? OF COURSE I'M NOT GOING TO FIGHT. WHY SHOULD I FIGHT?!

HOW CAN YOU SAY THAT? THE IRAQIS HAVE ALWAYS BEEN OUR ENEMIES. THEY WANT TO INVADE US.

AND WORSE, THEY DRIVE LIKE MANIACS...

THE ARABS NEVER LIKED THE PERSIANS. EVERYONE KNOWS THAT. THEY ATTACKED US 1400 YEARS AGO. THEY FORCED THEIR RELIGION ON US.

OK, ENOUGH OF THAT. THE REAL ISLAMIC INVASION HAS COME FROM OUR OWN GOVERNMENT.

TAJI!

MOM!

TAJI!?

DARLING

?

MOM

THE IRAQIS BOMBED US!

REALLY? WHEN?

JUST NOW!

WELL, I GUESS I SHOULD DRY OFF.

WAR ALWAYS TAKES YOU BY SURPRISE.

81

WE HAVE TO BOMB BAGHDAD!

TAKE YOUR FEET OFF THE TABLE, IT'S IMPOLITE.

BOMB BAGHDAD...YOU NEED PILOTS FOR THAT. AFTER THE GENERALS BLEW THEIR CHANCE AT A COUP D'ETAT, THEY WERE ALL JAILED OR EXECUTED...

WHAT'S THIS ABOUT? COUP D'ETAT? PILOTS IN JAIL? WHAT PILOTS?

I KNEW FIGHTER PILOTS. MY FRIEND PARDISSE'S FATHER WAS ONE.

SHE NEVER TOLD ME HER FATHER WAS IN PRISON! ALTHOUGH LAST YEAR SHE DIDN'T COME TO SCHOOL FOR A WHOLE MONTH.

THAT BASTARD SADDAM WAITED UNTIL WE WERE WEAK BEFORE ATTACKING!

PARDISSE ENTEZAMI'S DAD IS A FIGHTER PILOT. HE'S GOING TO GO BOMB BAGHDAD.

ENTEZAMI...ENTEZAMI... HE WAS ONE OF THE CONDEMNED. FIRST HE HAS TO GET OUT OF PRISON!

I'M GOING TO MY ROOM.

IT'S THE PITS! MY DAD IS A DEFEATIST. HE'S NO PATRIOT...

SUDDENLY, I HEARD THE IRANIAN NATIONAL ANTHEM COMING FROM THE TV. OUR STAR-SPANGLED BANNER.

OH IRAN, OUR GOLDEN COUNTRY. YOUR LAND IS THE WELLSPRING OF ART

IT HAD BEEN FORBIDDEN AND REPLACED BY THE NEW GOVERNMENT'S ISLAMIC HYMN...

IT HAD BEEN MORE THAN A YEAR SINCE WE'D HEARD IT...

LET THE EVIL THOUGHTS OF YOUR ENEMIES BE FAR FROM YOU

WE WERE OVERWHELMED...

WELCOME TO THE 8:00 NEWS. 140 IRANIAN F-14S CARRIED OUT BOMBING RAIDS ON BAGHDAD TONIGHT.

WELL, THERE'S YOUR PROOF THAT OUR ARMY IS STILL STRONG!

YOU CAN'T ALWAYS BELIEVE WHAT THEY SAY. 8 O'CLOCK. THE BBC IS BROADCASTING TOO. WHERE'S THE RADIO?

YOU DON'T BELIEVE ANYTHING! HERE'S THE RADIO!

BZZT...ZZZT...
ZZZT...

140 IRANIAN BOMBERS ATTACKED BAGHDAD TODAY...

HA! HA!

HOW'S THAT FEEL, SADDAM!

WE GOT THEM WHERE IT HURTS!

I WAS ALL WRONG ABOUT DAD. HE LOVED HIS COUNTRY AS MUCH AS I DID.

PRESIDENT BANISADR HAS ORDERED THE RELEASE OF THE MILITARY PILOTS JAILED AFTER THE FAILED COUP. THEY AGREED TO ATTACK IRAQ IF THE GOVERNMENT BROADCAST THE NATIONAL ANTHEM...

AS USUAL, MY DAD WAS RIGHT...

...THE REST OF THE NEWS WASN'T SO COOL...

IRANIAN LOSSES WERE VERY HEAVY... HALF OF THE PLANES IN THE MISSION HAVE NOT RETURNED.

I HOPE PARDISSE'S DAD ISN'T DEAD!

CALL HER.

I DON'T HAVE HER NUMBER.

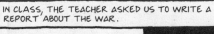

I HAD TO WAIT TWO WEEKS TO FIND OUT.

HEY! PARDISSE

I KNEW RIGHT AWAY, BUT I DIDN'T DARE ASK.

IN CLASS, THE TEACHER ASKED US TO WRITE A REPORT ABOUT THE WAR.

IT'S A DIFFICULT SUBJECT, BUT IT CONCERNS US ALL. THINK ABOUT IT CAREFULLY.

I DIDN'T NEED TO DO MUCH THINKING. I KNEW ALL ABOUT THE WAR.

YOU KNOW WHAT YOU'RE GOING TO SAY?

TOTALLY!

I WROTE FOUR PAGES ON THE HISTORICAL CONTEXT ENTITLED "THE ARAB CONQUEST AND OUR WAR."

I WAS VERY PROUD OF MYSELF.

...THIS WAR IS THE SAME AS THE ONE 1400 YEARS AGO...

BUT THE TEACHER DIDN'T SEEM TOO IMPRESSED.

THAT'S PRETTY GOOD, PAR-DISSE, COME TO THE BLACKBOARD.

...PARDISSE'S REPORT WAS BY FAR THE BEST. IT WAS A LETTER TO HER FATHER IN WHICH SHE PROMISED TO TAKE CARE OF HER MOTHER AND LITTLE BROTHER.

REST IN PEACE, DAD.

AT RECESS, I TRIED TO CONSOLE HER...

YOUR FATHER ACTED LIKE A GENUINE HERO, YOU SHOULD BE PROUD OF HIM!

I WISH HE WERE ALIVE AND IN JAIL RATHER THAN DEAD AND A HERO.

THOSE WERE HER EXACT WORDS TO ME.

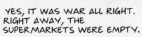

YES, IT WAS WAR ALL RIGHT. RIGHT AWAY, THE SUPERMARKETS WERE EMPTY.

I'M NOT SURE IT'S EVEN WORTH GETTING A CART.

I SAW IT FIRST!

LET GO OF THAT!

COME ON, STOP IT!

?

?

MIND YOUR OWN BUSINESS!

WHAT'S HER PROBLEM?

FORGET ABOUT IT, MOM!

IF STORES WERE CLOSED FOR A SINGLE DAY, YOU'D PROBABLY EAT EACH OTHER! AND YOU CALL YOURSELVES CIVILIZED PEOPLE! IF EVERYONE TOOK ONLY WHAT THEY NEEDED THERE WOULD BE ENOUGH TO GO AROUND!

AND IN THE PARKING LOT...

HOW MANY BOXES OF RICE DID WE GET?

UH...TWO!

HMM. WE'LL GO TO THE STORE ACROSS THE STREET AND TRY TO GET MORE. YOU NEVER KNOW!

?

THERE WASN'T MUCH AT THE GAS STATIONS EITHER.

DO YOU HAVE ANY JERRY CANS?

JERRY? CANS? WHY?

WHY DO YOU THINK? TO MAKE STRAWBERRY SODA!!!

DON'T TALK TO MY MOTHER LIKE THAT!

EVERY MORNING I HAVE TO DRIVE 40 MILES SO THAT YOU CAN HAVE A PEACEFUL LIFE. HOW AM I GOING TO DO THAT WITH NO CAR? HUH? THAT'S WHY I NEED CANS. FOR GASOLINE! CAN YOU UNDERSTAND THAT? THE CAR RUNS ON GAS!!!

LOOK, I AM SO SORRY, DARLING. I'VE BEEN RUNNING AROUND THE WHOLE DAY. I'VE GOT A SPLITTING HEADACHE. YOU KNOW WHAT? I'M JUST GOING TO FILL UP THE TANKS AND THEN WE'LL TRY TO FIND A RESTAURANT.

I HOPE YOU'RE PROUD OF YOURSELF.

AFTER WE MADE UP, WE WENT HOME WITH MY FATHER.

IT TOOK US UNTIL TWO IN THE MORNING. WE OBVIOUSLY DIDN'T GO TO ANY RESTAURANT.

WE DON'T FILL CANS. OTHERWISE THERE WON'T BE ENOUGH FOR EVERYONE.

ALRIGHT. TOO BAD. BUT DO YOU KNOW WHAT'S GOING ON? THE PRESS ISN'T SAYING ANYTHING.

OF COURSE THEY'RE NOT SAYING ANYTHING. IT'S A HUGE MESS!! IRAQ BOMBED THE REFINERY AT ABADAN!

MY GOD! MALI!

OH NO. OH GOD NO.

MALI WAS MY MOTHER'S CHILDHOOD FRIEND. SHE LIVED IN ABADAN WITH HER HUSBAND AND TWO KIDS.

QUICK! CALL THEM!

RING... RING... RING...

NO ONE'S ANSWERING!!

I TRIED HER PLACE TOO, BUT SHE'S DEAF!

DID YOU TRY HER MOTHER? SHE SHOULD KNOW WHAT HAPPENED!

AFTER ABADAN, EVERY BORDER TOWN WAS TARGETED BY BOMBERS. MOST OF THE PEOPLE LIVING IN THOSE AREAS HAD TO FLEE NORTHWARD, FAR FROM THE IRAQI MISSILES.

DING DONG

WHO COULD THAT BE AT THIS HOUR?

I HAVE NO IDEA!

CLIC!

MALI !!??!

EVERYTHING'S DESTROYED,

HEY, IT'LL BE OK, CALM DOWN...

LOOK AT THIS! THAT'S ALL I COULD SAVE

OH...

C'MON BOYS, I'LL FIX YOU SOME HOT CHOCOLATE.

I DON'T LIKE IT.

ME NEITHER.

FIRST WE WENT TO MY MOTHER'S HOUSE. WE KEPT RINGING THE DOORBELL, BUT SHE'S DEAF. I'M SORRY.

NO, YOU DID THE RIGHT THING COMING HERE.

THAT HOUSE COST A MILLION. A MILLION UP IN SMOKE! CAN YOU IMAGINE THAT?

...

MY FATHER WASN'T SO FOND OF MALI'S HUSBAND. HE THOUGHT HE WAS TOO MATERIALISTIC.

THEY DID HAVE A REALLY NICE HOUSE. WE SPENT OUR VACATION THERE A FEW YEARS EARLIER.

THE MARBLE ALONE COST ME 100,000.

I SEE...

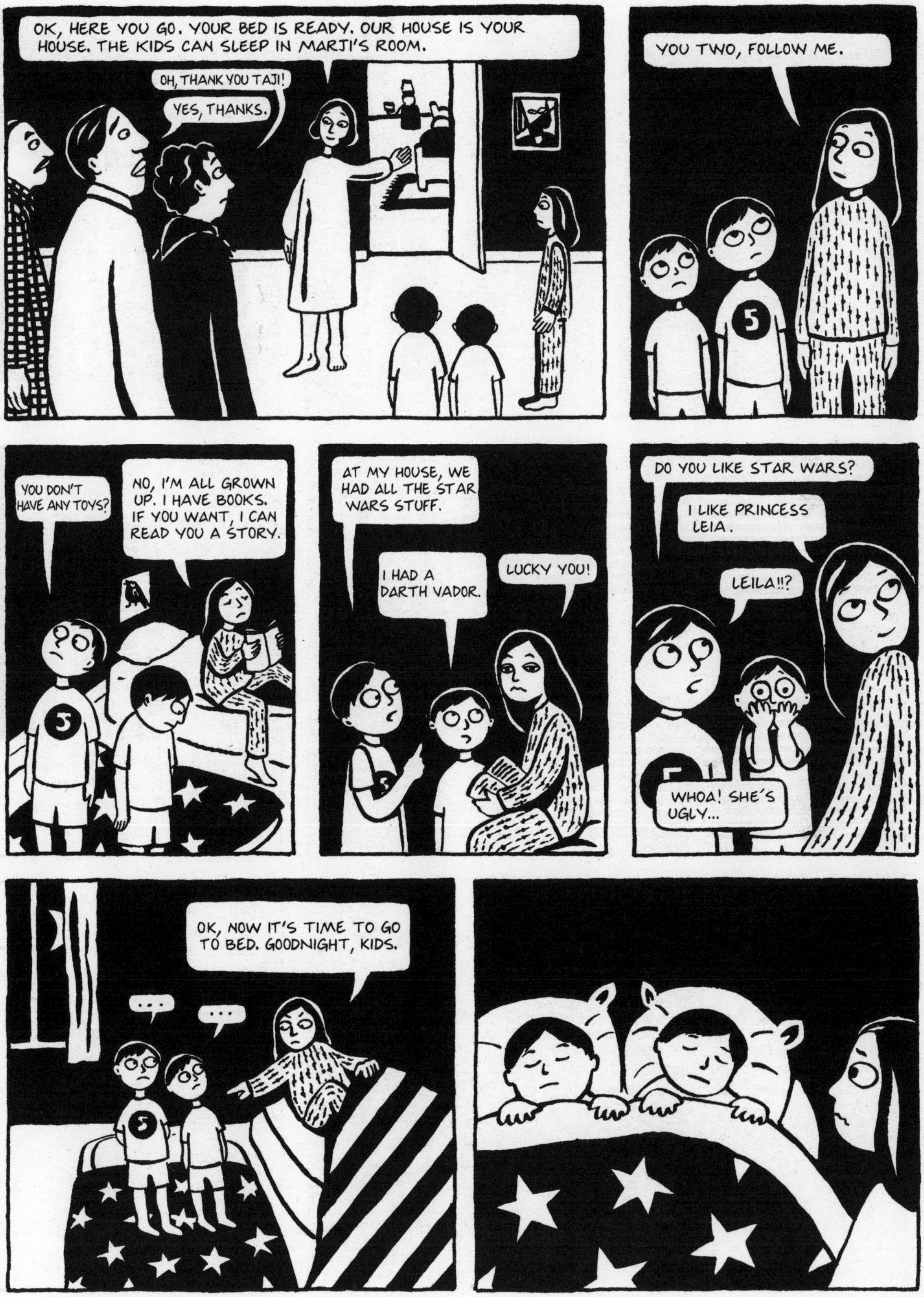
OK, HERE YOU GO. YOUR BED IS READY. OUR HOUSE IS YOUR HOUSE. THE KIDS CAN SLEEP IN MARJI'S ROOM.
OH, THANK YOU TAJI!
YES, THANKS.
YOU TWO, FOLLOW ME.
YOU DON'T HAVE ANY TOYS?
NO, I'M ALL GROWN UP. I HAVE BOOKS. IF YOU WANT, I CAN READ YOU A STORY.
AT MY HOUSE, WE HAD ALL THE STAR WARS STUFF.
I HAD A DARTH VADOR.
LUCKY YOU!
DO YOU LIKE STAR WARS?
I LIKE PRINCESS LEIA.
LEILA!!?
WHOA! SHE'S UGLY...
OK, NOW IT'S TIME TO GO TO BED. GOODNIGHT, KIDS.
...
...

MALI AND HER FAMILY SPENT A WEEK WITH US. THAT'S HOW LONG IT TOOK TO SELL THE JEWELRY AND START OVER AGAIN. MALI'S MOTHER WAS BITTER AND HARD TO DEAL WITH (AND DEAF). BUT THEY WERE HAPPY AT OUR PLACE. THEN, ONE DAY, WE WENT TO THE SUPERMARKET.

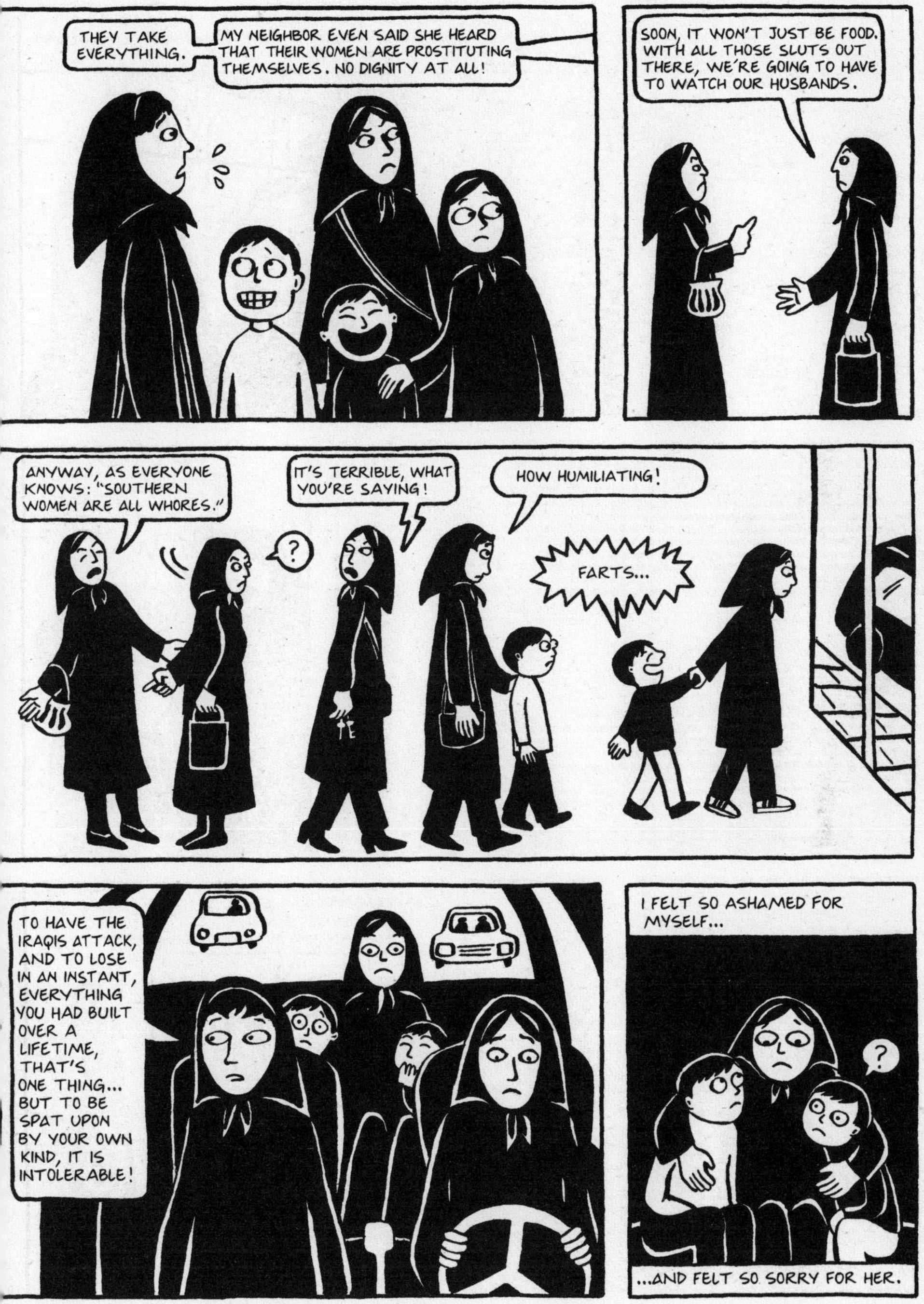
THEY TAKE EVERYTHING.
MY NEIGHBOR EVEN SAID SHE HEARD THAT THEIR WOMEN ARE PROSTITUTING THEMSELVES. NO DIGNITY AT ALL!
SOON, IT WON'T JUST BE FOOD. WITH ALL THOSE SLUTS OUT THERE, WE'RE GOING TO HAVE TO WATCH OUR HUSBANDS.
ANYWAY, AS EVERYONE KNOWS: "SOUTHERN WOMEN ARE ALL WHORES."
?
IT'S TERRIBLE, WHAT YOU'RE SAYING!
HOW HUMILIATING!
FARTS...
TO HAVE THE IRAQIS ATTACK, AND TO LOSE IN AN INSTANT, EVERYTHING YOU HAD BUILT OVER A LIFETIME, THAT'S ONE THING... BUT TO BE SPAT UPON BY YOUR OWN KIND, IT IS INTOLERABLE!
I FELT SO ASHAMED FOR MYSELF...
?
...AND FELT SO SORRY FOR HER.

THE KEY

THE IRAQI ARMY HAD CONQUERED THE CITY OF KHORRAMSHAHR. THEIR ARMS WERE MODERN, BUT WHERE IRAQ HAD QUALITY, WE HAD QUANTITY. COMPARED TO IRAQ, IRAN HAD A HUGE RESERVOIR OF POTENTIAL SOLDIERS. THE NUMBER OF WAR MARTYRS EMPHASIZED THAT DIFFERENCE.

TODAY'S MARTYRS

CAN YOU HELP ME STYLE MY HAIR?

HAVE YOU SEEN ALL THESE CASUALTIES?

HOW CAN I NOT SEE? THEY'RE DOING ALL THEY CAN TO SHOW HOW MANY PEOPLE HAVE DIED. THE STREETS ARE PACKED WITH NUPTIAL CHAMBERS.

ACCORDING TO SHIITE TRADITION, WHEN AN UNMARRIED MAN DIES, A NUPTIAL CHAMBER IS BUILT FOR HIM. THAT WAY, THE DEAD MAN CAN SYMBOLICALLY ATTAIN CARNAL KNOWLEDGE.

IT WAS OBVIOUS THAT MANY OF THE FIGHTERS DIED VIRGINS.

VRUUUUUUU

MOM, DON'T ALL THESE DEAD MEAN ANYTHING TO YOU?

OF COURSE THEY MEAN SOMETHING TO ME! BUT WE ARE STILL LIVING!

OUR COUNTRY HAS ALWAYS KNOWN WAR AND MARTYRS. SO, LIKE MY FATHER SAID: "WHEN A BIG WAVE COMES, LOWER YOUR HEAD AND LET IT PASS!"

THAT'S VERY PERSIAN. THE PHILOSOPHY OF RESIGNATION.

I AGREED WITH MY MOTHER. I TOO TRIED TO THINK ONLY OF LIFE. HOWEVER, IT WASN'T ALWAYS EASY: AT SCHOOL, THEY LINED US UP TWICE A DAY TO MOURN THE WAR DEAD. THEY PUT ON FUNERAL MARCHES, AND WE HAD TO BEAT OUR BREASTS.

I REMEMBER MY INITIATION. IT WAS THE FIRST DAY OF CLASS AFTER SUMMER VACATION.

WELCOME, GIRLS OF IRAN. THE WAR HAS TAKEN THE FLOWER OF OUR NATION'S YOUTH!

THEN THE LOUDSPEAKERS STARTED TO SING.

BABABABABA♪ ♫HEY TROOPS OF... BE ♪ READY, BE READY♫

LET'S GO CHILDREN, ON THE HEART!

WHACK! WHACK!

AND ALL TOGETHER, WE BEGAN THE SESSION.

IT WASN'T AS BAD AS ONE MIGHT THINK. WE'D SEEN IT BEFORE.

HITTING YOURSELF IS ONE OF THE COUNTRY'S RITUALS. DURING CERTAIN RELIGIOUS CEREMONIES, SOME PEOPLE FLAGELLATED THEMSELVES BRUTALLY.

SOMETIMES EVEN WITH CHAINS.

IT COULD GO VERY FAR.

SOMETIMES IT WAS CONSIDERED A MACHO THING.

AFTER A LITTLE WHILE, NO ONE TOOK THE TORTURE SESSIONS SERIOUSLY ANYMORE. AS FOR ME, I IMMEDIATELY STARTED MAKING FUN OF THEM.

THE MARTYRS! THE MARTYRS!

KILL ME!

SATRAPI! WHAT ARE YOU DOING ON THE GROUND?

I'M SUFFERING, CAN'T YOU SEE?

EVERY SITUATION OFFERED AN OPPORTUNITY FOR LAUGHS: LIKE WHEN WE HAD TO KNIT WINTER HOODS FOR THE SOLDIERS...

STOP THAT! OR I'LL CALL THE PRINCIPAL!!

...OR WHEN WE HAD TO DECORATE THE CLASSROOM FOR THE ANNIVERSARY OF THE REVOLUTION...

WHAT ARE THESE GARLANDS?

TOILET PAPER??

YOU'RE AS WORTHLESS AS YOUR DECORATIONS! YOU'RE WORTHLESS!! YOU HEAR ME?! WORTHLESS!!!...

POOPOO

WHO SAID THAT? WHO WAS IT? DOES SHE HAVE THE COURAGE TO STAND UP? IF NOT, YOU'LL ALL BE PUNISHED! WELL? WHO WAS IT??!!!?

WE WERE COMPLETELY UNITED.

YOU'RE ALL SUSPENDED FOR A WEEK!

I THINK THAT THE REASON WE WERE SO REBELLIOUS WAS THAT OUR GENERATION HAD KNOWN SECULAR SCHOOLS. OBVIOUSLY, THEY CALLED OUR PARENTS IN.

YOUR CHILDREN HAVE NO RESPECT FOR ANYTHING. NO SELF-CONTROL! THE BASIS OF EDUCATION COMES FROM THE FAMILY!

STOP RIGHT THERE. YOU'RE SAYING THAT WE DON'T KNOW HOW TO EDUCATE OUR CHILDREN?

LISTEN, WE'RE AT WAR. A LOT OF CHILDREN DON'T EVEN HAVE SCHOOL THESE DAYS. YOURS HAVE A RARE OPPORTUNITY. SO YOU SHOULD MAKE SURE THEY'RE WELL-BEHAVED!

WELL-BEHAVED? SO THEY CAN HIT THEMSELVES TWICE A DAY??

SO THEY CAN BE COVERED FROM HEAD TO TOE?

SO THAT THEY CAN BE FORBIDDEN TO PLAY LIKE THE KIDS THEY ARE ??

OH!

ANYWAY, THAT'S HOW IT IS! EITHER THEY OBEY THE LAW, OR THEY'RE EXPELLED!!

AND MAKE SURE THEY WEAR THEIR VEILS CORRECTLY...

IF HAIR IS AS STIMULATING AS YOU SAY, THEN YOU NEED TO SHAVE YOUR MUSTACHE!

MY FATHER ACTUALLY SAID THAT.

GIRLS HAD TO MAKE WINTER HOODS FOR THE SOLDIERS, BUT BOYS HAD TO PREPARE TO BECOME SOLDIERS.

HI MRS. NASRINE. YOU DON'T LOOK WELL.

MRS. NASRINE WAS OUR MAID.

SO, TELL ME, WHAT'S WRONG?

YOU OK?

NO, MY CHILD. I'M NOT OK.

YOU SEE THIS?

IT'S A PLASTIC KEY PAINTED GOLD.

THEY GAVE THIS TO MY SON AT SCHOOL. THEY TOLD THE BOYS THAT IF THEY WENT TO WAR AND WERE LUCKY ENOUGH TO DIE, THIS KEY WOULD GET THEM INTO HEAVEN.

MY GOD!

IT'S OK, CRY, LET YOURSELF GO.

I'LL MAKE SOME TEA.

I'VE SUFFERED SO MUCH. I RAISED MY FIVE KIDS WITH THE WATER OF MY TEARS, NOW THEY WANT TO TRADE THIS KEY FOR MY OLDEST SON...

ALL MY LIFE, I'VE BEEN FAITHFUL TO THE RELIGION. IF IT'S COME TO THIS... WELL, I CAN'T BELIEVE IN ANYTHING ANYMORE...

AND THE CHILD, WHAT DOES HE SAY?

THEY TOLD HIM THAT IN PARA- DISE THERE WILL BE PLENTY OF FOOD, WOMEN AND HOUSES MADE OF GOLD AND DIAMONDS.

WOMEN?

YEAH. WELL, HE'S FOURTEEN YEARS OLD. THAT'S EXCITING.

BRING HIM HERE, I'LL TALK TO HIM.

WELL, I'M OFF TO SCHOOL.

ON THE WAY, I THOUGHT OF MY COUSIN PEYMAN. HE WAS ALSO FOURTEEN.

WHEN I GOT BACK FROM SCHOOL...

LISTEN, CHILD, THOSE ARE JUST MADE-UP STORIES! WHAT HELL? WHAT PARADISE?

HI!

LISTEN INSTEAD OF STUFFING YOUR FACE!

THINK ABOUT WHEN YOU'RE GROWN UP. YOU WILL GO TO COLLEGE. YOU'LL BECOME SOMEBODY.

I'LL MARRY HER!

YOU IDIOT!

STOP, IT'S NO BIG DEAL!

WHAP!

I'M GOING TO MY ROOM.

HEY! PEYMAN?...WHAT?... NEXT WEEK YOU'RE HAVING A PARTY?...I'LL ASK MY MOM.

TELL ME, AT SCHOOL, DID THEY GIVE YOU THE KEYS TO PARADISE?

KEYS TO WHAT?

MOM, PEYMAN INVITED ME TO A PARTY. CAN I GO?

DING DONG

OOOH! SHAHAB!

HEY!

HI!

SHAHAB WAS ANOTHER COUSIN. HE HADN'T BEEN LUCKY: THE WAR STARTED JUST AS HE BEGAN HIS MILITARY SERVICE. THEY SENT HIM TO THE FRONT RIGHT AWAY.

I'M ON LEAVE.

COME IN, COME IN. I'LL MAKE SOME TEA.

I WAS JUST TALKING TO MY MAID. SHE SAID THEY'RE RECRUITING CHILDREN FOR THE FRONT. REALLY!!?

IT'S AWFUL. EVERY DAY I SEE BUSES FULL OF KIDS ARRIVING.

SHIT, YOU SEE THAT?

THEY COME FROM THE POOR AREAS, YOU CAN TELL...FIRST THEY CONVINCE THEM THAT THE AFTERLIFE IS EVEN BETTER THAN DISNEYLAND, THEN THEY PUT THEM IN A TRANCE WITH ALL THEIR SONGS...

IT'S NUTS! THEY HYPNOTIZE THEM AND JUST TOSS THEM INTO BATTLE. ABSOLUTE CARNAGE.

THE KEY TO PARADISE WAS FOR POOR PEOPLE. THOUSANDS OF YOUNG KIDS, PROMISED A BETTER LIFE, EXPLODED ON THE MINEFIELDS WITH THEIR KEYS AROUND THEIR NECKS.

MRS. NASRINE'S SON MANAGED TO AVOID THAT FATE, BUT LOTS OF OTHER KIDS FROM HIS NEIGHBORHOOD DIDN'T.

MEANWHILE, I GOT TO GO TO MY FIRST PARTY. NOT ONLY DID MY MOM LET ME GO, SHE ALSO KNITTED ME A SWEATER FULL OF HOLES AND MADE ME A NECKLACE WITH CHAINS AND NAILS. PUNK ROCK WAS IN.

I WAS LOOKING SHARP.

102

THE WINE

AFTER THE BORDER TOWNS, TEHRAN BECAME THE BOMBERS' MAIN TARGET. TOGETHER WITH THE OTHER PEOPLE IN OUR BUILDING, WE TURNED THE BASEMENT INTO A SHELTER. EVERY TIME THE SIREN RANG OUT, EVERYONE WOULD RUN DOWNSTAIRS...

PUT YOUR CIGARETTE OUT. THEY SAY THAT THE GLOW OF A CIGARETTE IS THE EASIEST THING TO SEE FROM THE SKY.

BUT WE'RE IN THE BASEMENT HERE!

AND ONCE IT WAS OVER...

WELL? WELL?

NO ONE'S ANSWERING!

I'M FINE!

OH THOSE POOR PEOPLE! LUCKY NOTHING HAPPENED TO YOU!

HE WANTS TO TALK TO YOU!

AFTER THE BOMBS AND THE INSTINCTIVE FEAR OF DEATH, YOU'D THINK OF THE VICTIMS AND ANOTHER KIND OF ANXIETY SEIZED YOU.

IT WASN'T JUST THE BASEMENTS. THE INTERIORS OF HOMES ALSO CHANGED. BUT IT WASN'T ONLY BECAUSE OF THE IRAQI PLANES.

MOM, WHAT'RE YOU DOING?

THE MASKING TAPE IS TO PROTECT AGAINST FLYING GLASS DURING A BOMBING AND THE BLACK CURTAINS ARE TO PROTECT US FROM OUR NEIGHBORS.

WHAT NEIGHBORS?

ACROSS THE STREET. THEY'RE TOTALLY DEVOTED TO THE NEW REGIME. A GLIMPSE OF WHAT GOES ON IN OUR HOUSE WOULD BE ENOUGH FOR THEM TO DENOUNCE US!

YOU KNOW TINOOSH'S DAD?

TINOOSH, YEAH. WHAT ABOUT HIM?

THE OTHER NIGHT, TWO GUARDIANS OF THE REVOLUTION PATROLS PAID THEM A VISIT.

SOMEONE TOLD US YOU WERE PLANNING A PARTY. YOU KNOW THAT IT'S STRICTLY FORBIDDEN!

UM...

...THEY FOUND RECORDS AND VIDEO-CASSETTES AT THEIR PLACE. A DECK OF CARDS, A CHESS SET. IN OTHER WORDS, EVERYTHING THAT'S BANNED.

GET YOUR ASS IN THE CAR. MOVE!

EXCUSE ME, SIR.

SHUT UP, SLUT!

...IT EARNED HIM SEVENTY-FIVE LASHES.

HIS WIFE CRIED SO MUCH THAT THEY FINALLY LET HER OFF WITH A HEFTY FINE. BUT HE CAN'T WALK ANYMORE...NOW YOU SEE WHY I'M PUTTING UP THE CURTAINS. WITH THE PARTIES WE HAVE ON THURSDAYS AND THE CARD GAMES ON MONDAYS, WE HAVE TO BE CAREFUL.

IN SPITE OF ALL THE DANGERS, THE PARTIES WENT ON. "WITHOUT THEM IT WOULDN'T BE PSYCHOLOGICALLY BEARABLE," SOME SAID. "WITHOUT PARTIES, WE MIGHT AS WELL JUST BURY OURSELVES NOW," ADDED THE OTHERS. MY UNCLE INVITED US TO HIS HOUSE TO CELEBRATE THE BIRTH OF MY COUSIN. EVERYONE WAS THERE. EVEN GRANDMA WAS DANCING.

DAMN! POWER OUTAGE!!

BE CAREFUL WHERE YOU STEP!!!

AWWW! NO MORE MUSIC!

DON'T WORRY ABOUT IT! I'LL GO GET THE ZARB.

A ZARB IS A KIND OF DRUM. MY FATHER PLAYED IT VERY WELL. LIKE A PRO.

WE HAD EVERYTHING. WELL, EVERYTHING THAT WAS FORBIDDEN. EVEN ALCOHOL, GALLONS OF IT.

MY UNCLE WAS THE VINTNER. HE HAD BUILT A GENUINE WINE-MAKING LAB IN HIS BASEMENT.

MRS. NASRINE, WHO WAS ALSO HIS CLEANING LADY, CRUSHED THE GRAPES.

GOD FORGIVE ME! GOD FORGIVE ME!

SUDDENLY, SIRENS STARTED TO WAIL...

...AND MY AUNT DID TOO.

IT'S ALRIGHT, STAY CALM!

AAAA...!

I FOUND MYSELF WITH THE NEWBORN BABY WE HAD BEEN CELEBRATING IN MY ARMS.

HER MOTHER HAD ALREADY ABANDONED HER.

SINCE THAT DAY, I'VE HAD DOUBTS ABOUT THE SO-CALLED "MATERNAL INSTINCT."

AFTER THE ALERT, WE WENT HOME.

SHE'S COMPLETELY NUTS! DID YOU SEE HOW SHE DROPPED THE BABY? THAT WAS PRETTY INCREDIBLE!

MY POOR BROTHER ISN'T EXACTLY SPOILED.

HALT!

HALT!

OPEN THE DOOR AND GET OUT!

ID, REGISTRATION AND DRIVER'S LICENSE.

OK. OK.

GO AHHH.

AHH...

BEEN DRINKING, HAVE WE!!?!!

NO, ABSOLUTELY NOT!

YOU THINK I'M STUPID?!!!... I CAN TELL BY YOUR TIE! PIECE OF WESTERNIZED TRASH!

I WON'T TAKE THAT FROM YOU. FOR TWENTY YEARS I'VE WORKED FOR THIS COUNTRY AND YOU DARE TO TALK TO ME LIKE THAT?

FORGIVE HIM.

SHUT UP!

FORGIVE HIM. LISTEN, I COULD BE YOUR MOTHER. HOW OLD ARE YOU? SIXTEEN?... MY DAUGHTER IS TWELVE... FORGIVE HIM...

YOU'RE LUCKY TO HAVE THIS WOMAN FOR YOUR WIFE, OTHERWISE YOU'D ALREADY BE IN HELL!

THANKS, THANKS SO MUCH!

YOU SAY YOU HAVEN'T BEEN DRINKING. WE'RE GOING TO SEE WHAT YOU HAVE AT HOME.

GRANDMA! MARJI! WHEN WE'RE HOME, GET OUT FIRST. I'LL TRY TO STALL HIM. FLUSH ALL THE ALCOHOL DOWN THE TOILET.

BUT HOW?

DON'T WORRY DEAR. I'M USED TO IT. WHEN YOUR FATHER WAS ALIVE, I WAS ALWAYS HIDING HIS TRACTS.

THEY FOLLOWED US ALL THE WAY HOME.

MUST YOU REALLY COME UPSTAIRS? OUR ELDERY NEIGHBOR HAS A HEART CONDITION. IF HE'S FRIGHTENED BY THE NOISE, IT COULD KILL HIM.

HURRY UP!

WHERE DO YOU TWO THINK YOU'RE GOING?

I HAVE DIABETES, MY BOY. IF I DON'T DRINK A LITTLE SYRUP, I'M GOING TO FAINT.

DIABETES, JUST LIKE MY MOTHER!

SO YOU UNDERSTAND IT'S URGENT!

GO AHEAD.

IT WAS A MIRACLE.

HURRY UP! I DON'T KNOW HOW MUCH LONGER YOUR FATHER CAN STALL THEM!

HURRY! HURRY!

AND THE FINAL TOUCH.

CLICK!

HERE THEY COME!

WHERE'S THE GUY?

WHERE INDEED! THEIR FAITH HAS NOTHING TO DO WITH IDEOLOGY! A FEW BILLS WERE ALL HE NEEDED TO FORGET THE WHOLE THING!!

HEY, YOU DIDN'T THROW IT ALL OUT?

YEP

NO MORE?

NOPE

MY GOD!...I NEED A PICK-ME-UP...

110

THE CIGARETTE

THE WAR HAD BEEN GOING ON FOR TWO YEARS. WE WERE USED TO IT. I WAS GROWING UP AND I EVEN HAD FRIENDS OLDER THAN ME.

YESTERDAY ON THE NEWS THEY SAID WE DESTROYED 13 IRAQI PLANES. RIGHT AFTER ON THE BBC, I HEARD THAT IN FACT THE IRAQIS HAD SHOT DOWN TWO OF OURS.

IT'S PERFECTLY CLEAR. EVERY DAY THEY TELL US THAT WE'VE DESTROYED TEN PLANES AND FIVE TANKS. IF YOU START FROM THE BEGINNING OF THE WAR, THAT MAKES SIX THOUSAND PLANES AND THREE THOUSAND TANKS DESTROYED. EVEN THE AMERICANS DON'T HAVE AN ARMY THIS BIG.

I GET IT. I'M GOING TO TELL MY DAD THAT ONE.

BRINGGG...

HEY, THERE'S THE BELL. DON'T YOU HAVE CLASS?

NO, WE'VE GOT PHYSICAL EDUCATION BUT WE'RE NOT GOING. WE'RE GOING FOR BURGERS.

BURGERS?

THEY ALSO HAVE HOT DOGS.

ALL YOU NEEDED WAS SOME MONEY.

YEAH! AT KANSAS ON JORDAN AVENUE.

DON'T LOOK AT ME LIKE THAT. WE'LL CLIMB THE WALL.

THE WALL??!!

HA HA HA HA! HA HA HA!

!!

IF I WANTED TO BE FRIENDS WITH 14-YEAR-OLDS, I HAD TO DO IT.

I WASN'T CHICKEN, SO I FOLLOWED THEM.

I HAD ALREADY BROKEN THE RULES ONCE BY GOING TO THE DEMONSTRATION IN '79. THIS WAS THE SECOND TIME.

JORDAN AVENUE WAS WHERE THE TEENAGERS FROM NORTH TEHRAN (THE NICE NEIGHBORHOODS) HUNG OUT. KANSAS WAS ITS TEMPLE.

IF SOME PUBLIC PLACES HAD SURVIVED THE REGIME'S REPRESSION, EITHER IT WAS TO LEAVE US A LITTLE FREE SPACE, OR ELSE IT WAS OUT OF IGNORANCE. PERSONALLY, THE LATTER THEORY SOUNDED MORE LIKELY: THEY PROBABLY HADN'T THE SLIGHTEST IDEA WHAT "KANSAS" WAS.

DID YOU SEE HIS HAIR? JUST LIKE ROD STEWART!

YEAH, IF HE GETS CAUGHT, HE'LL GET A BUZZ CUT!

KANS

...IN SPITE OF EVERYTHING, KIDS WERE TRYING TO LOOK HIP, EVEN UNDER RISK OF ARREST.

MY FRIENDS WEREN'T ACTUALLY THAT INTERESTED IN THE HAMBURGERS...

WE LET THE BOYS KNOW THAT THEY COULD FOLLOW US BY A FEW SIGNS.

FOLLOW THE OTHERS, I MEAN. I WAS TOO YOUNG TO INTEREST THEM.

WOOOOO

...THE SIRENS WENT OFF.

WHAT THE HELL ARE YOU DOING??

HIT THE DIRT!

WE HAD BEEN TOLD THAT IF WE WERE IN THE STREET DURING A BOMBING, WE SHOULD LIE DOWN IN THE GUTTER FOR SAFETY.

HA! YOU CHICKEN!

THE WONDERFUL DAY WAS SPOILED BY MY MOM.

SO HOW WAS SCHOOL?

OK. WHY?

YOU DARE TO LIE STRAIGHT TO MY FACE?

I'M NOT LYING!

SO MAYBE IT'S ME WHO CUT CLASS?

WHAT CLASS?

YOU TELL ME THE TRUTH RIGHT NOW OR ELSE YOU'LL BE PUNISHED TWICE!

MY MOTHER USED THE SAME TACTICS AS THE TORTURERS.

BUT ALL I HAD WAS RELIGION CLASS!

I DON'T GIVE A DAMN! YOU DON'T CUT CLASS!

AND YOU JUST LIED AGAIN! THE SCHOOL CALLED AND SAID YOU HAD GRAMMAR THIS AFTERNOON!

I HAD SAID RELIGION TO TRY TO MAKE MY MOTHER LESS ANGRY, BUT IT HADN'T WORKED.

THIS TIME I COVERED FOR YOU, BUT IT'S THE LAST TIME! NOW IS THE TIME FOR LEARNING. YOU HAVE YOUR WHOLE LIFE TO HAVE FUN! WHAT ARE YOU GOING TO BE WHEN YOU GROW UP?? IN THIS COUNTRY YOU HAVE TO KNOW EVERYTHING BETTER THAN ANYONE ELSE IF YOU'RE GOING TO SURVIVE!!

DIDN'T YOU MEET DAD WHEN YOU WERE FOURTEEN?

YOU'RE NOT FOURTEEN!

SO? I'M TWELVE!

DICTATOR! YOU ARE THE GUARDIAN OF THE REVOLUTION OF THIS HOUSE!

SOMEWHAT LATER...

THE IRANIAN ARMY HAS RETAKEN KHORRAMSHAHR...

...FOR THE FOURTH TIME THIS MONTH.

EVEN IF IT'S TRUE, WHAT DIFFERENCE DOES IT MAKE TO US?

MAY I GO TO THE BASEMENT, MA'AM?

YES, MISS SATRAPI.

THE BASEMENT WAS MY HIDEAWAY.

CLICK

AS IT TURNED OUT, THEY DID RETAKE KHORRAMSHAHR. WE ALL THOUGHT THAT THE WAR WOULD FINALLY END.

IN FACT, IRAQ PROPOSED A SETTLEMENT, AND SAUDI ARABIA WAS WILLING TO PAY FOR RECONSTRUCTION, TO RESTORE PEACE TO THE AREA.

BUT OUR GOVERNMENT WAS AGAINST IT.

THEY DECLARED:

WE REFUSE THIS IMPOSED PEACE!

WE SHALL CONQUER KARBALA*!

*A SHIITE HOLY CITY IN IRAQ

SO WE PLUNGED DEEPER INTO WAR...

THE WALLS WERE SUDDENLY COVERED WITH BELLIGERENT SLOGANS.

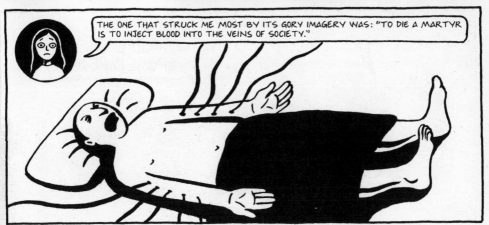

THE ONE THAT STRUCK ME MOST BY ITS GORY IMAGERY WAS: "TO DIE A MARTYR IS TO INJECT BLOOD INTO THE VEINS OF SOCIETY."

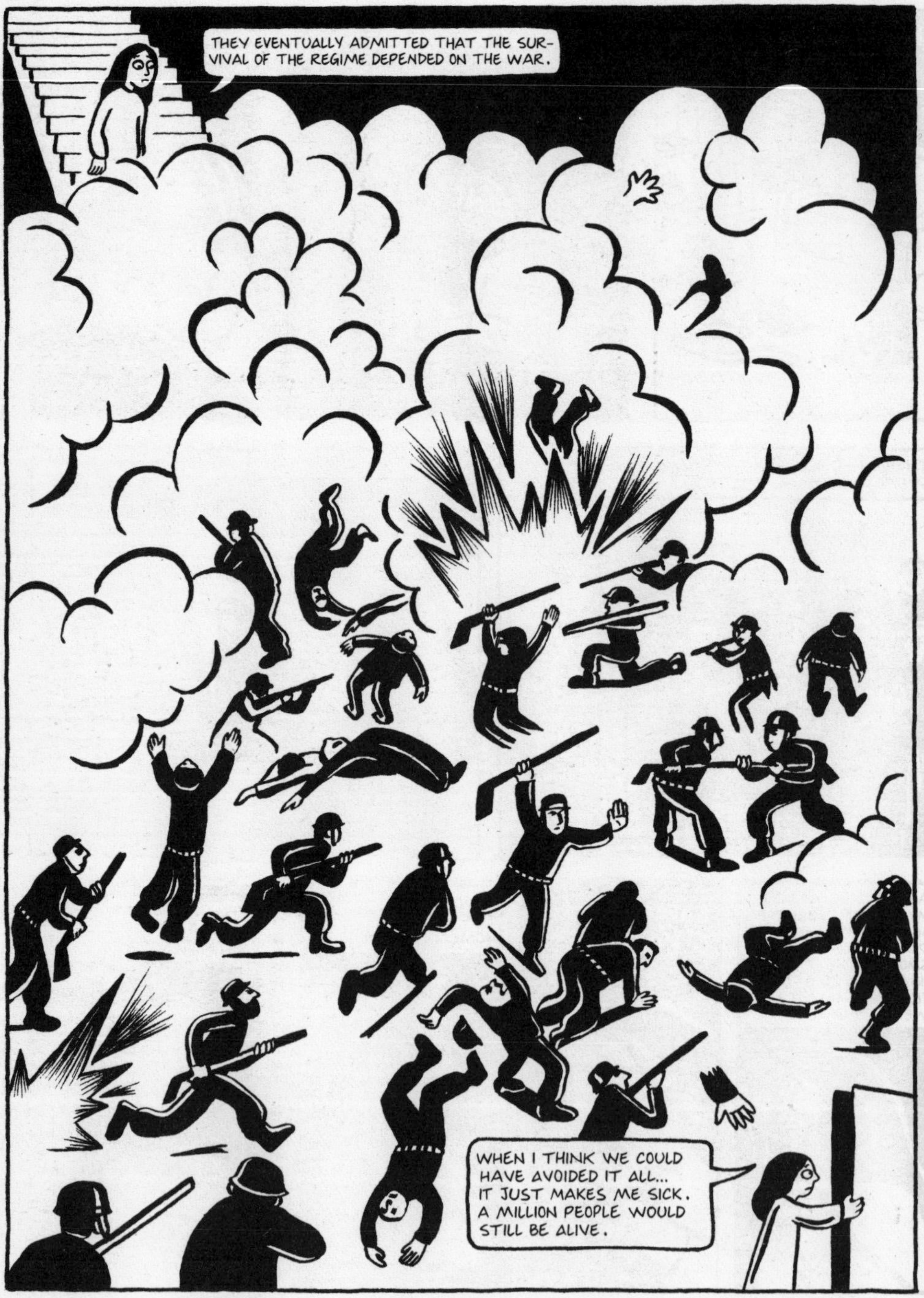
THEY EVENTUALLY ADMITTED THAT THE SURVIVAL OF THE REGIME DEPENDED ON THE WAR.
WHEN I THINK WE COULD HAVE AVOIDED IT ALL... IT JUST MAKES ME SICK. A MILLION PEOPLE WOULD STILL BE ALIVE.

NATURALLY, THE REGIME BECAME MORE REPRESSIVE.

IN THE NAME OF THAT WAR, THEY EXTERMINATED THE ENEMY WITHIN.

THOSE WHO OPPOSED THE REGIME WERE SYSTEMATICALLY ARRESTED...

AND EXECUTED TOGETHER.

AS FOR ME, I SEALED MY ACT OF REBELLION AGAINST MY MOTHER'S DICTATORSHIP BY SMOKING THE CIGARETTE I'D STOLEN FROM MY UNCLE TWO WEEKS EARLIER.

KOFFF! KOFFF! KOFFF!!!

IT WAS AWFUL. BUT THIS WAS NOT THE MOMENT TO GIVE IN.

WITH THIS FIRST CIGARETTE, I KISSED CHILDHOOD GOODBYE.

NOW I WAS A GROWN-UP.

THE PASSPORT

JULY 1982. WE WERE AT MY AUNT'S PLACE. THE INTERNAL WAR HAD BECOME A BIGGER ISSUE THAN THE WAR AGAINST IRAQ. ANYONE SHOWING THE SLIGHTEST RESISTANCE TO THE REGIME WAS PERSECUTED.

THERE MUST BE A LOT OF PEOPLE IN THE OPPOSITION IN OUR NEIGHBORHOOD. WE HEAR GUNSHOTS EVERY DAY.

TAHER, STOP SMOKING!

THE STRESS I GET FROM EVERY GUNSHOT I HEAR IS MUCH WORSE FOR ME THAN THE CIGARETTES.

SINCE HE HAD SENT HIS OLDEST SON TO HOLLAND, UNCLE TAHER HAD HAD TWO HEART ATTACKS. HE WAS ABSOLUTELY FORBIDDEN TO SMOKE.

THE BUTCHER TOLD ME HE'S SEEN KIDS EXECUTED IN THE STREET WITHOUT EVEN HAVING BEEN JUDGED. THE SHAME OF IT.

WHEN I THINK ABOUT IT, I'M GLAD THAT MY SON IS SAFELY ABROAD. BUT WITH THE BORDERS CLOSED, HOW AM I EVER GOING TO SEE HIM AGAIN?

THE BORDERS WERE CLOSED FOR THREE YEARS BETWEEN 1980 AND 1983.

HOW MANY TIMES DID I SAY TO MY WIFE, "COME ON, LET'S JOIN HIM." SHE DIDN'T WANT TO. SHE INVOKED HER COUNTRY, HER FAMILY, ETC, ETC.

ANYWAY, I'M ALREADY 59. BUT THOSE POOR 20-YEAR-OLDS WHO GET SLAUGHTERED. THEY KILL ME... THEY KILL ME!

MY UNCLE TAHER WAS SO SAD THAT IT HURT TO LOOK AT HIM. NO ONE DARED SAY A WORD.

SOME DAYS LATER.

WHAT ARE YOU THINKING?

ABOUT TAHER. HIS SON LEAVING HAS DONE HIM IN. I'VE NEVER SEEN HIM LIKE THAT.

CAN YOU IMAGINE? A THIRTEEN, FOURTEEN-YEAR-OLD CHILD, ALONE IN A COUNTRY WHERE HE DOESN'T EVEN SPEAK THE LANGUAGE?

TCH...AT FOURTEEN YOU DON'T NEED YOUR PARENTS ANYMORE!

GET REAL. UP TO A CERTAIN AGE, YOU NEED YOUR PARENTS, THEN LATER, THEY NEED YOU.

?

YOU'D BE BETTER OFF WITHOUT NAIL POLISH. YOU COULD GET ARRESTED.

I'LL PUT MY HANDS IN MY POCKETS.

PRETTY STUBBORN GIRL, HUH?

WHERE DO YOU SUPPOSE SHE GETS THAT?

SOMETIMES IT SCARES ME HOW BLUNT SHE IS.

IT'LL HELP HER LATER ON. YOU'LL SEE.

I AM SO LUCKY TO BE MARRIED TO A MAN LIKE YOU. YOU'RE SO SENSITIVE. THE KINDEST MAN ON EARTH.

HOW CAN YOU BE INSENSITIVE TO THE WOMAN YOU LOVE?

RRING... RRING...

IT ALWAYS RINGS AT THE WRONG TIME!

GOOD LORD, AGAIN!

WHAT?

UNCLE TAHER HAD JUST SUFFERED HIS THIRD HEART ATTACK. WE WERE OFF TO THE HOSPITAL.

RED CRESCENT TRUCKS WERE PULLED UP IN FRONT OF THE HOSPITAL, CALLING FOR PEOPLE TO GIVE BLOOD FOR THE WAR WOUNDED. THERE WERE SO MANY OF THEM.

GIVE BLOOD! GIVE BLOOD!!

GIVE BLOOD!

I FELT BOTH ANGRY AND EMBARRASSED...

ONCE INSIDE THE HOSPITAL I FELT EVEN WORSE.

I'M LOOKING FOR MR. TALISCHI'S ROOM.

TALISCHI...THAT'S 342, THIRD FLOOR, AT THE END OF THE HALL TO THE RIGHT.

342

SHHH

342

THEY THREW A GRENADE...THEY WANTED TO ARREST SOME COMMUNISTS WHO WERE HIDING NEAR OUR PLACE, AND THEY THREW A GRENADE...TAHER COULDN'T DEAL WITH IT... WHEN I CAME INTO THE LIVING ROOM, HE WAS LYING ON THE FLOOR...

342

HE NEEDS OPEN HEART SURGERY, BUT THEY'RE NOT EQUIPPED HERE. THEY TOLD ME THAT HE HAS TO BE SENT TO ENGLAND.

TO DO THAT, HE NEEDS A PERMIT. THEY GAVE ME THE NAME OF THE HOSPITAL DIRECTOR. IF HE AGREES, TAHER WILL GET A PASSPORT SO HE CAN GO.

SINCE THE BORDERS WERE CLOSED, ONLY VERY SICK PEOPLE (IF THEY GOT A PERMIT FROM THE HEALTH MINISTRY) WERE ALLOWED TO LEAVE.

IT'S ON THE 4TH FLOOR, NUMBER 406.

ONLY MY AUNT WAS ALLOWED IN. SHE HAD A BIG SURPRISE. THE DIRECTOR WAS HER FORMER WINDOW WASHER. SHE ACTED AS IF SHE DIDN'T RECOGNIZE HIM TO AVOID OFFENDING HIM.

MY HUSBAND HAD HIS THIRD HEART ATTACK. HE NEEDS MEDICAL CARE OUTSIDE THE COUNTRY.

HMM...

WE'LL DO OUR BEST. IF GOD WILLS IT, HE'LL GET BETTER. EVERYTHING DEPENDS ON GOD.

I NEED YOUR AUTHORIZATION SO HE CAN GET A PASSPORT!

IF GOD WILLS IT.

ALL THAT CREEPY WINDOW WASHER HAD TO DO TO BECOME DIRECTOR OF THE HOSPITAL WAS TO GROW A BEARD AND PUT ON A SUIT! THE FATE OF MY HUSBAND DEPENDS ON A WINDOW WASHER! NOW HE'S SO RELIGIOUS THAT HE WON'T LOOK A WOMAN IN THE EYE. THE PATHETIC FOOL!

AFTER THE DIRECTOR, WE WENT TO SEE THE CHIEF OF STAFF, DR. FATHI.

MA'AM, WE WILL DO WHAT WE CAN. WE ARE TERRIBLY STRAPPED AT THE MOMENT.

LOOK IN THIS ROOM. THEY'RE ALL VICTIMS OF CHEMICAL WEAPONS!

THE GERMANS SELL CHEMICAL WEAPONS TO IRAN AND IRAQ. THE WOUNDED ARE THEN SENT TO GERMANY TO BE TREATED. VERITABLE HUMAN GUINEA PIGS.

WHY ARE YOU TELLING ME THIS?! I COULDN'T CARE LESS. I WANT MY HUSBAND TO GET WELL!

CALM DOWN

CALM DOWN, DEAR. EVERYTHING WILL BE ALL RIGHT. DON'T WORRY.

WE'LL BE RIGHT BACK!

WE WENT TO SEE AN ACQUAIN-
TANCE OF MY FATHER'S, KHOSRO.
HIS BROTHER AND MY UNCLE ANOOSH
WERE IN PRISON TOGETHER DURING
THE REIGN OF THE SHAH.

EBI, THE BROTHER OF
ANOOSH? COME IN! COME IN!

SINCE THEY SHUT DOWN MY
PUBLISHING COMPANY, I'VE BEEN
PRINTING FAKE PASSPORTS. BIG
SELLERS. YOU WANT ONE?

NOT ME, MY
BROTHER-IN-LAW.

WHEN THEY LET HIM OUT, MY
BROTHER STARTED GOING TO
COUNTER-REVOLUTIONARY
DEMONSTRATIONS. HE TOLD ME THAT
THE CHIEF OF THE NEW EXECUTIONERS
WAS HIS TORTURER IN THE SHAH'S
PRISON. HE SAW IT WITH HIS OWN
EYES. HE SAID "KHOSRO, I CAN'T
TAKE ANY MORE." I MADE HIM A
FAKE PASSPORT AND HE SOUGHT
POLITICAL ASYLUM IN SWEDEN.

LOOK, EBI, A WHOLE MONTH'S
WORK, JUST FOR THE STAMP.

HOW MUCH TIME
WILL IT TAKE TO
MAKE A PASSPORT?

A WEEK.

CRR...

YOU CAN COME IN.
THEY'RE FRIENDS.

THIS IS NILOUFAR. HER BROTHER
WAS MY MESSENGER BOY. THEY
ARE LOOKING ALL OVER FOR HER
BECAUSE SHE'S A COMMUNIST. I
LET HER STAY IN MY BASEMENT.

SHE'S EIGHTEEN, THE SAME AGE
AS MY DAUGHTER, MANDANA.

KHOSRO'S DAUGHTER HAD LEFT
WITH HER MOTHER RIGHT
AFTER THE REVOLUTION.

THEY'VE BEEN SEARCHING
THE HOUSES OF EVERYONE
IN HER FAMILY. THIS IS THE
ONLY PLACE SHE'S SAFE.

123

AFTER NEGOTIATING A PRICE, THE EQUIVALENT OF ABOUT $200, KHOSRO AGREED TO MAKE A PASSPORT IN FIVE DAYS. WE WENT BACK TO THE HOSPITAL FEELING A LITTLE BETTER.

I SAW KHOSRO. HE CAN MAKE A PASSPORT FOR TAHER BY WEDNESDAY.

SO?

HE'S COME TO. HE WANTS TO SEE YOU.

SEE, IT'S NOT THE CIGARETTES THAT DID IT! IT WAS THAT DAMN GRENADE...

DON'T UPSET YOUR-SELF, TALK ABOUT SOMETHING ELSE.

LOOK AT HOW LITTLE MARJI IS GROWING UP. ONE DAY SHE'LL LEAVE AND YOU'LL SEE HOW HARD IT IS TO LOSE YOUR KIDS.

I HAVE ONLY ONE WISH, AND THAT'S TO SEE MY SON AGAIN, ONE LAST TIME.

124

TWO DAYS LATER, NILOUFAR, THE EIGHTEEN-YEAR-OLD COMMUNIST, WAS SPOTTED.

ARRESTED...

AND EXECUTED.

KHOSRO FOUND HIS HOUSE RANSACKED...

FLED ACROSS THE MOUNTAINS TO TURKEY...

AND SOUGHT ASYLUM WITH HIS BROTHER IN SWEDEN.

HE NEVER GOT TO MAKE THE PASSPORT.

THREE WEEKS AFTER THESE EVENTS, UNCLE TAHER WAS BURIED. HIS REAL PASSPORT ARRIVED THE SAME DAY...

...HE NEVER GOT TO SEE HIS SON...

A YEAR AFTER MY UNCLE DIED, THE BORDERS WERE REOPENED. MY PARENTS RAN TO GET PASSPORTS.

LOOK AT THE LAST PAGE: "IT IS STRICTLY FORBIDDEN TO TRAVEL IN OCCUPIED PALESTINE WITH THIS DOCUMENT."

MY GOD. JUST LOOK AT ME IN THIS PICTURE, WITH THE SCARF ON MY HEAD.

CAN I SEE?

SHE SURE DIDN'T LOOK VERY HAPPY. IN FACT, SHE WAS UNRECOGNIZABLE.

AS SOON AS I GET MY PASSPORT, WE'LL GO ON A BIG TRIP!

WELL, ACTUALLY...

WE WANT TO SPEND SOME TIME TOGETHER, JUST THE TWO OF US, FOR A FEW DAYS.

WHERE?

TURKEY.

BAH...TURKEY'S FOR THE BIRDS. ONLY UNCOOL PEOPLE GO TO TURKEY. IF YOU'RE TAKING A TRIP, WHY NOT GO TO EUROPE OR THE UNITED STATES?!...

IF YOU WANT US TO BRING YOU BACK SOME PRESENTS, JUST ASK.

WHAT CAN YOU BRING ME BACK FROM TURKEY? SHISH-KEBABS?

LISTEN MARJI, WHERE DO YOU THINK ALL THE HIP STUFF YOU LIKE COMES FROM?

DURING THE WAR, THERE WERE NO IMPORTS FROM THE WEST.

A DENIM JACKET, CHOCOLATE, A POSTER, NO, TWO POSTERS. ONE OF KIM WILDE AND ONE OF IRON MAIDEN.

IRON MAIDEN? THOSE FOUR BRUTES?

THEY'RE NOT BRUTES. I REALLY LIKE WHAT THEY DO.

YOU LIKE THAT?

I LOVE IT.

SEE, MOM?

FIRST THING AFTER THEY GOT TO ISTANBUL, THEY WENT TO BUY THE POSTERS.

I'M GLAD WE FOUND JUST WHAT SHE WANTED!

ABSOLUTELY! IT'S SO HARD FOR KIDS IN IRAN. THE POOR THINGS.

TELL ME THE TRUTH, YOU REALLY LIKE IRON MAIDEN?

ABSOLUTELY!

YOU HYPOCRITE!

I WONDER HOW WE'RE GOING TO GET THEM PAST CUSTOMS!

I'VE BEEN WONDERING MYSELF. THEY'RE ENORMOUS.

AS SOON AS THEY WERE IN THE HOTEL, THEY SET TO FINDING A WAY.

WE COULD FOLD THEM AND HIDE THEM IN THE LINING OF THE SUITCASE!

FOLD THEM? THAT WILL LEAVE MARKS. SHE'LL BE DISAPPOINTED.

WE COULD JUST CARRY THEM UNDER OUR ARMS AND ACT NATURAL.

UNDER OUR ARMS? COME ON!

AND THEN MY MOTHER HAD A GREAT IDEA...

TAKE OFF YOUR COAT.

SHE TORE OUT THE LINING.

THEN, SHE PLACED THE TWO POSTERS BEHIND IT...

...AND THEN SEWED IT BACK IN.

ARRIVING AT TEHRAN'S MEHRABAD AIRPORT...

I'M WALKING LIKE FRANKENSTEIN.

NO YOU'RE NOT. YOU LOOK COMPLETELY NATURAL.

PLACE YOUR BAGS ON THE TABLE.

STAY CALM!

SO, WHAT HAVE YOU GOT WITH YOU? ALCOHOL? PLAYING CARDS? MUSIC? FILM? CHESS SET? MAGAZINES?...

NOTHING. JUST PERSONAL AFFAIRS.

YOU'RE SURE YOU'VE GOT NOTHING ILLEGAL?

NOPE.

NO, NO.

YOU REALIZE THAT IF I FIND ANYTHING ILLEGAL, I'LL...

SIR, PLEASE, DO WE REALLY LOOK LIKE SMUGGLERS?

....

...ALRIGHT. TAKE YOUR LUGGAGE AND GO!

CUSTOM

?

EXIT خروج →

MOM! DAD!

129

BACK HOME...

HERE. THIS IS FOR YOU. NIKE'S LATEST MODEL.

AND THIS...

WOW! MICHAEL JACKSON!

AND HERE'S YOUR DENIM JACKET.

COOL!

WHAT ABOUT MY POSTERS?

EBI! BRING YOUR COAT!

?

BE CAREFUL!

I WANTED POSTERS, NOT PHOTOS!!

YOU JUST WAIT!

CRRAK

FAR OUT!!

DAD, YOU'RE A GENIUS!

THANK YOUR MOTHER. IT WAS HER IDEA.

!!

THANK YOU MOM! SO, HOW WAS TURKEY?

GREAT! IT WAS A LITTLE COLD, BUT IT WAS NICE.

I LOVED TURKEY.

I PUT MY POSTERS UP IN MY ROOM.

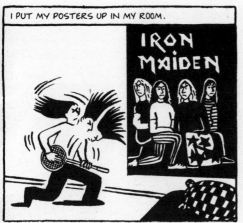

I PUT MY 1983 NIKES ON...

...AND MY DENIM JACKET WITH THE MICHAEL JACKSON BUTTON, AND OF COURSE, MY HEADSCARF.

SO WHAT DO YOU THINK?

NICE! VERY CUTE!

OK, I'M GOING OUT.

WHERE?

TO BUY SOME TAPES.

WHERE?

NOT FAR. ON GANDHI AVENUE.

BE BACK IN AN HOUR!

I'LL BE BACK IN TWO HOURS.

FOR AN IRANIAN MOTHER, MY MOM WAS VERY PERMISSIVE. I ONLY KNEW TWO OR THREE OTHER GIRLS WHO COULD GO OUT ALONE AT THIRTEEN.

FOR A YEAR NOW, THE FOOD SHORTAGE HAD BEEN RESOLVED BY THE GROWTH OF THE BLACK MARKET. HOWEVER, FINDING TAPES WAS A LITTLE MORE COMPLICATED. ON GANDHI AVENUE YOU COULD FIND THEM SOMETIMES.

ESTEVIE VONDER — ABBA, BEE GEES — YAZOO — JULIO IGLESIAS, — PINK FLOYD — JIKAEL MACKSON — VIDEOS, MUSIC, CARDS, LIPSTICK, NAIL POLISH, CHESS SET, PANTYHOSE, CHOCOLATE, ...,...

I BOUGHT TWO TAPES: KIM WILDE AND CAMEL.

HOW MUCH?

110 TUMANS.

♪ WE'RE THE KIDS IN AMERICA ♪ WHOA...

YOU! STOP!

THEY WERE GUARDIANS OF THE REVOLUTION, THE WOMEN'S BRANCH. THIS GROUP HAD BEEN ADDED IN 1982, TO ARREST WOMEN WHO WERE IMPROPERLY VEILED. (LIKE ME, FOR EXAMPLE.)

THEIR JOB WAS TO PUT US BACK ON THE STRAIGHT AND NARROW BY EXPLAINING THE DUTIES OF MUSLIM WOMEN.

WHY ARE YOU WEARING THOSE "PUNK" SHOES?

WHAT PUNK SHOES?

THOSE!

BUT THESE ARE SNEAKERS!

SHUT UP! THEY'RE PUNK.

IT WAS OBVIOUS THAT SHE HAD NO IDEA WHAT PUNK WAS.

THERE WAS NO ALTERNATIVE. I HAD TO LIE.

I WEAR THESE BECAUSE I PLAY BASKETBALL.

I'M ON MY SCHOOL'S TEAM.

OH SURE. I CAN TELL BY YOUR HEIGHT!

AND YOU WEAR THIS JACKET FOR BASKETBALL TOO??

WHAT DO I SEE HERE? MICHAEL JACKSON! THAT SYMBOL OF DECADENCE?

NO, IT'S MALCOLM X, THE LEADER OF BLACK MUSLIMS IN AMERICA.

DON'T GIVE ME THAT! IT'S MICHAEL JACKSON!

WHO? I DON'T KNOW HIM.

BACK THEN, MICHAEL JACKSON WAS STILL BLACK.

LOWER YOUR SCARF, YOU LITTLE WHORE!

AREN'T YOU ASHAMED TO WEAR TIGHT JEANS LIKE THESE??

THEY SHRANK!!

GO ON, GET IN THE CAR. WE'RE TAKING YOU DOWN TO THE COMMITTEE.

THE COMMITTEE WAS THE HQ OF THE GUARDIANS OF THE REVOLUTION.

AT THE COMMITTEE, THEY DIDN'T HAVE TO INFORM MY PARENTS. THEY COULD DETAIN ME FOR HOURS, OR FOR DAYS. I COULD BE WHIPPED. IN SHORT, ANYTHING COULD HAPPEN TO ME. IT WAS TIME FOR ACTION.

I'M SORRY MA'AM! I'LL NEVER DO IT AGAIN...

GET IN THE CAR!

MA'AM, MY MOTHER'S DEAD. MY STEPMOTHER IS REALLY CRUEL AND IF I DON'T GO HOME RIGHT AWAY, SHE'LL KILL ME...

SHE'LL BURN ME WITH THE CLOTHES IRON!

SHE'LL MAKE MY FATHER PUT ME IN AN ORPHANAGE

MAYBE SHE BELIEVED ME, MAYBE SHE JUST PRETENDED TO. BUT, MIRACULOUSLY, SHE LET ME GO.

BACK HOME...

MARJI! WHAT HAPPENED? HAVE YOU BEEN CRYING?

NO MOM. I'M JUST TIRED. I'M GOING TO MY ROOM.

THERE WAS NO WAY I COULD TELL THE TRUTH. SHE NEVER WOULD HAVE LET ME GO OUT ALONE AGAIN.

I GOT OFF PRETTY EASY, CONSIDERING. THE GUARDIANS OF THE REVOLUTION DIDN'T FIND MY TAPES.

♫ WE'RE THE KIDS IN AMERICA WHOAO ♫

TO EACH HIS OWN WAY OF CALMING DOWN.

THE SHABBAT

TO KEEP US FROM FORGETTING THAT WE WERE AT WAR, IRAQ OPTED FOR A NEW STRATEGY...

I HEARD THEY'RE GOING TO USE BALLISTIC MISSILES AGAINST US.

WHAT ARE YOU SAYING? WE'RE NOT AT WAR WITH THE SOVIET UNION. I DON'T BELIEVE THE IRAQIS HAVE WEAPONS LIKE THAT.

FROM THE IRAQI BORDER TO TEHRAN IT'S THOUSANDS OF MILES. MISSILES THAT CAN GO THAT FAR COST A FORTUNE!

WELL, THAT'S WHAT THE RUMORS SAY!

WE IRANIANS ARE OLYMPIC CHAMPIONS WHEN IT COMES TO GOSSIP.

SHE'S RIGHT. WE LOVE TO EXAGGERATE.

YOU SEEM TO HAVE THE OPPOSITE SYMPTOM.

WHY DO YOU SAY THAT?

EVEN WHEN YOU SEE SOMETHING WITH YOUR OWN EYES, YOU NEED CONFIRMATION FROM THE BBC.

MY NATURAL OPTIMISM JUST LEADS ME TO BE SKEPTICAL.

MOM'S PESSIMISM SOON WON OUT OVER DAD'S OPTIMISM. IT TURNED OUT THAT THE IRAQIS DID HAVE MISSILES. THEY WERE CALLED "SCUDS" AND TEHRAN BECAME THEIR TARGET.

NOW THAT TEHRAN WAS UNDER ATTACK, MANY FLED. THE CITY WAS DESERTED. AS FOR US, WE STAYED. NOT JUST OUT OF FATALISM. IF THERE WAS TO BE A FUTURE, IN MY PARENTS' EYES, THAT FUTURE WAS LINKED TO MY FRENCH EDUCATION. AND TEHRAN WAS THE ONLY PLACE I COULD GET IT.

SOME PEOPLE, MORE CIRCUMSPECT, TOOK SHELTER IN THE BASEMENTS OF BIG HOTELS, WELL-KNOWN FOR THEIR SAFETY. APPARENTLY, THEIR REINFORCED CONCRETE STRUCTURES WERE BOMBPROOF.

ONE EXAMPLE WAS OUR NEIGHBORS, THE BABA-LEVYS. THEY WERE AMONG THE FEW JEWISH FAMILIES THAT HAD STAYED AFTER THE REVOLUTION. MR. BABA-LEVY SAID THEIR ANCESTORS HAD COME THREE THOUSAND YEARS AGO, AND IRAN WAS THEIR HOME.

...THEIR DAUGHTER NEDA WAS A QUIET GIRL WHO DIDN'T PLAY MUCH, BUT WE WOULD TALK ABOUT ROMANCE FROM TIME TO TIME.

...ONE DAY A BLOND PRINCE WITH BLUE EYES WILL COME AND TAKE ME TO HIS CASTLE...

OH YEAH! ME TOO!

SO LIFE WENT ON...

...ON ONE DAY, LIKE ANY OTHER:

MOM, CAN I HAVE SOME MONEY? I WANT TO GET SOME JEANS AND ESPADRILLES.

HOW MUCH?

OH, 1000, 1200 TUMANS.

1000 TUMANS?

YEP, THAT'S HOW MUCH THEY COST.

I SEE.

OUR CURRENCY HAD LOST ALL ITS VALUE. IT WAS SEVEN TUMANS TO THE DOLLAR WHEN THE SHAH WAS STILL AROUND. FOUR YEARS LATER IT WAS 110 TUMANS TO THE DOLLAR. FOR MY MOTHER, THE CHANGE WAS SO SUDDEN THAT SHE HAD A HARD TIME ACCEPTING IT.

I WENT WITH MY FRIEND SHADI.

SO, HOW DO THEY LOOK?

THEY LOOK SUPER!

OK, I'LL TAKE THE JEANS, AND THESE EARRINGS.

AND I'LL TAKE THAT RING, THERE!

WE WERE IN THE MIDST OF SHOPPING EUPHORIA, WHEN SUDDENLY...

BOOM!!!

A MISSILE HAS JUST EXPLODED IN THE TAVANIR NEIGHBORHOOD.

WHAT!

TAVANIR WAS WHERE I LIVED.

THE JEANS!

IF SOMEONE HAD TIMED ME, I THINK I WOULD HAVE BEAT THE WORLD SPEED RECORD.

TAXI!

FASTER! PLEASE HURRY...

A CROWD HAD GATHERED IN FRONT OF MY STREET! THE BOMB HAD HIT MY STREET!

MA'AM, WHICH BUILDING WAS HIT?

APPARENTLY, IT EXPLODED AT THE END OF THE STREET.

MY BUILDING AND THE BABA-LEVY'S WERE AT THE END OF THE STREET.

LET ME THROUGH.

ONE CHANCE IN TWO THAT IT WAS OUR BUILDING.

PLEASE, LET ME THROUGH.

YOU CAN'T GO BEYOND THIS POINT!

...I LIVE HERE...

AND HE LET ME THROUGH.

I DIDN'T WANT TO LOOK UP. I LOOKED AT MY TREMBLING LEGS. I COULDN'T GO FORWARD, LIKE IN A NIGHTMARE.

LET THEM BE ALIVE. LET THEM BE ALIVE. LET THEM...

MARJI

MARJI!

MOM!

YOU'RE ALL RIGHT? DAD'S ALL RIGHT? GRANDMA'S ALL RIGHT?

EVERYONE'S OK. I WAS THE ONLY ONE HOME.

OH, MOM.

...

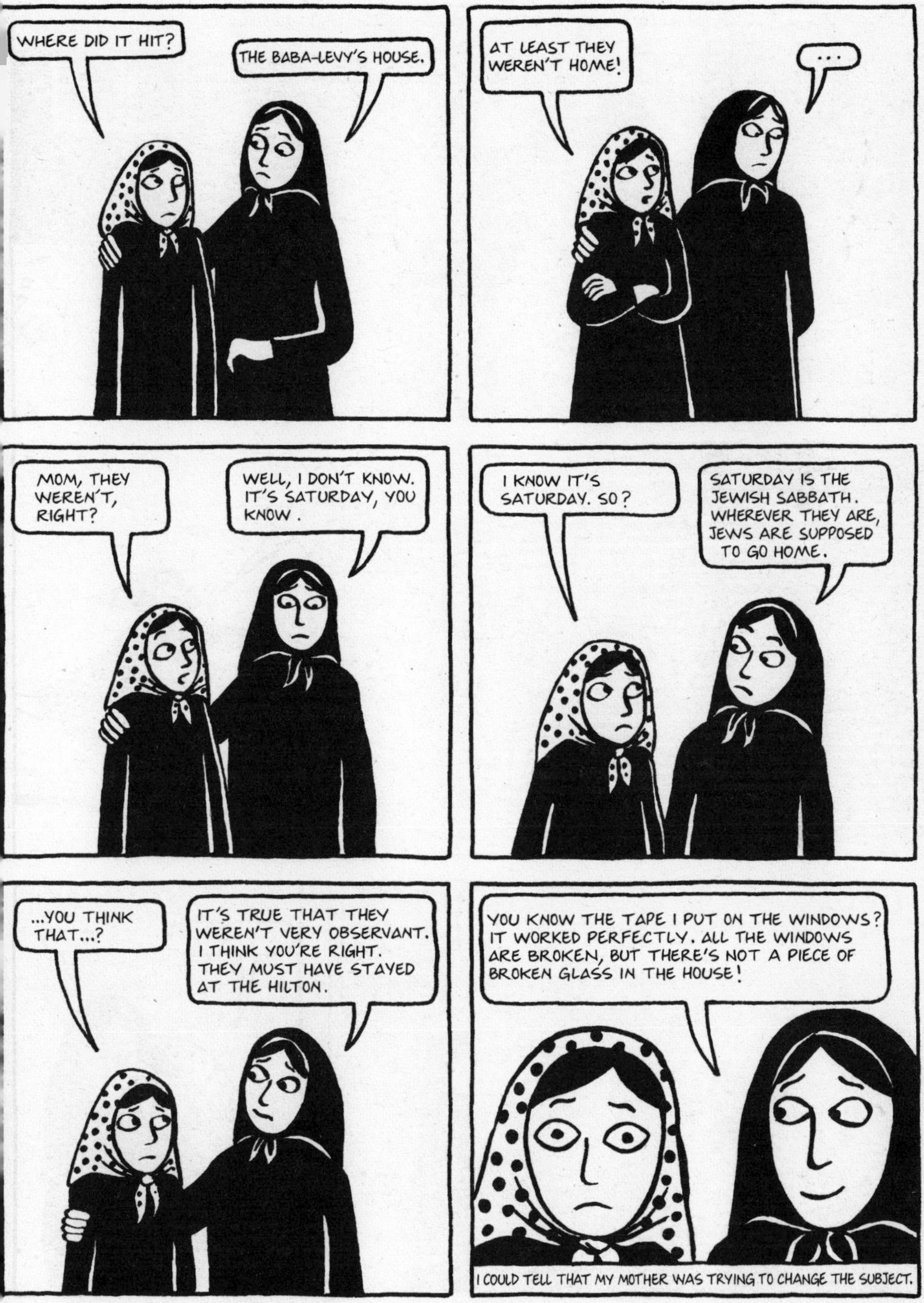
WHERE DID IT HIT?
THE BABA-LEVY'S HOUSE.
AT LEAST THEY WEREN'T HOME!
...
MOM, THEY WEREN'T, RIGHT?
WELL, I DON'T KNOW. IT'S SATURDAY, YOU KNOW.
I KNOW IT'S SATURDAY. SO?
SATURDAY IS THE JEWISH SABBATH. WHEREVER THEY ARE, JEWS ARE SUPPOSED TO GO HOME.
...YOU THINK THAT...?
IT'S TRUE THAT THEY WEREN'T VERY OBSERVANT. I THINK YOU'RE RIGHT. THEY MUST HAVE STAYED AT THE HILTON.
YOU KNOW THE TAPE I PUT ON THE WINDOWS? IT WORKED PERFECTLY. ALL THE WINDOWS ARE BROKEN, BUT THERE'S NOT A PIECE OF BROKEN GLASS IN THE HOUSE!
I COULD TELL THAT MY MOTHER WAS TRYING TO CHANGE THE SUBJECT.

WHEN WE WALKED PAST THE BABA-LEVY'S HOUSE, WHICH WAS COMPLETELY DESTROYED, I COULD FEEL THAT SHE WAS DISCREETLY PULLING ME AWAY. SOMETHING TOLD ME THAT THE BABA-LEVYS HAD BEEN AT HOME. SOMETHING CAUGHT MY ATTENTION.

I SAW A TURQUOISE BRACELET. IT WAS NEDA'S. HER AUNT HAD GIVEN IT TO HER FOR HER FOURTEENTH BIRTHDAY...

THE BRACELET WAS STILL ATTACHED TO... I DON'T KNOW WHAT...

NO SCREAM IN THE WORLD COULD HAVE RELIEVED MY SUFFERING AND MY ANGER.

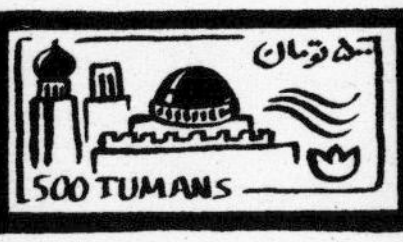
500 TUMANS

THE DOWRY

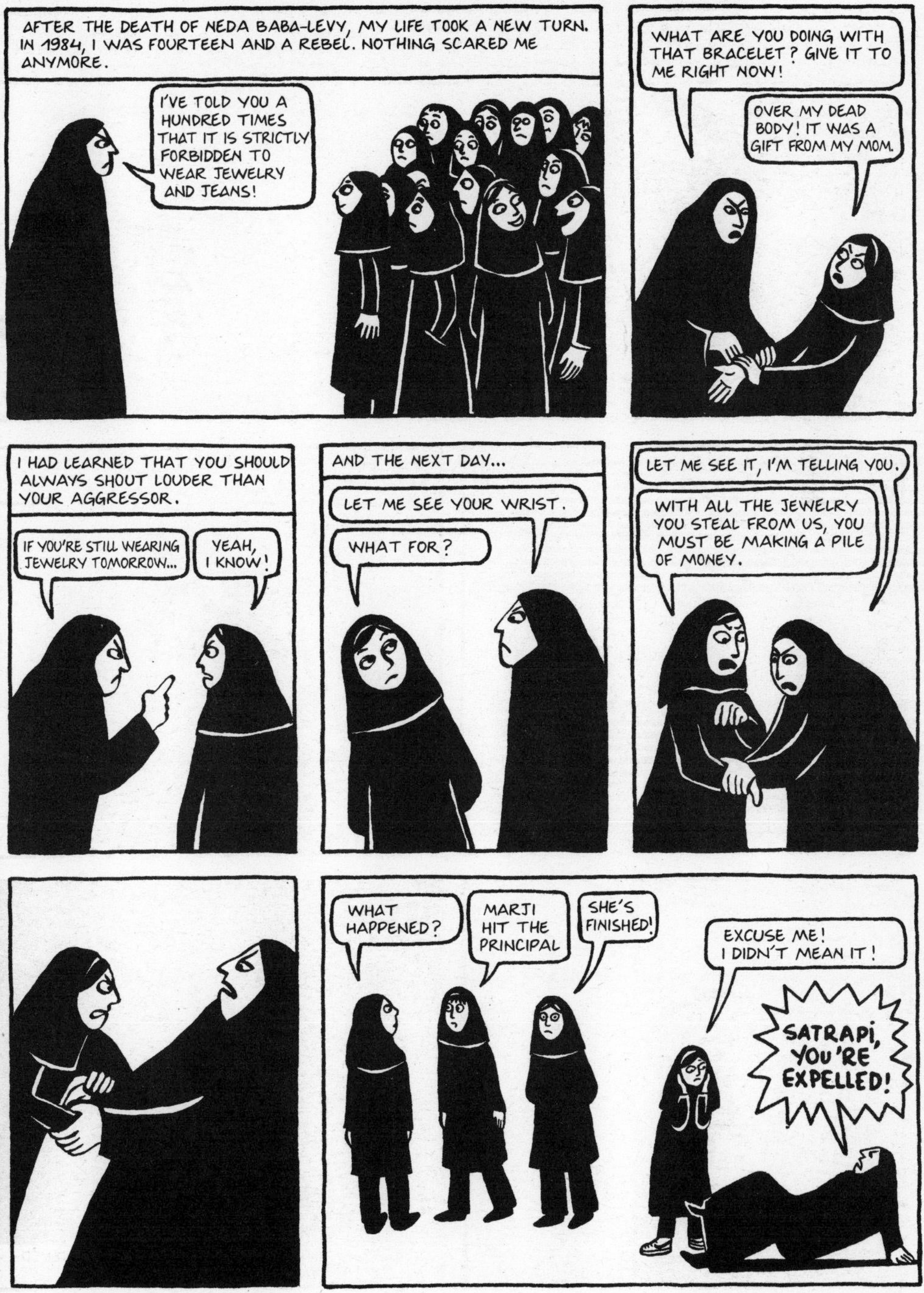
AFTER THE DEATH OF NEDA BABA-LEVY, MY LIFE TOOK A NEW TURN. IN 1984, I WAS FOURTEEN AND A REBEL. NOTHING SCARED ME ANYMORE.
I'VE TOLD YOU A HUNDRED TIMES THAT IT IS STRICTLY FORBIDDEN TO WEAR JEWELRY AND JEANS!
WHAT ARE YOU DOING WITH THAT BRACELET? GIVE IT TO ME RIGHT NOW!
OVER MY DEAD BODY! IT WAS A GIFT FROM MY MOM.
I HAD LEARNED THAT YOU SHOULD ALWAYS SHOUT LOUDER THAN YOUR AGGRESSOR.
IF YOU'RE STILL WEARING JEWELRY TOMORROW...
YEAH, I KNOW!
AND THE NEXT DAY...
LET ME SEE YOUR WRIST.
WHAT FOR?
LET ME SEE IT, I'M TELLING YOU.
WITH ALL THE JEWELRY YOU STEAL FROM US, YOU MUST BE MAKING A PILE OF MONEY.
WHAT HAPPENED?
MARJI HIT THE PRINCIPAL
SHE'S FINISHED!
EXCUSE ME! I DIDN'T MEAN IT!
SATRAPI, YOU'RE EXPELLED!

AFTER I WAS EXPELLED, IT WAS A REAL STRUGGLE TO FIND ANOTHER SCHOOL THAT WOULD ACCEPT ME. HITTING THE PRINCIPAL WAS A VERITABLE CRIME. BUT THANKS TO MY AUNT, WHO KNEW SOME BUREAUCRATS IN THE EDUCATION SYSTEM, THEY MANAGED TO PLACE ME IN ANOTHER SCHOOL. AND THERE...

SINCE THE ISLAMIC REPUBLIC WAS FOUNDED, WE NO LONGER HAVE POLITICAL PRISONERS.

MA'AM!

MY UNCLE WAS IMPRISONED BY THE SHAH'S REGIME, BUT IT WAS THE ISLAMIC REGIME THAT ORDERED HIS EXECUTION.

YOU SAY THAT WE DON'T HAVE POLITICAL PRISONERS ANYMORE. BUT WE'VE GONE FROM 3000 PRISONERS UNDER THE SHAH TO 300,000 UNDER YOUR REGIME.

HOW DARE YOU LIE TO US LIKE THAT?

OH, SATRAPI!

CLAP!
CLAP!
CLAP!
CLAP!
CLAP!
CLAP!
CLAP!
CLAP!
CLAP!

OBVIOUSLY, THAT EVENING MY FATHER GOT A PHONE CALL.

YES. OF COURSE...YES...

WHO IS IT?

IT WAS THE PRINCIPAL OF MARJI'S SCHOOL. APPARENTLY SHE TOLD OFF THE RELIGION TEACHER. SHE GETS THAT FROM HER UNCLE.

MAYBE YOU'D LIKE HER TO END UP LIKE HIM TOO? EXECUTED?

YOU KNOW WHAT THEY DO TO THE YOUNG GIRLS THEY ARREST?

YOU KNOW WHAT HAPPENED TO NILOUFAR? THE GIRL YOU MET AT KHOSRO'S HOUSE? THE MAN WHO MADE PASSPORTS?

YOU KNOW THAT IT'S AGAINST THE LAW TO KILL A VIRGIN...

SO A GUARDIAN OF THE REVOLUTION MARRIES HER...

...AND TAKES HER VIRGINITY BEFORE EXECUTING HER. DO YOU UNDERSTAND WHAT THAT MEANS???

IF SOMEONE SO MUCH AS TOUCHES A HAIR ON YOUR HEAD, I'LL KILL HIM!

BUT HOW DO YOU KNOW THAT FOR SURE? MAYBE THEY JUST EXECUTED HER!

NO. YOUR MOTHER'S RIGHT. TRADITIONALLY, WHEN A GIRL GETS MARRIED, THE HUSBAND IS SUPPOSED TO PAY HER A DOWRY.

IF THE GIRL DIES, THE HUSBAND HAS TO GIVE THE DOWRY TO HER FAMILY.

THAT'S WHAT HAPPENED WITH NILOUFAR. AFTER SHE WAS EXECUTED, TO MAKE SURE HER AWFUL FATE WAS UNDERSTOOD, THEY SENT 500 TUMANS* TO HER PARENTS.

500 TUMANS FOR THE LIFE AND VIRGINITY OF AN INNOCENT GIRL.

*EQUIVALENT TO $5.00

I HAD NO IDEA.

ALL NIGHT LONG, I THOUGHT OF THAT PHRASE: "TO DIE A MARTYR IS TO INJECT BLOOD INTO THE VEINS OF SOCIETY." NILOUFAR WAS A REAL MARTYR, AND HER BLOOD CERTAINLY DID NOT FEED OUR SOCIETY'S VEINS.

ONE WEEK LATER...

MARJI, CAN YOU COME HERE FOR A FEW MINUTES? WE WANT TO TALK TO YOU.

I WENT TO SEE THE PRINCIPAL TODAY. SHE ASSURED ME THAT SHE HAD NOT SENT A REPORT THIS TIME. BUT CONSIDERING THE PERSON YOU ARE AND THE EDUCATION YOU'VE RECEIVED, WE THOUGHT THAT IT WOULD BE BETTER IF YOU LEFT IRAN.

WHAT?

YOUR MOTHER AND I HAVE DECIDED TO SEND YOU TO AUSTRIA.

WHY AUSTRIA?

FIRST OF ALL, BECAUSE IT'S EASIER TO GET AN AUSTRIAN VISA, AND SECOND BECAUSE MY BEST FRIEND LIVES IN VIENNA. DO YOU REMEMBER HER? ZOZO? SHERINE'S MOM?

YEAH, YEAH. BUT I DON'T SPEAK GERMAN!

THERE'S A FRENCH SCHOOL IN VIENNA. ONE OF THE BEST IN EUROPE!

AND WHAT ARE YOU GOING TO DO THERE?

YOU'RE GOING ON AHEAD OF US. WE HAVE SOME BUSINESS TO TAKE CARE OF. WE'LL JOIN YOU A FEW MONTHS FROM NOW!

BUT I'M ONLY FOURTEEN! YOU TRUST ME?

YOU'RE FOURTEEN AND I KNOW HOW I BROUGHT YOU UP. ABOVE ALL, I TRUST YOUR EDUCATION.

YOU'RE THE SAME PERSON WHO WENT ON VACATION TO FRANCE ALL BY YOURSELF, REMEMBER?

BEFORE THE REVOLUTION, MY PARENTS SENT ME TO SUMMER CAMP IN FRANCE. MY MOTHER DIDN'T WANT ME TO GROW UP LIKE AN ONLY CHILD.

IT'S TRUE, THAT WAS GREAT...REAL INDEPENDENCE.

WE LOVE YOU SO MUCH THAT WE WANT YOU TO GO.

WE FEEL IT'S BETTER FOR YOU TO BE FAR AWAY AND HAPPY THAN CLOSE BY AND MISERABLE. JUDGING BY THE SITUATION HERE, YOU'LL BE BETTER OFF SOMEWHERE ELSE.

AT THAT POINT, I STARTED TO HAVE MY DOUBTS. WHY SAY THOSE THINGS IF THEY WERE COMING TOO?

WE ADORE YOU!

DON'T EVER FORGET WHO YOU ARE!

NO. I WON'T EVER FORGET.

148

I REPEATED WHAT THEY HAD TOLD ME OVER AND OVER IN MY HEAD. I WAS PRETTY SURE THEY WEREN'T COMING TO VIENNA.

I STAYED UP ALL NIGHT AND WONDERED IF THE MOON SHONE AS BRIGHTLY IN VIENNA.

THE NEXT DAY I FILLED A JAR WITH SOIL FROM OUR GARDEN. IRANIAN SOIL.

I TOOK DOWN ALL OF MY POSTERS.

I INVITED MY GIRLFRIENDS OVER TO SAY GOODBYE.

HERE. I'M GIVING YOU MY MOST PRECIOUS THINGS, SO THAT YOU WON'T FORGET ME.

I NEVER REALIZED HOW MUCH THEY LOVED ME.

AND I UNDERSTOOD HOW IMPORTANT THEY WERE TO ME.

ON THE EVE OF MY DEPARTURE, MY GRANDMOTHER CAME TO SPEND THE NIGHT AT OUR HOUSE.

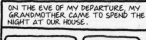

CAN I SLEEP WITH YOU?

THAT'S WHY I'M HERE!

I WATCHED MY GRANDMA UNDRESS. EACH MORNING, SHE PICKED JASMINE FLOWERS TO PUT IN HER BRA SO THAT SHE WOULD SMELL NICE. WHEN SHE UNDRESSED, YOU COULD SEE THE FLOWERS FALL FROM HER BREASTS.

IT WAS SOMETHING TO SEE

GRANDMA, HOW DO YOU HAVE SUCH ROUND BREASTS AT YOUR AGE?

EVERY MORNING AND NIGHT, I SOAK THEM IN A BOWL OF ICE WATER FOR TEN MINUTES.

SHE ACTUALLY DID, AND I KNEW IT. I JUST WANTED TO HEAR HER SAY IT.

I'LL MISS YOU.

OH, I'LL COME SEE YOU.

SHE TOO WAS LYING TO ME.

LISTEN, I DON'T WANT TO PREACH, BUT LET ME GIVE YOU SOME ADVICE THAT WILL ALWAYS HELP YOU.

IN LIFE YOU'LL MEET A LOT OF JERKS. IF THEY HURT YOU, TELL YOURSELF THAT IT'S BECAUSE THEY'RE STUPID. THAT WILL HELP KEEP YOU FROM REACTING TO THEIR CRUELTY. BECAUSE THERE IS NOTHING WORSE THAN BITTERNESS AND VENGEANCE... ALWAYS KEEP YOUR DIGNITY AND BE TRUE TO YOURSELF.

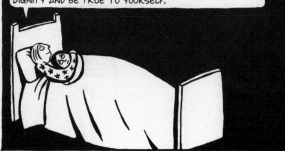

I SMELLED MY GRANDMA'S BOSOM. IT SMELLED GOOD. I'LL NEVER FORGET THAT SMELL.

AND THE NEXT MORNING.

WAKE UP! IT'S SEVEN O'CLOCK. WE'VE GOT TO GO.

?

I WILL ALWAYS BE TRUE TO MYSELF.

I'M NOT COMING ALONG.

DON'T EVER FORGET WHAT I TOLD YOU.

GRANDMA

HERE WE ARE!

THERE WAS A HUGE LINE. LOTS OF PEOPLE WERE LEAVING THE COUNTRY.

ESPECIALLY YOUNG BOYS. CONSIDERED FUTURE SOLDIERS, THEY WERE FORBIDDEN TO LEAVE THE COUNTRY AFTER THEY TURNED THIRTEEN.

MEHRABAD AIRPORT

YOU'LL SEE. EVERYTHING WILL BE OK.

DON'T CRY. THINK OF YOUR FUTURE.

EUROPE AWAITS YOU.

AS SOON AS YOU GET TO VIENNA, GO AND EAT A SACHERTORTE. IT'S THE MOST DELICIOUS CHOCOLATE CAKE.

AND IN SIX MONTHS, WE'LL COME SEE YOU.

WHAT I HAD FEARED WAS TRUE. MAYBE THEY'D COME TO VISIT, BUT WE'D NEVER LIVE TOGETHER AGAIN.

NO TEARS. YOU'RE A BIG GIRL.

YOU'VE GOT TO GO NOW. DON'T FORGET WHO YOU ARE AND WHERE YOU COME FROM.

I LOVE YOU!

152

I COULDN'T BEAR LOOKING AT THEM THERE BEHIND THE GLASS. NOTHING'S WORSE THAN SAYING GOODBYE. IT'S A LITTLE LIKE DYING.

GO ON, GO ON.

CLOSE YOUR SUITCASE, YOU CAN GO.

I COULDN'T JUST GO.

I TURNED AROUND TO SEE THEM ONE LAST TIME.

IT WOULD HAVE BEEN BETTER TO JUST GO.

CREDITS

Translation of first part: Mattias Ripa
Translation of second part: Blake Ferris
Supervision of translation: Marjane Satrapi and Carol Bernstein
Lettering: Eve Deluze
Additional hand lettering: Céline Merrien

THANKS TO

L'Association
David B.
Jean-Christophe Menu
Emile Bravo
Christophe Blain
Guillaume Dumora
Fanny Dalle-Rive
Nicolas Leroy
Matthieu Wahiche
Charlotte Miquel

PERSEPOLIS 2

The Story of a Return

THE SOUP

NOVEMBER 1984. I AM IN AUSTRIA. I HAD COME HERE WITH THE IDEA OF LEAVING A RELIGIOUS IRAN FOR AN OPEN AND SECULAR EUROPE AND THAT ZOZO, MY MOTHER'S BEST FRIEND, WOULD LOVE ME LIKE HER OWN DAUGHTER.

ONLY HERE I AM! SHE LEFT ME AT A BOARDING HOUSE RUN BY NUNS.

MY ROOM WAS SMALL, AND FOR THE FIRST TIME IN MY LIFE I HAD TO SHARE MY SPACE WITH ANOTHER PERSON.

I HADN'T MET HER YET. I ONLY KNEW THAT HER NAME WAS LUCIA.

I WONDERED WHAT SHE WOULD LOOK LIKE.

EUROPE, THE ALPS, SWITZERLAND, AUSTRIA... FROM THIS I DEDUCED THAT SHE WOULD BE LIKE HEIDI.

THIS WAS OKAY WITH ME. I REALLY LIKED HEIDI.

I HAD BEEN IN VIENNA ELEVEN DAYS. ZOZO AND HER DAUGHTER SHIRIN, WHOM I HAD KNOWN DURING MY CHILDHOOD, HAD COME TO GET ME AT THE AIRPORT.

SHIRIN WAS AS I REMEMBERED HER. HOWEVER, I DETECTED SOMETHING UNKIND IN THE LOOK HER MOTHER GAVE ME.

YOU HAVEN'T CHANGED MUCH. WELL, YES! NOW YOU HAVE LONG HAIR!!

YOU HAVEN'T EITHER. YOU'RE THE SAME.

IT'S GOING TO BE COOL TO GO TO SCHOOL WITHOUT A VEIL, TO NOT HAVE TO BEAT ONESELF EVERY DAY FOR THE WAR MARTYRS...

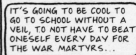

HAVE YOU SEEN THESE? THEY'RE REALLY FASHIONABLE. THEY'RE TO PROTECT YOUR EARS FROM THE COLD. DO YOU WANT TO TRY THEM ON?

NO THANKS!

THIS IS MY RASPBERRY-SCENTED PEN, BUT I HAVE STRAWBERRY AND BLACKBERRY ONES, TOO.

DO YOU WANT TO PUT ON SOME LIPSTICK? I LOVE PEARLY PINK. IT'S VERY IN!!!

HMPHH...

WHAT A TRAITOR! WHILE PEOPLE WERE DYING IN OUR COUNTRY, SHE WAS TALKING TO ME ABOUT TRIVIAL THINGS.

...I LIVED WITH THEM FOR TEN DAYS. THERE WERE FIGHTS DAILY.

HI SWEETHEART! HERE, THESE ARE FOR YOU!

YOU INCOMPETENT IDIOT! I WORK MYSELF TO THE BONE SO THAT YOU CAN THROW MONEY AWAY ON FLOWERS!

BUT ZOZO, IT'S OUR WEDDING ANNIVERSARY.

YOU CAN GIVE ME WHATEVER YOU WANT THE DAY YOU'VE EARNED SOME MONEY. I'VE HAD ENOUGH!!

IN TEHRAN, ZOZO WAS HER HUSBAND HOUSHANG'S SECRETARY,

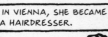
IN VIENNA, SHE BECAME A HAIRDRESSER.

IT WAS SHE, BY THE WAY, WHO CUT OFF MY LONG HAIR.

AS FOR HOUSHANG, ZOZO'S HUSBAND, HE WAS A CEO IN IRAN,

BUT IN AUSTRIA, HE WAS NOTHING.

THANKS TO A DOZEN BAD INVESTMENTS, HOUSHANG HAD LOST ALL HIS CAPITAL. "YOU GAMBLED IT AWAY!" I HEARD THAT IN THE COURSE OF ONE OF THEIR HABITUAL QUARRELS.

I SAW YOU AT THE CAFÉ WITH THOSE TWO BASTARDS! THEY'D HAVE TO STEAL THE CLOTHES OFF YOUR BACK FOR YOU TO RECOGNIZE THEIR INGRATITUDE!

I WAS ASHAMED. I'D NEVER HEARD MY PARENTS BICKER OVER MONEY.

PROBABLY BECAUSE MY FATHER WASN'T INCOMPETENT ...

AND AFTER THESE TEN DAYS...

MARJANE, I SPOKE TO YOUR MOTHER.

OUR APARTMENT, AS YOU'VE NO DOUBT NOTICED, IS TOO SMALL. I FOUND YOU A BOARDING HOUSE IN A BEAUTIFUL PART OF VIENNA, NEAR RATHAUS.

IT'S RUN BY NUNS. THE MOTHER SUPERIOR AND SEVERAL OF THE SISTERS SPEAK FLUENT FRENCH.

WHEN DO WE GO?

RIGHT AWAY. GO PACK YOUR BAG.

NUNS. I WAS ACQUAINTED WITH THEM. I WAS AT THE ÉCOLE JEANNE D'ARC* IN TEHRAN. THE NUNS I ENCOUNTERED THERE WERE FEROCIOUS.

YOU'LL COME SEE US ON WEEKENDS. WE'LL GO ICE-SKATING.

YEAH, YEAH...

DESPITE EVERYTHING, I WAS HAPPY TO LEAVE THEIR HOUSE. IN THIS WAY, I'D BE RID OF ZOZO THE MEAN AND SHIRIN THE INANE.

* JOAN OF ARC SCHOOL

THE ONLY ONE I WAS GOING TO MISS WAS HOUSHANG. I SAW IN HIM A PROTECTOR.

TAKE CARE OF YOURSELF.

YES, UNCLE HOUSHANG.

HE SAW IN ME AN ALLY.

OKAY! THAT'S ENOUGH. LET'S GO!

AND WE LEFT...

HERE'S YOUR NEW HOME.

IT'S IMPERATIVE THAT YOU BE BACK BY 9:30. AFTER THAT THE DOOR WILL BE LOCKED.

HERE, MADEMOISELLE. THIS IS YOUR ROOM. YOU'LL SHARE IT WITH LUCIA. SHE'S ARRIVING THIS AFTERNOON.

YOU'LL SEE, YOU'LL BE HAPPY WITH US. WHICH DENOMINATION ARE YOU?

NONE.

OH!

THE SHARED KITCHEN,

THE SHOWERS,

FOR YOUR SHOPPING, YOU CAN GO TO "ALDI." GO OUT AND TURN LEFT, LINKS!*

LINKS!

NOW I HAD A REAL INDEPENDENT ADULT LIFE. I WAS GOING TO FEED MYSELF, DO MY OWN LAUNDRY...

I HEADED STRAIGHT FOR THE SUPERMARKET TO BUY GROCERIES LIKE A WOMAN.

*ALDI IS A SUPERMARKET AND LINKS MEANS LEFT IN GERMAN.

IT HAD BEEN FOUR YEARS SINCE I'D SEEN SUCH A WELL-STOCKED STORE.

THE FIRST AISLE I HEADED FOR WAS THE ONE WITH SCENTED DETERGENTS.

WE COULDN'T FIND THEM IN IRAN ANYMORE.

I FILLED THE CART WITH ALL KINDS OF PRODUCTS.

EVEN TODAY, AFTER ALL THIS TIME, YOU CAN ALWAYS FIND AT LEAST A DOZEN BOXES OF GOOD-SMELLING LAUNDRY POWDER IN MY HOUSE.

GIVEN MY RESTRICTED BUDGET, I TOOK TWO BOXES OF PASTA.

I DIDN'T KNOW YET THAT THIS WOULD BE MY ONLY FOOD DURING THE FOUR YEARS TO COME.

I HANDED OVER A 100 SHILLING BILL. LUCKILY, IT WAS ENOUGH, OTHERWISE I WOULD HAVE BEEN ASHAMED.

ACHT UND NEUNZIG DREIZIG BITTE!

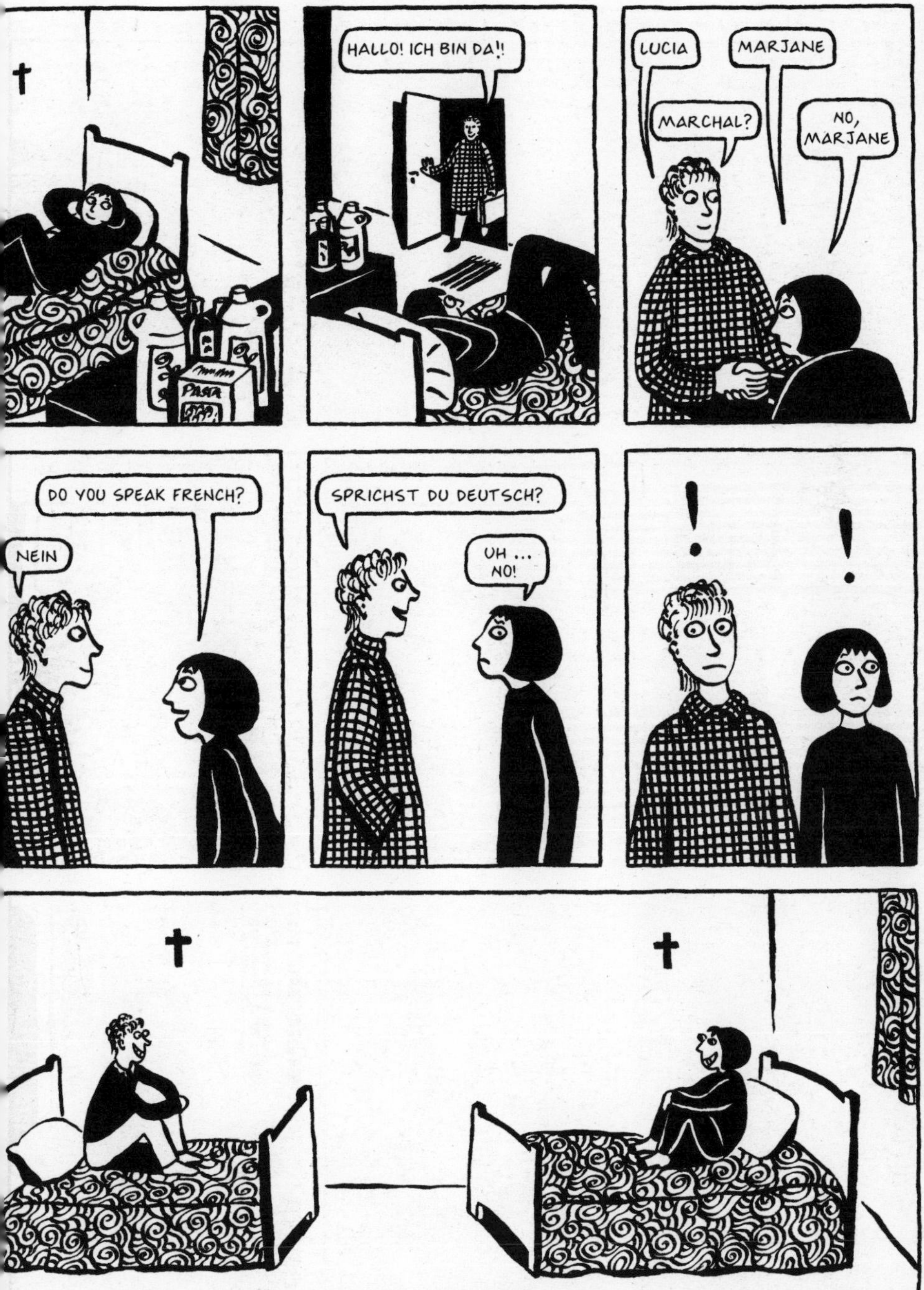
HALLO! ICH BIN DA!!
LUCIA
MARJANE
MARCHAL?
NO, MARJANE
DO YOU SPEAK FRENCH?
NEIN
SPRICHST DU DEUTSCH?
UH ... NO!
!
!

I OFFERED HER SOME OF THE PISTACHIOS I'D BROUGHT WITH ME, A PRESENT FROM MY UNCLE. THEY ARE A SPECIALTY OF IRAN THAT IS OFTEN GIVEN WHEN SOMEONE IS GOING ABROAD. WE CONSIDER OUR PISTACHIOS TO BE THE WORLD'S BEST. . .

MMM...

... AS WE CONSIDER MANY OF OUR THINGS TO BE.

LUCIA MADE ME A KNORR SOUP, "CREAM OF MUSHROOM."

mmm...

I DIDN'T LIKE IT MUCH.

MAGST DU FERNSEHEN?

FERNSEHEN?

FENS, FUNS, FENR, .. FENÊTRE*!!!

* WINDOW IN FRENCH.

FERNSEHEN?

NEIN! HI HI HI ... DAS IST FENSTER!

WARTE MAL!

DAS IST EIN FERNSEHEN.

AH! TV! IT'S THE SAME THING.

TV!

FERNSEHEN! YA! YA! FERNSEHEN!

I WAS HAPPY. I WAS SPEAKING GERMAN.

SO WE WENT TO THE TV ROOM, WHICH WAS ON THE GROUND FLOOR.

HALLO!

EVERYONE WAS WATCHING A MOVIE. THEY SEEMED TO BE ENJOYING THEMSELVES. EXCEPT ME! I WAS HEARING "ACHS" AND "OCHS," "ICHS" AND "MICHS," BUT NOTHING THAT I COULD UNDERSTAND.

HA!

HA! HA! HA! HA! HA!

!!!

Hi! Hi! Hi!

?!

I DECIDED TO LEAVE DISCREETLY.

BYE BYE LUCIA.

SHE DIDN'T EVEN ANSWER ME.

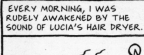
TYROL

EVERY MORNING, I WAS RUDELY AWAKENED BY THE SOUND OF LUCIA'S HAIR DRYER.

IT WAS MY VERY OWN ALARM CLOCK. SET FOR 6:30 ON THE DOT.

MORNING!

YEAH, RIGHT.

HALLO!

WOKEN BY A HAIR DRYER TO THEN RETURN TO A SCHOOL WHERE I HAD NO FRIENDS.

HI!

HI!

HI!

HI!

HI!

BUT IT WAS TO BE EXPECTED. I WAS ARRIVING IN THE MIDDLE OF THE TRIMESTER AND CLIQUES HAD ALREADY FORMED.

AND THEN THERE WAS THE FIRST MATH TEST. I DISTINGUISHED MYSELF BY MY HIGH LEVEL.

SATRAPI! BRAVO! EXCELLENT WORK. JUST ONE MISTAKE COST YOU HALF A POINT. YOU GOT A 19.5 OUT OF 20.

OH SHIT!

THIS GRADE WON ME A CERTAIN AMOUNT OF ATTENTION. I WAS VERY POPULAR WHEN IT CAME TO MATH HOMEWORK.

THEN I BEGAN TO DRAW CARICATURES OF THE TEACHERS. I HAD GOTTEN INTO THIS HABIT WITH MY TEACHERS IN IRAN.

THE DIFFERENCE BEING THAT THEY WERE ALL VEILED, THEREFORE MUCH EASIER TO DRAW.

THESE PORTRAITS ALSO BROUGHT ME SOME GOODWILL.

BESIDES, MY MISTAKES IN FRENCH MADE ME SOMEONE OF INTEREST. IT HAD BEEN THREE YEARS SINCE I'D PRACTICED MY FRENCH, AFTER THE CLOSING OF THE BILINGUAL SCHOOLS BY THE ISLAMIC GOVERNMENT.

WHAT DO YOU CALL THAT THING, YOU KNOW, LIKE A RULER?*

WHAT THING?

OH, THAT THING! YOU KNOW, A DICK!

OH, RIGHT! WE CALL IT A DICK.

A DICK?

CAN YOU LEND ME YOUR DICK?

?!!

HA! HA! HA! HA!

WELL, AT LEAST I EXISTED.

* I MEANT A TRIANGLE.

THINGS EVOLVED. AFTER SOME TIME, JULIE, THE SULLEN GIRL IN THE SECOND ROW, TOOK AN INTEREST IN ME. SHE WAS AN EIGHTEEN-YEAR-OLD FRENCH GIRL, IN A CLASS WHERE THE AVERAGE AGE WAS FOURTEEN.

I UNDERSTOOD LATER THAT HER RESERVE CAME FROM THE FACT THAT SHE CONSIDERED THE OTHERS TO BE SPOILED CHILDREN. BUT I WAS DIFFERENT. I HAD KNOWN WAR.

SHE INTRODUCED ME TO MOMO. HE WAS TWO YEARS OLDER.

THIS IS MARJANE. SHE'S IRANIAN. SHE'S KNOWN WAR.

WAR?

DELIGHTED!

YOU'VE ALREADY SEEN LOTS OF DEAD PEOPLE?

UM... A FEW.

COOL!

MOMO GREETED PEOPLE IN HIS OWN WAY.

MMM...

...MMM

SO IT WAS HE WHO KISSED ME ON THE MOUTH FOR THE FIRST TIME.

...THROUGH MOMO, I GOT TO KNOW THIERRY AND OLIVIER, TWO SWISS ORPHANS WHO WERE LIVING IN AUSTRIA WITH THEIR UNCLE, A DIPLOMAT.

I'M ALSO A BIT OF AN ORPHAN.

YOUR PARENTS ARE DEAD?

NO, THEY'RE IN IRAN.

THE FACT THAT I WAS LIVING WITHOUT MY PARENTS ALSO SUITED JULIE.

AN ECCENTRIC, A PUNK, TWO ORPHANS AND A THIRD-WORLDER, WE MADE QUITE A GROUP OF FRIENDS. THEY WERE REALLY INTERESTED IN MY STORY. ESPECIALLY MOMO! HE WAS FASCINATED BY DEATH.

CHRISTMAS VACATION WAS APPROACHING. EVERYONE WAS TALKING ABOUT THEIR PLANS.

I'M GOING TO BE BORED OUT OF MY MIND WITH MY PARENTS IN NICE.

FIJI

BORA BORA

CHICAGO

CHRISTMAS IS AN AMERICAN INVENTION. A SANTA CLAUS DECKED OUT IN RED AND WHITE WAS COCA-COLA'S MASCOT.

IT'S GOOD FOR BUSINESS.

BARCELONA

HONDURAS

I'M GOING BACK TO FRANCE TO SEE MY FATHER.

I'M GOING TO MY GRAND-MOTHER'S IN SALZBURG. SHE'S THE ONLY ONE IN MY FAMILY WHO'S STILL BEARABLE.

WE'RE GOING TO BE BORED CRAZY IN THE ALPS.

YEAH, WE'RE GOING SKIING. IT'LL BE COOL!

YOU KNOW, IN IRAN WE DON'T CELEBRATE CHRISTMAS . . .

YOU'RE GOING SKIING? THAT'S SO GREAT!

IT'S NO BIG DEAL.

our new year is march 21, the . . .

YES.

I'LL BE IN ANNECY. WE'LL BE NEIGHBORS. WE COULD MAYBE SEE EACH OTHER.

FRIDAY, DECEMBER 22, 1984. THE STREETS WERE PACKED. THE HOLIDAY FRENZY HAD INFECTED EVERYONE. I THOUGHT OF THIERRY WHEN HE TALKED ABOUT IT BEING "GOOD FOR BUSINESS."

MY STREET, THOUGH, WAS DESERTED. THERE WEREN'T ANY STORES.

WHAT AM I GOING TO DO ALL ALONE FOR TWO WEEKS? EVEN THE BOARDING HOUSE WILL BE EMPTY.

WHEN I GOT BACK, I FOUND LUCIA. STILL FAITHFUL TO HER POST.

ARE YOU OKAY?

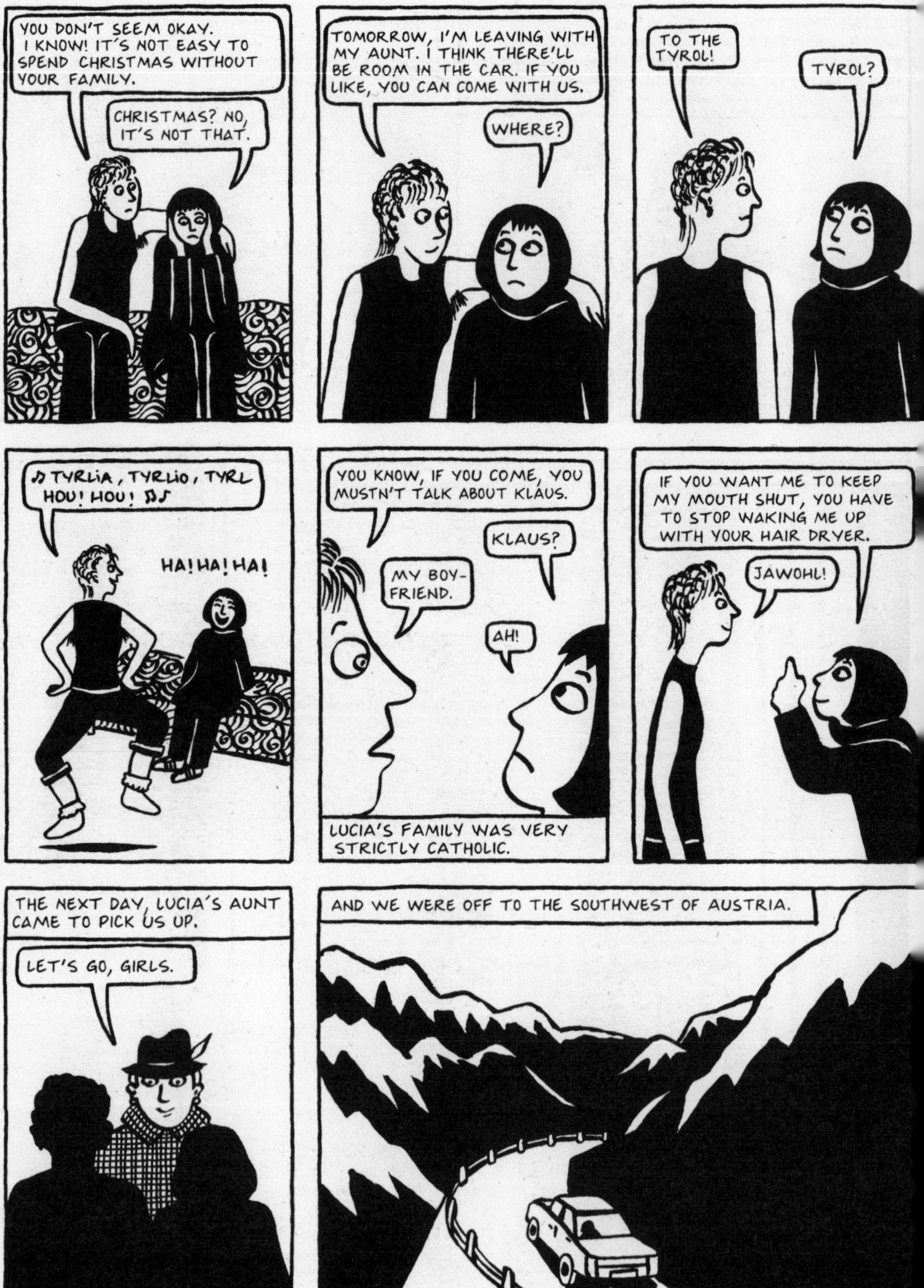
YOU DON'T SEEM OKAY. I KNOW! IT'S NOT EASY TO SPEND CHRISTMAS WITHOUT YOUR FAMILY.
CHRISTMAS? NO, IT'S NOT THAT.
TOMORROW, I'M LEAVING WITH MY AUNT. I THINK THERE'LL BE ROOM IN THE CAR. IF YOU LIKE, YOU CAN COME WITH US.
WHERE?
TO THE TYROL!
TYROL?
♪ TYRLiA, TYRLiO, TYRL HOU! HOU! ♫♪
HA! HA! HA!
YOU KNOW, IF YOU COME, YOU MUSTN'T TALK ABOUT KLAUS.
KLAUS?
MY BOY-FRIEND.
AH!
LUCIA'S FAMILY WAS VERY STRICTLY CATHOLIC.
IF YOU WANT ME TO KEEP MY MOUTH SHUT, YOU HAVE TO STOP WAKING ME UP WITH YOUR HAIR DRYER.
JAWOHL!
THE NEXT DAY, LUCIA'S AUNT CAME TO PICK US UP.
LET'S GO, GIRLS.
AND WE WERE OFF TO THE SOUTHWEST OF AUSTRIA.

LUCIA'S PARENTS WERE INCREDIBLE. THEY WERE UNLIKE ANYONE I'D EVER MET. HER TYROLEAN AUSTRIAN FATHER WORE PANTS MADE OF LEATHER. HER TYROLEAN ITALIAN MOTHER HAD A MUSTACHE. ONLY HER SISTER REMINDED ME OF HEIDI.

AFTEKH DINNEKH, WE AKH GOING TO CHUKKH.

ΔΔΔ!!!

JΔ!

THEIR GERMAN WAS DIFFICULT TO UNDERSTAND.

AND INDEED WE WENT TO CHURCH FOR MIDNIGHT MASS.

IT ENDED AT THREE IN THE MORNING!

173

LUCIA'S FAMILY HAD NEVER SEEN ANY IRANIANS. I WAS THEREFORE INVITED OVER EVERY DAY BY AN UNCLE AND AN AUNT WHO WANTED TO GET TO KNOW ME.

IT'S GOOD? YOU LIKE?

YES.

MY GERMAN WAS RUDIMENTARY, THEIRS UNUSUAL. A COUSIN WHO HAD SPENT FOUR YEARS IN FRANCOPHONE SWITZERLAND ENJOYED ACTING AS MY TRANSLATOR.

SHE SAYS THAT SHE ATE WELL.

SHE SAYS THAT SHE LIKES TYROL A LOT.

DESSERT!

SHE SAYS THAT TYROLEANS ARE VERY NICE.

THEY SAY THAT THEY LIKE YOU TOO.

WE SPOKE OF EVERYTHING.

IT'S WONDERFUL TO HAVE INTERNATIONAL FRIENDS.

JAAA

AS OPPOSED TO MY SCHOOL FRIENDS' FAVORITE SUBJECTS OF CONVERSATION, WE NEVER TOUCHED ON WAR, OR DEATH.

FINALLY THE DAY OF DEPARTURE ARRIVED.

YOU KNOW, I'M A CABINETMAKER. I MADE THIS FRAME ESPECIALLY FOR YOU.

SCHATZI,* A CANDIED APPLE AND SOME FRUIT FOR THE ROAD.

I HAD A NEW SET OF PARENTS ...

* DEAR

... LUCIA WAS MY SISTER.

AFTER THIS TRIP, I NEVER COMPLAINED ABOUT HER HAIR DRYER.

 # PASTA

Panel 1:
BAKUNIN WAS AGAINST MARX.

WHO'S BAKUNIN?

Panel 2:
WHAT? YOU DON'T KNOW BAKUNIN?

...

HE WAS AN ANARCHIST.

Panel 3:
NO! HE WAS THE ANARCHIST!

WELL... LONG LIVE VACATIONS.

MORE VACATION??

?

FOR ME, NOT GOING TO SCHOOL WAS SYNONYMOUS WITH SOLITUDE, ESPECIALLY NOW THAT LUCIA WAS SPENDING ALL HER TIME WITH HER BOYFRIEND, KLAUS.

Panel 4:
DO YOU HAVE A PROBLEM WITH VACATION?

NO! BUT YOU SEE, AT HOME, WE HAD TWO WEEKS OF REST FOR THE NEW YEAR AND AFTER THAT WE HAD TO WAIT UNTIL SUMMER.

Panel 5:
YOU'LL GET USED TO IT. THANKS TO THE LEFT, THERE ARE HOLIDAYS IN EUROPE. WE ARE NOT FORCED TO WORK ALL THE TIME.

AND YOUR POINT ...?

Panel 6:
IF, AT THE BEGINNING OF THE CENTURY, THE ANARCHISTS HAD TRIUMPHED, WE WOULDN'T WORK AT ALL. MAN ISN'T MADE FOR WORK.

Panel 7:
COME ON, RELAX, TAKE ADVANTAGE! CULTIVATE YOURSELF! YOU DON'T EVEN KNOW BAKUNIN!

ASSHOLE ...

Panel 8:
AND YOU, ARE YOU GOING SKIING?

YEAH... AS USUAL.

THIS CRETIN MOMO WASN'T ALTOGETHER WRONG. I NEEDED TO FIT IN, AND FOR THAT I NEEDED TO EDUCATE MYSELF.

Panel 9:
SO, I CREATED A REASON.

WHERE ARE YOU GOING ON VACATION?

NOWHERE. I'M GOING TO READ. I LOVE READING.

IN FACT, IT WAS A USEFUL ANSWER TO THE PERENNIAL QUESTION "WHERE ARE YOU GOING?," ALL THE WHILE GIVING ME A ROLE.

SO THEY WENT OFF SKIING AND I SET MYSELF TO READING. I STARTED WITH BAKUNIN. I LEARNED THAT HE WAS RUSSIAN, THAT HE HAD BEEN EXCLUDED FROM THE FIRST INTERNATIONAL* AND THAT HE REJECTED ALL AUTHORITY, ESPECIALLY THAT OF THE STATE.

ASIDE FROM THAT, I DIDN'T UNDERSTAND MUCH OF HIS PHILOSOPHY, AS SURELY MOMO DIDN'T EITHER.

* FIRST INTERNATIONAL CONFERENCE OF COMMUNIST COOPERATORS.

THEN, I STUDIED THE HISTORY OF THE COMMUNE.

I CONCLUDED THAT THE FRENCH RIGHT OF THIS EPOCH WERE WORTHY OF MY COUNTRY'S FUNDAMENTALISTS.

THEN, I TURNED MY ATTENTION TO SARTRE, MY COMRADES' FAVORITE AUTHOR.

"THE NOTION OF CONSCIOUSNESS COMES FROM MAN'S LIVED EXPERIENCE."

I FOUND HIM A LITTLE ANNOYING...

WHEN I'D HAD ENOUGH OF READING, I WENT TO THE SUPERMARKET.

IT WAS SO COLD THAT I HAD THE BRIGHT IDEA OF WEARING MY SKI SUIT, BROUGHT FROM TEHRAN, TO GO OUT.

DECKED OUT LIKE THIS IN VIENNA, I FELT LIKE I WAS ON THE SLOPES OF INNSBRUCK, CLOSE TO MY FRIENDS.

I WAS SO BORED THAT TO BUY FOUR DIFFERENT PRODUCTS, I WOULD GO TO THE SUPERMARKET AT LEAST FOUR TIMES.

MY BOARDING HOUSE

THE SUPERMARKET

IF I'D HAD ANYTHING FUN TO DO, I DON'T THINK I WOULD EVER HAVE READ AS MUCH AS I DID.

TO EDUCATE MYSELF, I HAD TO UNDERSTAND EVERYTHING. STARTING WITH MYSELF, ME, MARJI, THE WOMAN. SO I THREW MYSELF INTO READING MY MOTHER'S FAVORITE BOOK.

"THE MANDARINS," BY SIMONE DE BAVAR.

NO! BEAUVOIR.

SHE HAD READ ME SOME EXCERPTS, BUT I WAS A LITTLE YOUNG.

...??

I READ "THE SECOND SEX." SIMONE EXPLAINED THAT IF WOMEN PEED STANDING UP, THEIR PERCEPTION OF LIFE WOULD CHANGE.

SO I TRIED. IT RAN LIGHTLY DOWN MY LEFT LEG. IT WAS A LITTLE DISGUSTING.

SEATED, IT WAS MUCH SIMPLER. AND, AS AN IRANIAN WOMAN, BEFORE LEARNING TO URINATE LIKE A MAN, I NEEDED TO LEARN TO BECOME A LIBERATED AND EMANCIPATED WOMAN.

AND THEN CAME THE DAY. THE FAMOUS DAY IN THE MONTH OF FEBRUARY WHEN I WAS PREPARING MY ETERNAL SPAGHETTI.

I WAS VERY HUNGRY. SO HUNGRY THAT ONE PLATE WOULDN'T HAVE BEEN ENOUGH.

I WENT DOWNSTAIRS WITH MY POT TO WATCH TV IN THE REFECTORY.

I LOVED THAT. AT MY PARENTS' HOUSE, IT WAS STRICTLY FORBIDDEN. "INSPECTOR DERRICK" WAS ON. THE NUNS LIKED IT A LOT.

WHEN SUDDENLY THE MOTHER SUPERIOR BLOCKED MY LINE OF VISION.

A LITTLE RESTRAINT, MADEMOISELLE!

BUT HERE, EVERYONE EATS WHILE WATCHING TV.

BUT NOT IN A POT! WHAT KIND OF MANNERS ARE THESE?

IT'S TRUE WHAT THEY SAY ABOUT IRANIANS. THEY HAVE NO EDUCATION.

IT'S TRUE WHAT THEY SAY ABOUT YOU, TOO. YOU WERE ALL PROSTITUTES BEFORE BECOMING NUNS!

THE MOTHER SUPERIOR NO LONGER WANTED TO SEE ME, SO I WAS CALLED BEFORE HER ASSISTANT.

APPROACH!

IT'S UNACCEPTABLE, WHAT YOU SAID TO MOTHER BRIDGET!

AND WHAT SHE SAID TO ME, YOU FIND THAT ACCEPTABLE?

YOU'RE EXPELLED. I'M GOING TO CALL YOUR MOTHER'S FRIEND TO COME GET YOU.

DON'T BOTHER. I HAVE FRIENDS WHO WILL BE HAPPY TO TAKE CARE OF ME.

I WAS THINKING OF JULIE.

YOU SHOULD BE ASHAMED OF YOURSELF!

SO SHOULD YOU!

SHUT UP, YOU INSOLENT GIRL. AS YOU'VE PAID, YOU CAN STAY UNTIL THE END OF THE MONTH.

...

YOU HAVE NOTHING TO SAY TO ME?

...

خر احمق به شعور

EXCUSE ME?

I SAID THANK YOU!

IN EVERY RELIGION, YOU FIND THE SAME EXTREMISTS.

I DIDN'T WAIT FOR THE END OF THE MONTH. A FEW DAYS LATER, I CALLED JULIE.

THEY THREW ME OUT. I DON'T KNOW WHAT TO DO.

HOLD ON A MINUTE. I'M GOING TO ASK MY MOTHER IF YOU CAN COME LIVE HERE.

SHE SAYS THAT SHE IS THRILLED TO HAVE YOU!

OH JULIE! THANKS!!

I REPACKED MY BAG.

I SAID GOODBYE TO LUCIA, WHOM I NEVER SAW AGAIN.

THE SISTERS SENT A LETTER TO MY PARENTS.

EXPLAINING TO THEM THAT, HUMILIATED TO HAVE BEEN CAUGHT RED-HANDED STEALING A FRUIT YOGURT, I HAD DECIDED TO LEAVE THE BOARDING HOUSE OF MY OWN VOLITION.

BUT WHAT IN THE WORLD CAN THIS MEAN? SHE HATES FRUIT YOGURT.

I DON'T UNDERSTAND.

HAPPILY, MY PARENTS KNEW MY TASTES.

OH, THOSE LIARS!... THEY COULD HAVE AT LEAST FOUND A BETTER EXCUSE.

READING WASN'T ENOUGH. TO FIT IN, I STILL HAD A LONG WAY TO GO.

 # THE PILL

MY NEW HOME WAS A LOT MORE COMFORTABLE THAN THE BOARDING HOUSE. I SHARED JULIE'S ROOM.

DO YOU WANT ME TO GO WORK SOMEWHERE ELSE?

STAY PUT, I JUST CAME BY TO GET MY JACKET.

WOULD YOU BELIEVE I HAVE A DATE WITH ERNST, THE OWNER OF CAFÉ SCHELTER.

THE OWNER?

BUT HOW OLD IS THIS OWNER?

TWENTY-SIX.

TWENTY-SIX??

YES ... MATURE, THE WAY I LIKE THEM.

OK, I'M OFF.

DID YOU DO YOUR HOMEWORK?

BYE, MOM!

JULIE, WHERE ARE YOU GOING?

AND THE SISTERS WHO FOUND ME INSOLENT ... IF ONLY THEY'D SEEN JULIE.

IN MY CULTURE, PARENTS WERE SACRED. WE AT LEAST OWED THEM AN ANSWER.

ARMELLE, WOULD YOU LIKE A CUP OF TEA?

YES.

TO BEHAVE LIKE THIS TOWARD ONE'S OWN MOTHER MADE ME INDIGNANT.

I REALLY LIKED ARMELLE. SHE WAS GENTLE AND DISCREET. IN FACT, A LITTLE TOO MUCH SO. COMPARED TO MY MOTHER, SHE LACKED AUTHORITY.

DON'T PUT TOO MUCH IN. WHEN THE TEA IS STRONG, IT LOSES ITS FLAVOR.

I KNOW, AT HOME WE DRINK TEA ALL DAY LONG.

OF COURSE... HOW SILLY OF ME! TEA, INDIA, PERSIA, RUSSIA, SAMOVARS...

ARMELLE WAS VERY CULTURED EVEN IF SHE DIDN'T KNOW BAKUNIN. LACAN WAS HER THING. SHE WAS PASSIONATE ABOUT HIM.

YOU KNOW, HE OPENED UP THE FIELD OF PSYCHOANALYSIS WITH STRUCTURAL LINGUISTICS.

HE MANAGED TO ISOLATE THE REGISTERS OF THE SYMBOLIC IMAGINATION AND REALITY.

HE IS ONE OF THE FIRST TO HAVE UNDERTAKEN GROUP THERAPY!

A WOMAN AND A MAN DON'T THINK ALIKE, DON'T FUNCTION ALIKE, DON'T WRITE ALIKE. WOMEN'S LITERATURE BLAH, BLAH, BLAH, MEN'S LITERATURE, BLAH, BLAH, BLAH, BLAH,...

I LISTENED OUT OF POLITENESS.

... AND ALSO BECAUSE SHE WAS THE ONLY ONE WHO KNEW IRAN. SHE UNDERSTOOD MY NOSTALGIA FOR THE CASPIAN SEA. SHE WAS ALSO THE ONLY ONE TO HAVE SEEN A SAMOVAR.

AND THEN, SHE WAS THE ONE WHO HAD CALLED MY PARENTS TO REASSURE THEM.

JULIE AND I DISCUSSED A LOT BEFORE BED.

I THINK YOUR MOTHER IS VERY NICE.

SHE CAN BE REALLY UNBEARABLE WHEN SHE WANTS TO BE.

BUT SHE REALLY LIKES YOU, TOO. THANKS TO YOU, SHE GOES EASIER ON ME. SHE THINKS THAT YOU'RE A GOOD INFLUENCE ON ME.

WHAT KIND OF GOOD INFLUENCE?

OH, YOU'RE THE PURE, TIMID, INNOCENT VIRGIN WHO DOES HER HOMEWORK. I'M NOT LIKE THAT. I'VE BEEN HAVING SEX FOR FIVE YEARS.

I'VE ALREADY SLEPT WITH EIGHTEEN GUYS: FABRICE, OLIVIER, LAURENT, LUC, JEAN-MARC, ANOTHER LAURENT, SEBASTIEN, . . .

I WAS SHOCKED. IN MY COUNTRY, EVEN WHEN YOU HAD SEX BEFORE MARRIAGE, YOU HID IT.

AT FIRST WE USED CONDOMS, BUT THE GUY FEELS LESS.

"FEELS LESS" WHAT?

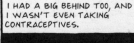

WELL, THE VAGINA!

THE VVV...??!!:

NOW I'M ON THE PILL. THAT'S WHY I HAVE SUCH A BIG BUTT.

I HAD A BIG BEHIND TOO, AND I WASN'T EVEN TAKING CONTRACEPTIVES.

ARMELLE HAD A GOOD JOB AT THE UNITED NATIONS. SHE TRAVELED FREQUENTLY.

I STOCKED THE REFRIGERATOR. STUDY HARD! JULIE, DON'T CUT CLASS!!

OKAY.

WHEN I GET BACK I WANT THE HOUSE TO BE CLEAN AND TIDY.

YES, MA'AM.

HOW LONG WILL YOU BE GONE?

SIX DAYS. IF YOU NEED ANYTHING, CALL MARTIN.

MARTIN AND ARMELLE GOT TO KNOW EACH OTHER IN VIENNA. THEY WORKED TOGETHER, WERE BOTH DIVORCED AND CARRIED ON A PLATONIC RELATIONSHIP.

IT WAS JULIE WHO HAD EXPLAINED IT TO ME.

I DON'T THINK THEY'RE SLEEPING TOGETHER. IF THEY WERE, I WOULD KNOW.

WHAT DO YOU KNOW ABOUT IT?

YOU'VE SEEN HOW ANNOYING SHE IS... IT'S FOR SURE! SHE'S NOT FUCKING.

I DIDN'T YET HAVE ANY EXPERIENCE THAT WOULD HAVE ALLOWED ME TO MAKE THE CONNECTION BETWEEN ARMELLE'S CHARACTER AND HER SEX LIFE.

HAVE A GOOD TRIP!

NO SOONER WAS HER MOTHER GONE...

...THAN JULIE ORGANIZED A PARTY FOR THE DAY AFTER WITH HER FRIENDS FROM THE CAFÉ SCHELTER.

THE NIGHT OF THE PARTY.

HOW DO I LOOK?

NOT SO GOOD.

WAIT, I'M GOING TO MAKE YOU UP. YOU'LL SEE.

SHE DID MY HAIR AND DREW ON A THICK LINE OF BLACK EYELINER THAT, FROM THEN ON, BECAME MY USUAL MAKEUP.

I THOUGHT I LOOKED VERY BEAUTIFUL.

WHAT ARE YOU DOING, JULIE? YOU'RE PUTTING PERFUME THERE?

THERE! IT HAS A NAME! IT'S CALLED A SEX, A PUSSY, A MINOU ...

MINOU? THAT'S MY AUNT'S NAME.

GOOD FOR HER!

PLUS, MINOU IN PERSIAN MEANS PARADISE!

HA! HA! HA!

GENTLEMEN! WELCOME TO PARADISE.

HA! HA! HA!

DO YOU HAVE ANY GOOD MUSIC?

YES, I HAVE ALL OF PINK FLOYD.

I KNEW PINK FLOYD. MY PARENTS LISTENED TO THEM WHENEVER WE WENT ON A TRIP.

TO ME, IT WASN'T EXACTLY PARTY MUSIC.

AND THE PARTY WAS NOT WHAT I IMAGINED. IN IRAN, AT PARTIES, EVERYONE WOULD DANCE AND EAT. IN VIENNA, PEOPLE PREFERRED TO LIE AROUND AND SMOKE.

AND THEN, I WAS TURNED OFF BY ALL THESE PUBLIC DISPLAYS OF AFFECTION. WHAT DO YOU EXPECT, I CAME FROM A TRADITIONALIST COUNTRY.

AROUND FOUR IN THE MORNING, THE LAST GUESTS FINALLY LEFT. I WAS SO SLEEPY.

I WANTED TO REMOVE MY MAKE-UP, BUT IT WASN'T COMING OFF WITH WATER.

I WENT TO ASK JULIE FOR SOME MAKEUP REMOVER, BUT APPARENTLY SHE AND ERNST WERE ALREADY ASLEEP IN OUR ROOM.

WHEN SUDDENLY

AH!
AH!!
OH!
OH!
AHH!
AH!

OH, OH, OH!
AH, AH!
OH YES!
OH! AH! YES!

MY GOD, THEY WERE IN THE MIDDLE OF . . .

. . . HAVING SEX!

I RUSHED TO THE LIVING ROOM TO PROTECT MYSELF FROM I DON'T KNOW WHAT, BEHIND MY BEST FRIEND, A BOOK.

IT GOES WITHOUT SAYING THAT I DIDN'T UNDERSTAND A WORD I READ.

SEVERAL MINUTES LATER, I MADE OUT IN THE DARK THE SILHOUETTE OF A NAKED MAN,

FOLLOWED BY ONE OF A NAKED WOMAN,

THEN A MAN AND WOMAN HALF-NAKED!

HELLO!

HI!

UH...

I COULDN'T BELIEVE MY EYES...

...I'D NEVER SEEN THAT!

IT REMINDED ME OF THE DAY, EIGHT YEARS BEFORE, IN THE CAR WITH MY DAD.

DAD! WHAT ARE BALLS?

WHAT? WE SAY TESTICLE. A MAN'S SEX IS MADE OF TWO BALLS AND A PENIS. THESE BALLS ARE CALLED TESTICLES.

BALLS? BALLS, LIKE THESE?

AND, A LITTLE RED, MY FATHER ANSWERED SERIOUSLY.

NO, MORE LIKE THIS. THEY'RE NOT TENNIS BALLS. THEY'RE MORE LIKE PING-PONG BALLS.

AH, PING-PONG BALLS! HA! HA! HA! HA! HA! HA!

I DON'T BELIEVE IT. YOU... YOU... YOU'RE STONED!!!

BUT THAT'S SO COOL!

SHE'S TRIPPING. GO ON WOLFY, WHY DON'T YOU PUT SOME MUSIC ON?

WOLFY?

SO HE WASN'T ERNST, THE OWNER OF CAFÉ SCHELTER! JULIE HAD JUST SLEPT WITH HER NINETEENTH GUY.

THAT NIGHT, I REALLY UNDERSTOOD THE MEANING OF "THE SEXUAL REVOLUTION."

IT WAS MY FIRST BIG STEP TOWARD ASSIMILATING INTO WESTERN CULTURE.

THE VEGETABLE

MY MENTAL TRANSFORMATION WAS FOLLOWED BY MY PHYSICAL METAMORPHOSIS.

BETWEEN THE AGES OF FIFTEEN AND SIXTEEN, I GREW SEVEN INCHES. IT WAS IMPRESSIVE.

ME AT FIFTEEN

ME AT SIXTEEN

MY HEAD ALSO CHANGED IN ITS OWN WAY. FIRST, MY FACE GOT LONGER.

THEN MY RIGHT EYE GREW,

FOLLOWED SWIFTLY BY MY CHIN WHICH DOUBLED IN LENGTH.

THEN IT WAS MY MOUTH,

MY RIGHT HAND,

MY LEFT FOOT.

(EVEN TODAY, IT'S HALF A SIZE BIGGER THAN MY RIGHT FOOT.)

OF COURSE MY NOSE TRIPLED ITS SIZE.

AND WAS DECORATED BY A LARGE BEAUTY MARK.

WHICH I THOUGHT HIDEOUS AT THE TIME.

THEN MY CHIN ADVANCED MAJESTICALLY,

ONLY TO RETREAT TO ITS ORIGINAL POSITION SEVERAL MONTHS LATER.

FINALLY MY CHEST DEVELOPED

AND MY CENTER OF GRAVITY WAS BALANCED OUT BY THE POUNDS ON MY BUTT.

IN SHORT, I WAS IN AN UGLY STAGE SEEMINGLY WITHOUT END.

AS IF MY NATURAL DEFORMITY WASN'T ENOUGH, I TRIED A FEW NEW HAIRCUTS. A LITTLE SNIP OF THE SCISSORS ON THE LEFT.

AND A WEEK LATER, A LITTLE SNIP OF THE SCISSORS ON THE RIGHT.

I LOOKED LIKE COSETTE IN "LES MISÉRABLES."

SO I COATED MY HAIR WITH GEL,

I ADDED A THICK LINE OF EYELINER,

A FEW SAFETY PINS,

WHICH WERE REPLACED BY A SCARF. IT SOFTENED THE LOOK.

IT WAS BEGINNING TO LOOK LIKE SOMETHING.

HAVE YOU SEEN HOW BEAUTIFUL SHE IS NOW?

... UH ...

TO MY ENORMOUS SURPRISE, MY NEW LOOK EVEN PLEASED THE HALL MONITORS. IT SHOULD BE SAID THAT THEY WERE VERY YOUNG.

YOU CHANGE YOUR HAIRSTYLE EVERY DAY. WHO CUTS YOUR HAIR? — I DO.

IF I PAY YOU, WILL YOU CUT MY HAIR, TOO?

THAT'S HOW I BECAME THE SCHOOL'S OFFICIAL HAIRCUTTER.

IT HELPED ME EARN A LITTLE SPENDING MONEY.

MY RELATIONSHIP WITH THE SCHOOL'S LACKEYS DIDN'T PLEASE MY FRIENDS MUCH.

SO, YOU SEEM TO BE ON AWFULLY GOOD TERMS WITH THE PEONS.

NOT REALLY! I JUST CUT THEIR HAIR.

THAT'S NOT ALL YOU DO FOR THEM. YOU KISS THEIR ASSES FROM TIME TO TIME.

I DO NOT. I THINK THEY'RE NICE, THAT'S ALL.

PEONS, THEY'RE PEONS. THEY HAVE A FIXED PSYCHOLOGICAL PROFILE. THEY ARE THIRSTY FOR POWER AND ARE LOOKING TO CONTROL US.

YEAH, LIKE THE COPS.

EXACTLY! LIFE IS PAIN. PAIN IS EVERYTHING. EVERYTHING IS NOTHINGNESS. THEREFORE LIFE IS NOTHINGNESS. WHEN MAN RECOGNIZES THIS HOLE, HE CAN NO LONGER LIVE LIKE AN EARTHWORM, INVENTING GAMES OF LEADERS AND FOLLOWERS TO FORGET HIS FICKLENESS.

WHATEVER! EXISTENCE IS NOT ABSURD. THERE ARE PEOPLE WHO BELIEVE IN IT AND WHO GIVE THEIR LIVES FOR VALUES LIKE LIBERTY.

WHAT RUBBISH! EVEN THAT, IT'S A DISTRACTION FROM BOREDOM.

SO MY UNCLE DIED TO DISTRACT HIMSELF?

...

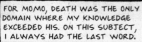

FOR MOMO, DEATH WAS THE ONLY DOMAIN WHERE MY KNOWLEDGE EXCEEDED HIS. ON THIS SUBJECT, I ALWAYS HAD THE LAST WORD.

NOBLE COMBAT, BLAH BLAH BLAH ...

OK! ARE WE GOING TO SMOKE A JOINT?

SURE!

IT WAS ALWAYS THIERRY WHO ROLLED THE JOINTS WHILE WE KEPT AN EYE OUT FOR THE MONITORS SO WE WOULDN'T BE CAUGHT BY SURPRISE.

HERE!

I DIDN'T LIKE TO SMOKE, BUT I DID IT OUT OF SOLIDARITY. AT THE TIME, TO ME, GRASS AND HEROIN WERE THE SAME THING.

EACH TIME I WAS OFFERED A JOINT, I REMEMBERED THIS CONVERSATION MY PARENTS HAD ABOUT MY COUSIN KAMRAN.

POOR BOY, HE'S STUCK HIMSELF SO MANY TIMES HE'S BEGUN TO LOOK LIKE A VEGETABLE.

THIS KIND OF THING ALWAYS HAPPENS TO THE MOST FRAGILE ONES.

BECOMING A VEGETABLE WAS OUT OF THE QUESTION.

SO I PRETENDED TO PARTICIPATE, BUT I NEVER INHALED THE SMOKE.

AND AS SOON AS MY FRIENDS' BACKS WERE TURNED, I STUCK MY FINGERS IN MY EYES TO MAKE THEM GOOD AND RED.

THEN, I IMITATED THEIR LAUGHTER.

I WAS QUITE BELIEVABLE.

194

THE HARDER I TRIED TO ASSIMILATE, THE MORE I HAD THE FEELING THAT I WAS DISTANCING
MYSELF FROM MY CULTURE, BETRAYING MY PARENTS AND MY ORIGINS, THAT I WAS PLAYING A
GAME BY SOMEBODY ELSE'S RULES.

EACH TELEPHONE CALL FROM MY PARENTS REMINDED ME OF MY COWARDICE AND MY BETRAYAL. I WAS
AT ONCE HAPPY TO HEAR THEIR VOICES AND ASHAMED TO TALK TO THEM.

- YES, I'M DOING FINE. I'M GETTING GOOD GRADES.

- FRIENDS? OF COURSE, LOTS!

- DAD . . .

- DAD, I LOVE YOU!

- YOU HAVE SOME GOOD FRIENDS?

- THAT DOESN'T SURPRISE ME, YOU ALWAYS HAD
  A TALENT FOR COMMUNICATING WITH PEOPLE!

- EAT ORANGES. THEY'RE FULL OF VITAMIN C.

- US TOO, WE ADORE YOU. YOU'RE THE CHILD ALL
  PARENTS DREAM OF HAVING!

IF ONLY THEY KNEW . . . IF THEY KNEW THAT THEIR DAUGHTER WAS MADE UP LIKE A PUNK,
THAT SHE SMOKED JOINTS TO MAKE A GOOD IMPRESSION, THAT SHE HAD SEEN MEN IN THEIR
UNDERWEAR WHILE THEY WERE BEING BOMBED EVERY DAY, THEY WOULDN'T CALL ME THEIR
DREAM CHILD.

I FELT SO GUILTY THAT WHENEVER THERE WAS NEWS ABOUT IRAN, I CHANGED THE CHANNEL.

IRAN-IRAK KRIEG

IT WAS TOO UNBEARABLE.

DID YOU WATCH TV YESTERDAY? YOU MUST BE WORRIED.

NO, IT'S OKAY! I TALKED TO MY PARENTS. THEY'RE FINE.

I WAS LYING. I KNEW NOTHING AND I DIDN'T WANT TO KNOW MORE.

I WANTED TO FORGET EVERYTHING, TO MAKE MY PAST DISAPPEAR, BUT MY UNCONSCIOUS CAUGHT UP WITH ME.

I EVEN MANAGED TO DENY MY NATIONALITY.

DURING A PARTY AT SCHOOL.

HI, I'M MARC. I GRADUATED LAST YEAR. YOU'RE NEW! WHAT'S YOUR NAME?

MARJANE. I'VE BEEN HERE A YEAR.

AND WHERE ARE YOU FROM MARIE-JEANNE?

I'M FRENCH.

OH REALLY? YOU HAVE A FUNNY ACCENT FOR A FRENCH GIRL.

OH! I HAVE TO FIND MY FRIENDS. BYE.

I SHOULD SAY THAT AT THE TIME, IRAN WAS THE EPITOME OF EVIL AND TO BE IRANIAN WAS A HEAVY BURDEN TO BEAR.

IT WAS EASIER TO LIE THAN TO ASSUME THAT BURDEN.

WHO'S THAT GUY?

MARC? HE'S ANNA'S BROTHER, THE GIRL IN THE STRIPED SWEAT-ER. HE'S A JERK FROM BOURGE. YOU SHOULDN'T TALK TO THOSE PEOPLE.

AND WHEN I GOT BACK THAT NIGHT, I REMEMBERED THAT LINE MY GRANDMOTHER TOLD ME: "ALWAYS KEEP YOUR DIGNITY AND BE TRUE TO YOURSELF!"

OH GRANDMA ...

UNFORTUNATELY, IT ALL CAME OUT IN THE END. A FEW DAYS LATER IN A CAFÉ NEAR SCHOOL.

SHE TOLD MY BROTHER THAT SHE WAS FRENCH.

AND YOUR BROTHER BELIEVED HER?

WHAT DO YOU THINK? HAVE YOU HEARD THE WAY SHE TALKS?

HAVE YOU SEEN HER FACE?

BUT YOUR BROTHER WAS HITTING ON HER OR WHAT?

OF COURSE NOT!!

AH, THAT'S A RELIEF. CONSIDERING HOW UGLY SHE IS, IT WOULD BE REALLY UNFAIR IF SHE GOT A GUY LIKE MARC.

HA, HA, HA! I WOULD COMMIT SUICIDE IF MY BROTHER WAS GOING OUT WITH A COW LIKE THAT!

I DON'T KNOW IF YOU'VE NOTICED, BUT SHE NEVER TALKS ABOUT EITHER HER COUNTRY OR HER PARENTS.

WELL, OF COURSE! SHE LIES WHEN SHE SAYS THAT SHE'S KNOWN WAR. IT'S ALL TO MAKE HERSELF SEEM INTERESTING.

ANYWAY, HER PARENTS CLEARLY DON'T CARE ABOUT HER, OR THEY WOULDN'T HAVE SENT HER ALONE.

THAT WAS TOO MUCH. I SAW RED.

YOU ARE GOING TO SHUT UP OR I AM GOING TO MAKE YOU! **I AM IRANIAN AND PROUD OF IT!**

SHE IS COMPLETELY CRAZY.

I WANTED TO DIE.

CAFÉ~

WHERE WERE MY PARENTS TO TAKE ME IN THEIR ARMS, TO REASSURE ME?

BUT REALLY, I HAD NOTHING TO CRY ABOUT.

I HAD JUST REDEEMED MYSELF.

FOR THE FIRST TIME IN A YEAR, I FELT PROUD.

I FINALLY UNDERSTOOD WHAT MY GRANDMOTHER MEANT. IF I WASN'T COMFORTABLE WITH MYSELF, I WOULD NEVER BE COMFORTABLE.

THE HORSE

JULIE AND HER MOTHER HAD LEFT VIENNA. NOW I WAS LIVING IN A WOHNGEMEINSCHAFT. THE WOHNGEMEINSCHAFT IS A COMMUNAL APARTMENT. I COULD STAY FOR FOUR MONTHS.

THE WINDOW OF MY ROOM.

MY ROOM.

IT WAS FULL OF LIGHT. I HAD A DOUBLE-BED, A BUREAU, AND A DESK. FOR THE FIRST TIME IN A LONG TIME I HAD MY OWN SPACE.

IT WAS REALLY NICE.

MY EIGHT HOUSEMATES WERE EIGHT MEN, ALL HOMOSEXUALS.

FRANZ

ANDREAS

MARKUS

KLAUS

JAN

DIETER

ME

MARTIN

MANFRED

I HAD BEEN IN AUSTRIA FOR OVER A YEAR AND A HALF. I HAD ABANDONED MY PUNK LOOK. I NO LONGER WANTED TO BE MARGINAL.

MARJANE! IT'S YOUR MOTHER ON THE PHONE.

I'M COMING!

WHAT??

OH, MY MOTHER, MY MOTHER!

WHAT ABOUT YOUR MOTHER?

SHE'S COMING TO SEE ME!

THAT'S GREAT!

WHEN?

IN TWO WEEKS.

EVEN THOUGH IT HAD BEEN NINETEEN MONTHS SINCE I HAD SEEN MY MOTHER, THE FIFTEEN DAYS OF WAITING WERE VERY LONG. THE DAY OF HER ARRIVAL, I BATHED LIKE NEVER BEFORE.

I IRONED MY CLOTHES FOR THE FIRST TIME,

I MADE MYSELF AS BEAUTIFUL AS I COULD BEFORE GOING TO MEET HER AT THE AIRPORT.

I SAW FROM AFAR A WOMAN WHO LOOKED LIKE HER, THE SAME SILHOUETTE, THE SAME WALK, BUT WITH GRAY HAIR. MY MOTHER WAS A BRUNETTE.

WHEN THIS WOMAN GOT CLOSE, THERE WASN'T ANY DOUBT. IT WAS REALLY HER. BEFORE I LEFT HOME, MOM ONLY HAD A FEW GRAY HAIRS. IT'S INCREDIBLE WHAT TIME DOES TO YOU.

MOM! MOM!

I DIDN'T KNOW IF SHE HADN'T RECOGNIZED ME, OR HADN'T HEARD ME.

IN ANY CASE, SHE DIDN'T STOP.

MOM!

MARJI?

SHE HADN'T RECOGNIZED ME, AND WITH GOOD REASON: I'D ALMOST DOUBLED IN HEIGHT AND SIZE.

OH MY DEAR, YOU ARE SO TALL!

DUTY FREE SHOP

MOM! MOM, YOU'VE GONE GRAY!

IT FELT STRANGE TO TAKE HER IN MY ARMS. OUR PROPORTIONS HAD BEEN REVERSED.

WITH THE OTHERS' PERMISSION, BROUGHT HER TO STAY WITH ME.

I LIVE HERE. YOU'LL SEE, YOU'LL LIKE IT. MY HOUSEMATES ARE VERY NICE. THEY'RE VERY EXCITED AT THE THOUGHT OF MEETING YOU.

HI

HELLO
WELCOME
HI

HALLO

HOW ARE YOU?

MAKE YOUR-SELF AT HOME.

THIS IS MY ROOM. WE'LL SHARE THE SAME BED.

IT'S NICE . . . I HADN'T UNDERSTOOD THAT YOUR HOUSEMATES WERE MEN.

IT'S AMAZING HOW YOU'VE GROWN.

I DIDN'T REPEAT THAT SHE, TOO, HAD CHANGED. AT HER AGE, YOU DON'T GROW UP, YOU GROW OLD.

IN PERSIAN GRAMMAR, THERE'S NO GENDER. MASCULINE AND FEMININE ARE INTERCHANGEABLE.

JUST LIKE THAT YOU LIVE WITH EIGHT MEN.

DON'T WORRY MOM! THEY'RE ALL HOMOSEXUALS.

HOMOSEXUALS??

I HAD TOLD HER THAT TO REASSURE HER AND I THINK THAT, DESPITE THE SHOCK, SHE WAS APPEASED.

BESIDES, I SURPRISED HER ONE DAY IN THE MIDST OF TEACHING "I LOVE YOU" IN PERSIAN TO FRANZ, WHO HAD JUST MET AN IRANIAN GUY.

DOUSTET DARAM, OUU . . . YOU UNDERSTAND? OUU . . :

DOSTET DARAM

NO! OUU . . .

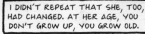

203

RECOUNTING NINETEEN MONTHS IN A FEW DAYS ISN'T EASY. WE HAD TO TALK A LOT TO MAKE UP FOR LOST TIME. OUR CONVERSATIONS WERE ALWAYS DISJOINTED.

TELL ME, HOW'S DAD? WHAT'S HE DOING?

OH, HE TAKES CARE OF THE GAS IN TEHRAN'S BUILDINGS.

IT FRUSTRATES HIM A LITTLE. YOU KNOW, YOUR FATHER SPECIALIZED IN THE CONSTRUCTION OF STEEL FACTORIES, BUT DURING WARTIME THERE'S NO POINT IN BUILDING.

IS HE HAPPY ANYWAY?

YES, HE'S OKAY. HE MISSES YOU ENORMOUSLY, BUT HE'S HAPPY THAT YOU'RE LIVING HERE, FAR FROM THE PROBLEMS.

MOM, WHERE'S YOUR NECKLACE?

MY MOTHER ALWAYS WORE A GOLDEN PENDANT THAT DAD HAD GIVEN HER FOR THEIR TENTH WEDDING ANNIVERSARY.

I LEFT IT IN IRAN. YOU SEE, WE DON'T HAVE THE RIGHT TO TAKE ANYTHING OF VALUE OUT OF THE COUNTRY.

I LEARNED LATER THAT SHE HAD LIED TO ME.

YOU DON'T LIKE WHAT I MADE?

NO, NO, I LOVE IT. I'M JUST NOT VERY HUNGRY.

THERE AGAIN, SHE WAS LYING. AFTER THIS DAY, SHE NEVER AGAIN LET ME DO THE COOKING.

HERE - A LETTER FROM YOUR FATHER. I'M NOT THE ONE WHO OPENED IT, IT'S THE CUSTOMS IN TEHRAN. THEY CHECK EVERYTHING!

IN THE LETTER, HE WAS OVERJOYED BY THE THOUGHT THAT I HAD A PEACEFUL LIFE IN VIENNA.

IF YOU ONLY KNEW...

I HAD THE IMPRESSION THAT HE DIDN'T REALIZE WHAT I WAS ENDURING.

WE OFTEN WENT WALKING, MY MOTHER AND I.

HOW'S OUR COUNTRY DOING?

SIGH! STILL THE SAME, BOMBINGS, ARRESTS, WE'RE SO USED TO IT THAT THE CALM HERE MAKES ME A LITTLE NERVOUS.

DO YOU REMEMBER OUR NEIGHBORS, THE KIANIS? THEY BOUGHT A HOUSE IN DEMAVEND.* WHEN WE HEAR THAT THERE'S GOING TO BE AN AIR STRIKE, WE TAKE REFUGE AT THEIR HOUSE. THE AIR IS VERY PURE UP THERE. WE HAVE A GOOD TIME.

* A MOUNTAINOUS CITY NORTH OF TEHRAN.

HOW GOOD IT FEELS TO WALK WITHOUT A VEIL ON MY HEAD, WITHOUT THE WORRY OF BEING ARRESTED OVER TWO LOCKS OF HAIR OR MY NAIL POLISH.

SHE NEVER ASKED ME ANY QUESTIONS ABOUT MY SITUATION. CERTAINLY OUT OF A SENSE OF RESTRAINT AND ALSO BECAUSE SHE WAS SCARED OF THE ANSWERS. IF SHE HAD SACRIFICED HERSELF SO THAT I COULD LIVE FREELY, THE LEAST I COULD DO WAS BEHAVE WELL.

SO WHEN WORDS FAILED US, GESTURES CAME TO OUR AID.

I LOVE MY MOM.

SHE LOVES YOU, TOO.

I'M HAPPY TO SEE YOU SO WELL-SETTLED HERE. NOW YOU MUST MAKE AN EFFORT, YOU MUST BECOME SOMEBODY. I DON'T CARE WHAT YOU DO LATER, ONLY TRY TO BE THE BEST. EVEN IF YOU BECOME A CABARET DANCER, BETTER THAT YOU DANCE AT THE LIDO THAN IN A HOLE IN THE WALL.

WHILE WE'RE ON THE SUBJECT, DID YOU KNOW YOUR UNCLE MASSOUD IS LIVING IN GERMANY?

IN GERMANY? BUT THAT'S NEXT DOOR. HE DIDN'T WANT TO COME VISIT US?

HE'S VERY DEPRESSED. IN IRAN, HE WAS SOMEBODY: "MR. CHARTERED ACCOUNTANT!" IN GERMANY, THEY THINK HE'S A TURK . . . AT OUR AGE, IT'S DIFFICULT TO START OVER AT ZERO.

I REMEMBER THE DAYS WHEN WE TRAVELED AROUND EUROPE. IT WAS ENOUGH TO CARRY AN IRANIAN PASSPORT, THEY ROLLED OUT THE RED CARPET. WE WERE RICH BEFORE. NOW AS SOON AS THEY LEARN OUR NATIONALITY, THEY GO THROUGH EVERYTHING, AS THOUGH WE WERE ALL TERRORISTS. THEY TREAT US AS THOUGH WE HAVE THE PLAGUE.

A FEW DAYS LATER AT THE CAFÉ HAWELKA.

GIVE ME A CIGARETTE.

!?

DON'T PLAY THE INNOCENT WITH ME, I KNOW YOU SMOKE!

WHAT MAKES YOU THINK THAT?

YOU SMELL LIKE SMOKE AND I SAW A PACKET OF CAMELS IN YOUR BAG!

YOU WENT THROUGH MY THINGS??

I'D BEEN LIVING ALONE TOO LONG TO ACCEPT ANY INVASION OF MY PRIVACY.

COME ON... GIVE ME THAT CIGARETTE!

I DECIDED TO LET IT GO. I KNEW SHE WAS LEAVING IN TWENTY DAYS AND I DIDN'T WANT TO REGRET ANYTHING.

HERE, HERE'S YOUR CIGARETTE.

IT'S MAYBE RIDICULOUS TO ASK YOU THIS QUESTION NOW, BUT WHAT REALLY HAPPENED WITH THE NUNS?

LIKE I TOLD YOU.

THEY SAID THAT IRANIANS DON'T HAVE ANY EDUCATION AND I ANSWERED BACK THAT THEY WERE ALL PROSTITUTES.

WELL DONE!

UNDER NORMAL CIRCUMSTANCES, SHE WOULD SURELY HAVE REPRIMANDED ME FOR INSULTING PEOPLE.

YOU WON'T DO IT AGAIN, RIGHT?

OF COURSE NOT.

WHEN YOU SEE YOUR PARENTS RARELY, ALL IS FORGIVEN.

206

MY STAY AT THE WOHNGE-MEINSCHAFT WAS TEMPORARY. I HAD TO FIND NEW LODGINGS.

MARJI, I PASSED BY THE UNIVERSITY. I SAW AN AD FOR A ROOM IN THE THIRTEENTH QUARTER.

WE WENT THERE THAT AFTERNOON. HANSE NIESE WEG 1.

HALLO! I'M FRAU DOCTOR HELLER.

MRS. SATRAPI.

* SHE'S SO FAT!

HERE... THE RENT IS TWO THOUSAND SHILLINGS*. SHE CAN USE THE KITCHEN AND THE BATHROOM WHICH SHE'LL SHARE WITH THREE ROOMMATES, TWO ENGLISH MUSICIANS AND AN AMERICAN ARCHITECTURE STUDENT.

* 150 DOLLARS.

ALL THE TERMS SUITED US.

TAKE GOOD CARE OF MY DAUGHTER.

OF COURSE, MRS. SATRAPI, OF COURSE.

AND AT THE TRAM STOP.

WHAT DID YOU THINK OF THE TEA?

LIKE HORSE PISS!

HER TOO, SHE LOOKED LIKE A HORSE!

MPFRR

MMF

HORSE PISS FROM A HORSE-FACE!!

EVEN TODAY THIS INFANTILE JOKE BRINGS TEARS TO OUR EYES.

I SPENT TWENTY-SEVEN DAYS BY HER SIDE. I TASTED THE HEAVENLY FOOD OF MY COUNTRY, PREPARED BY MY MOTHER. IT WAS A CHANGE FROM PASTA.

SHE STROKED MY HAIR EVERY NIGHT TO PUT ME TO SLEEP.

IT RELAXED ME TO TALK TO HER. IT HAD BEEN SO LONG SINCE I'D BEEN ABLE TO TALK TO SOMEONE WITHOUT HAVING TO EXPLAIN MY CULTURE.

THE EVE OF HER DEPARTURE.

MY DEAR, YOU WON'T INSULT DR. HELLER, RIGHT?

I PROMISE.

BUY YOURSELF FRUITS AND VEGETABLES. YOU MUST EAT WELL. IT'S NOT FOR NOTHING THAT WE SAY "A HEALTHY MIND IN A HEALTHY BODY!"

LOOK! I MADE SOME SKETCHES INSPIRED BY OUR WINDOW-SHOPPING. I'LL MAKE YOU SOME OUTFITS. YOU'RE IN NEED OF SOME NEW ONES.

EVER SINCE MY ARRIVAL IN AUSTRIA, I HADN'T BOUGHT MYSELF ANYTHING AND, GIVEN MY GROWTH SPURT, MY CLOTHES NO LONGER FIT ME.

THEN CAME THE DREADED DAY OF DEPARTURE. I WAS SAD BUT, WELL, I'D BEGUN TO GET USED TO SEPARATIONS.

MY MOTHER LEFT.

I'M SURE THAT SHE UNDERSTOOD THE MISERY OF MY ISOLATION EVEN IF SHE KEPT A STRAIGHT FACE AND GAVE NOTHING AWAY. SHE LEFT ME WITH A BAG OF AFFECTION THAT SUSTAINED ME FOR SEVERAL MONTHS.

HIDE AND SEEK

FRAU DOCTOR HELLER'S HOUSE WAS AN OLD VILLA, BUILT BY HER FATHER, A 1930S SCULPTOR OF SOME RENOWN. THE BIG TERRACE THAT LOOKED OUT ON THE GARDEN WAS MY FAVORITE PLACE. I SPENT SOME VERY PLEASANT MOMENTS THERE.

ONLY THE EXCREMENT OF VICTOR, FRAU DOCTOR HELLER'S DOG, DISTURBED THIS HARMONY.

ON AVERAGE, HE DEFECATED ONCE A WEEK ON MY BED.

DOCTOR HELLER!

DO YOU HAVE ANY IDEA? IT'S THE FIFTH TIME IN A MONTH! IT'S UNACCEPTABLE! WHY DON'T YOU TRAIN HIM?

YES, WELL! I'M GOING TO HAVE THE SHEETS CHANGED.

I OFTEN FORGOT THAT HE WAS TOO OLD TO LEARN ANYTHING.

YOU ARE REALLY VERY UPTIGHT!

?!

ALL MY FRIENDS HAD LEFT OUR SCHOOL. JULIE WAS IN SPAIN, THIERRY AND OLIVIER HAD GONE BACK TO SWITZERLAND AND MOMO HAD BEEN EXPELLED. I WAS ALONE AT SCHOOL, BUT I DIDN'T CARE.

MY LACK OF INTEREST IN OTHERS MADE ME MORE INTERESTING.

HOW'S IT GOING, MARJANE?

FINE, FINE!

EVER SINCE I'D SEEN MY MOTHER, I DIDN'T NEED ANYONE.

WELL, ALMOST.

DO YOU WANT TO WALK HOME TOGETHER?

NO. MY BOYFRIEND'S COMING TO GET ME.

HIS NAME WAS ENRIQUE. I'D MET HIM THROUGH DIETER, ONE OF MY FORMER HOUSEMATES.

ENRIQUE WAS HALF-AUSTRIAN, HALF-SPANISH.

WHAT DO YOU SAY ABOUT GOING TO AN ANARCHIST PARTY THIS WEEKEND?

OF COURSE! I'D LOVE TO.

ENRIQUE WAS TWENTY AND PLAYED THE PIANO.

I LIKED HIM A LOT.

THERE'LL BE ABOUT TWENTY OF US, IT'LL BE COOL.

DO YOU KNOW ALL OF THEM?

YES.

LEARNING THAT HE KNEW REAL ANARCHISTS ONLY INTENSIFIED MY FEELINGS FOR HIM.

'A REVOLUTIONARY ANARCHISTS' PARTY!" IT REMINDED ME OF THE COMMITMENT AND THE
BATTLES OF MY CHILDHOOD IN IRAN. EVEN BETTER, IT WOULD PERHAPS ALLOW ME TO BETTER
UNDERSTAND BAKUNIN.

DOWN WITH
THE BOURGEOISIE

LONG LIVE
BAKUNIN

I WAS COUNTING THE HOURS.

FINALLY THE BIG DAY ARRIVED.

AFTER AN HOUR AND A HALF ON THE ROAD, WE ARRIVED IN THE MIDDLE OF THE FOREST.

IN THE DISTANCE I SAW A GROUP OF ADULTS CHASING ONE ANOTHER AND SHOUTING:

YOU'RE IT!

YOU'LL NEVER GET ME!

CATCH ME IF YOU CAN!

!?

WHAT A DISAPPOINTMENT... MY ENTHUSIASM WAS QUICKLY REPLACED BY A FEELING OF DISGUST AND PROFOUND CONTEMPT.

SO THESE ARE THE ANARCHISTS?

WHAT DO YOU THINK?

. . .

AT THIS INSTANT, MY LOVE FOR ENRIQUE SUFFERED A DEVAS-TATING BLOW.

COME, WE'RE GOING TO JOIN IN THE GAME.

. . .

COME ON, YOU'LL SEE, WE'LL HAVE A GOOD TIME!

I'M NOT REALLY IN THE MOOD FOR A PARTY.

ENRIQUE INSISTED. I FINALLY GAVE IN.

WE PLAYED HIDE-AND-SEEK.

THEN VOLLEYBALL.

TO WRAP UP THE PARTY, WE GRILLED SAUSAGES WHILE SINGING JANIS JOPLIN.

THE SAUSAGES AND THE MUSIC WERE GOOD... I WAS IN LOVE AGAIN.

THEN WE WENT INSIDE TO GO TO SLEEP.

GOOD NIGHT ALL.

SWEET DREAMS!

WE'RE ALL GOING TO SLEEP HERE?

IT EMBARRASSED ME TO SLEEP WITH ENRIQUE IN FRONT OF ALL THESE PEOPLE. I CAME FROM A CULTURE WHERE EVEN KISSING IN PUBLIC WAS CONSIDERED A SEXUAL ACT.

HERE, MARJANE, LET ME INTRODUCE YOU TO INGRID.

DELIGHTED TO MEET YOU, MARJANE. THERE'S A ROOM UPSTAIRS. YOU CAN SLEEP THERE IF YOU LIKE.

YES, THANKS, THAT'S KIND OF YOU.

SHE'S VERY CUTE, YOUR GIRLFRIEND.

I KNOW.

GOOD NIGHT, LOVE-BIRDS.

UNTIL THAT NIGHT, MY RELATIONSHIP WITH ENRIQUE WAS STRICTLY PLATONIC. I HAD GROWN UP IN A COUNTRY WHERE THE SEX ACT WAS NEVER CONSUMMATED UNTIL AFTER MARRIAGE. FOR ENRIQUE, IT WASN'T A PROBLEM. WE SATISFIED OURSELVES WITH TENDER KISSES.

BUT THIS NIGHT WAS DIFFERENT. I FELT READY TO LOSE MY INNOCENCE.

AND TOO BAD IF NO IRANIAN EVER MARRIES ME. I LIVE IN EUROPE AND I'LL MARRY A EUROPEAN!

I DIDN'T WANT TO BE A TIMID VIRGIN ANY LONGER.

UNFORTUNATELY, THE NEXT MORNING I WAS AS MUCH A VIRGIN AND AS TIMID AS THE NIGHT BEFORE.

NEVERTHELESS I HAD TRIED MY BEST.

IT'S MY FAULT! I'M SO UNBELIEVABLY UGLY. I'M SURE THAT'S WHY HE DIDN'T WANT ME.

I DIDN'T SEE ANY OTHER EXPLANATION.

I'M UGLY. I SMELL. I'M TERRIBLE. I'M HAIRY!

I WENT TO JOIN HIM SO WE COULD TALK.

?!!?   INGRID!

I HAD JUST FOUND ANOTHER EXPLANATION: "HE WAS IN LOVE WITH INGRID."

HI, MY SWEETPEA. I DIDN'T WANT TO WAKE YOU. YOU WERE SLEEPING SO PEACE-FULLY. ARE YOU OKAY?

YES.

I HAVE SOME THINGS TO DO. SEE YOU LATER.

SEE YOU.

WHY ARE YOU SO SAD?

I KNOW. COME, I NEED TO TALK TO YOU.

HE'S GOING TO TELL ME THAT HE'S MARRYING THAT FAT COW.

COME...

HE'S GOING TO TELL ME THAT SHE IS THE LOVE OF HIS LIFE, THAT I'M LIKE A SISTER TO HIM.

MARJANE, I ADORE YOU. THANKS TO YOU, I'VE DISCOVERED SOMETHING VERY IMPORTANT.

I'M LISTENING.

I HAVEN'T TOLD ANYONE. I WANTED TO SHARE THIS SECRET WITH YOU FIRST.

IT'S TRUE? YOU DIDN'T EVEN TELL INGRID?

NO!

HERE IT IS: I THINK I'M GAY.

WHAT? YOU, TOO?

IT WAS INCONCEIVABLE. FIRST MY EIGHT HOUSEMATES AND NOW MY BOYFRIEND. TO THINK THAT ALL THE MEN I KNEW FOUND LOVE AMONGST THEMSELVES.

IF IT DIDN'T WORK WITH YOU, IT WOULDN'T WORK WITH ANYONE!

I NEVER REALLY KNEW WHO I WAS. YOU REMOVED ALL MY DOUBTS.

I SWEAR, IT'S NOT YOU. I THINK YOU'RE PRETTY, ATTRACTIVE, SWEET; IT'S ME, I PROMISE YOU, IT'S ME.

NEVERTHELESS, SOMEWHERE INSIDE, I WAS REASSURED. IT WAS EASIER TO ACCEPT THAT HE WAS GAY THAN THAT HE HAD A PREFERENCE FOR INGRID OR HE FOUND ME UGLY.

I'M HAPPY FOR YOU.

WHAT ELSE COULD I SAY?

PROMISE ME THAT WE'LL ALWAYS BE FRIENDS.

I PROMISE.

I GAVE MY WORD, BUT I WAS TOO YOUNG TO KEEP IT. THIS CHASTE LOVE AFFAIR FRUSTRATED ME MORE THAN IT SATISFIED ME. I WANTED TO LOVE AND BE LOVED FOR REAL.

I LOST TOUCH WITH ENRIQUE BUT HIS ANARCHIST FRIENDS ADOPTED ME. MY LIFE WAS SPLIT BETWEEN THEM, MY SCHOOL, AND FRAU DOCTOR HELLER'S HOUSE.

FRENCH HIGH SCHOOL OF VIENNA

THE COMMUNAL LIFE WENT HAND IN HAND WITH THE USE OF ALL KINDS OF MOOD ENHANCERS: WEED, HASH, . . .

I TRIPPED EVERY WEEKEND, AND YOU COULD SEE IT ON MY FACE.

MY PHYSICS TEACHER, YONNEL ARROUAS, WAS WORRIED ABOUT ME.

MARJANE, ARE YOU OKAY? YOU CAN TALK TO ME IF YOU'D LIKE.

· · ·

AT HOME, THERE'S A WAR. I'M SCARED FOR MY PARENTS. I'M ALONE AND I FEEL GUILTY. I DON'T HAVE MUCH MONEY. MY UNCLE WAS ASSASSINATED. I SAW MY NEIGHBOR DIE IN A BOMBING. . .

I SENSED THAT HE DIDN'T BELIEVE ME. HE MUST HAVE THOUGHT THAT I WAS EXAGGERATING.

I PERSISTED ANYWAY. I NEEDED TO TALK SO MUCH.

THEN, I LIVE IN THIS CRAZY WO-MAN'S HOUSE, MY BOYFRIEND...

ENOUGH, IT'S OKAY. WOULD YOU LIKE TO COME OVER FOR LUNCH AT OUR HOUSE ON SATURDAY? MY MOTHER WILL BE THERE, TOO.

I ACCEPTED.

AT HIS HOUSE, I PLAYED WITH HIS TWINS, JOHANNA AND CAROLINE.

mariane! mariane! mariane! mariane!

cucu!

I SPENT A LONG TIME TALK-ING TO MRS. ARROUAS, MY TEACHER'S MOTHER, A FRENCHWOMAN OF JEWISH-MOROCCAN ORIGINS.

I UNDERSTAND HOW HARD IT IS FOR YOU. YOU HAVE TO MAKE THREE TIMES THE EFFORT OF ANYONE ELSE TO SUCCEED! THAT'S THE IMMIGRANT LOT!! IT WAS THE SAME FOR ME, WHEN I ARRIVED IN FRANCE.

BE STRONG. ALL WILL GO WELL FOR YOU. I HOPE TO SEE YOU SOON.

BUT WE NEVER SAW EACH OTHER AGAIN. YONNEL'S WIFE DIDN'T LIKE ME. SHE MUST HAVE THOUGHT THAT I WAS MAKING UP STORIES. SO I WAS NEVER AGAIN INVITED OVER.

AFTER MY ROMANTIC DISAPPOINTMENT WITH ENRIQUE, I UNDERSTOOD JULIE BETTER WHEN SHE TALKED ABOUT THE NEGATIVE EFFECTS OF A PLATONIC AFFAIR ON HER MOTHER. I HAD GRASPED THE NECESSITY OF A CARNAL RELATIONSHIP. BUT AFTER THIS INCIDENT, WHAT WAS I TO DO? I FELT EVEN MORE UNLOVABLE AND HAD EVEN LESS SELF-CONFIDENCE.

AND THEN ONE DAY A NEW STUDENT ARRIVED IN MY CLASS. HIS NAME WAS JEAN-PAUL. I LIKED HIM.

MARJANE, WOULD YOU LIKE TO GRAB A DRINK THIS WEEKEND?

YOU AND ME?

WHO ELSE?

WHEN?

WELL, THIS WEEKEND. SATURDAY PERHAPS.

WE ARRANGED TO MEET AT CAFÉ DE L'EUROPE AT SIX O'CLOCK.

I PUT ON MY BEST CLOTHES. I WAS SO EXCITED THAT I GOT THERE AN HOUR EARLY.

HE WAS HALF AN HOUR LATE.

AT LAST!

HI! WHAT ARE YOU READING?

OH, IT'S YOU! I HADN'T NOTICED.

HAVE YOU BEEN HERE LONG?

NO, I JUST GOT HERE.

...

...

218

I REALLY LIKED HIM.

SO, HOW ARE YOU?

FINE, FINE, AND YOU?

I'M OKAY. IT'S JUST ... YOU KNOW, I'M EXPERIENCING A GREAT LACK OF AFFECTION.

I WAS HOPING TO MOVE HIM ENOUGH THAT HE'D TAKE MY HAND, CONSPICUOUSLY PLACED ON THE TABLE, WHILE SAYING, "DON'T WORRY, I'LL TAKE CARE OF YOU."

INSTEAD, HE SAID:

EVERYTHING COMES TO HE WHO WAITS.

I DIDN'T REALLY UNDERSTAND WHAT HE WAS TRYING TO SAY.

... SO I WAITED ...

AND AFTER TEN MINUTES OF WAITING,

LISTEN, I DIDN'T GET OUR LAST MATH CLASS ON LOGARITHMS VERY WELL. I HAVE SOME QUESTIONS TO ASK YOU.

??!!!

I HAD TO REMAIN DIGNIFIED. I EXPLAINED EVERYTHING AS NATURALLY AS POSSIBLE.

FOR EXAMPLE THE LOGARITHM OF 100 EQUALS 2 BECAUSE 10^2 EQUALS 100, ...

WE WERE TOGETHER UNTIL NINE O'CLOCK, TALKING ABOUT FUNC-TIONS AND TRIGONOMETRY.

THIS WAS VERY NICE. THANKS, AND SEE YOU SOON.

WHAT DID YOU THINK, YOU STUPID GIRL? YOU THINK THAT A GUY LIKE HIM COULD BE INTERES-TED IN A GIRL LIKE YOU??

WHAT AN IMBECILE! HOW COULD I HAVE BEEN SO DELUSIONAL?

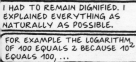

THE FOLLOWING WEEKEND, I WAS BACK AT THE COMMUNE.

WHERE WERE YOU THE PAST TWO WEEKS? WHY DIDN'T YOU COME SEE US?

ONE OF MY TEACHERS INVITED ME OVER, AND LAST WEEK I SAW A FRIEND.

INGRID, MY FORMER ENEMY, HAD NOW BECOME A GREAT FRIEND. SHE TAUGHT ME TRANSCENDENTAL MEDITATION. WITH HER, I SPENT MY TIME EITHER MEDITATING,

OR TRIPPING.

I DIDN'T ALWAYS LIKE IT, BUT I BY FAR PREFERRED BORING MYSELF WITH HER TO HAVING TO CONFRONT MY SOLITUDE AND MY DISAPPOINTMENTS.

LITTLE BY LITTLE, I BECAME THE PORTRAIT OF DORIAN GRAY. THE MORE TIME PASSED, THE MORE I WAS MARKED.

BUT THIS KIND OF DECADENCE WAS PLEASING TO SOME. AND THAT'S HOW I MET THE FIRST GREAT LOVE OF MY LIFE.

HEY! MARJANE!

HIS NAME WAS MARKUS. HE WAS STUDYING LITERATURE. AT LEAST I WAS SURE THAT HE DIDN'T WANT TO SEE ME BECAUSE OF HIS MATH PROBLEMS.

WHAT ARE YOU DOING ON SATURDAY?

I'M GOING TO SEE MY FRIENDS IN THE COUNTRY. WHY?

DO YOU WANT TO GO TO A CLUB?

SURE, WHY NOT?

THIS TIME I DIDN'T MAKE ANY EFFORT AT ALL: I DIDN'T PUT ON MY BEST CLOTHES AND I ARRIVED AN HOUR LATE.

I HAD GIVEN UP. I THOUGHT THAT YOU WOULDN'T COME. I'M HAPPY THAT YOU'RE HERE. DO YOU WANT TO DANCE?

NO, I DON'T LIKE DANCING. ACTUALLY, I DON'T LIKE CLUBS.

WE DANCED ANYWAY.

YOU'RE SO BEAUTIFUL TONIGHT!

WHAT A LIAR.

ASIDE FROM THE FACT THAT WE WERE BOTH ONLY CHILDREN, WE DIDN'T HAVE ANYTHING IN COMMON. I WAS UNCOMFORTABLE.

HAPPILY, THIS PATHETIC SITUATION DIDN'T LAST LONG. THE CLUB CLOSED AT 2:30 IN THE MORNING.

IF YOU WANT, I CAN TAKE YOU HOME, BUT I NEED TO FILL UP FIRST. SHALL WE SPLIT IT?

OKAY.

NOTHING SURPRISED ME ANYMORE. EVEN PAYING FOR GAS SO THAT MY WHITE KNIGHT COULD DRIVE ME HOME SEEMED COMPLETELY NORMAL.

YOU KNOW WHAT I LOVE ABOUT YOU, YOUR REBELLIOUS SIDE AND YOUR NATURAL NONCHALANCE.

THANKS

THEN . . .

THINGS ALWAYS HAPPEN WHEN YOU LEAST EXPECT. IT WAS HAPPINESS.

I FINALLY HAD A REAL BOYFRIEND. I WAS OVER THE MOON. ONE NIGHT AT MARKUS' HOUSE,

I'M GOING TO WRITE A PLAY.

OH YEAH, I'D LOVE TO BE IN IT.

WHEN SUDDENLY,

WAS MACHT SIE HIER? SIE MUSS RAUS GEHEN!

IT WAS HIS MOTHER. MARKUS DIDN'T HAVE A FATHER. SHE THOUGHT I DIDN'T UNDERSTAND GERMAN. SHE WAS SAYING THAT I HAD TO GO "RAUS," OUTSIDE.

I'D ALREADY HEARD THIS THREATENING WORD YELLED AT ME IN THE METRO.

DU SCHEIß AUSLÄNDERIN, GEH RAUS!

IT WAS AN OLD MAN WHO SAID "DIRTY FOREIGNER, GET OUT!" I HAD HEARD IT ANOTHER TIME IN THE STREET. BUT I TRIED TO MAKE LIGHT OF IT. I THOUGHT THAT IT WAS JUST THE REACTION OF A NASTY OLD MAN.

BUT THIS, THIS WAS DIFFERENT. IT WAS NEITHER AN OLD MAN DESTROYED BY THE WAR, NOR A YOUNG IDIOT. IT WAS MY BOYFRIEND'S MOTHER WHO ATTACKED ME. SHE WAS SAYING THAT I WAS TAKING ADVANTAGE OF MARKUS AND HIS SITUATION TO OBTAIN AN AUSTRIAN PASSPORT, THAT I WAS A WITCH.

I THINK SHE'D NEVER LOOKED AT HERSELF IN THE MIRROR.

LAß UNS IN RUHE!

SHE ORDERED ME TO LEAVE THEM ALONE, HER AND HER SON.

RAUS! ICH SAGE RAUS!!

THEN THREW ME OUT.

GO ON HOME. I'LL COME SEE YOU TOMORROW AT YOUR HOUSE.

MARKUS MUST HAVE BEEN SUFFERING MORE THAN I. HE HAD TO SACRIFICE HIS RELATIONSHIP WITH HIS MOTHER TO CONTINUE TO SEE ME. I DIDN'T WANT TO ADD TO IT. SO I SAID NOTHING ...

AT MY HOUSE, IT WASN'T MUCH BETTER.

YOU DON'T HAVE ANYTHING TO SMOKE?

NO, NOW THAT I DON'T SEE INGRID ...

IT'S SO STUPID! MY MOTHER CUT OFF MY ALLOWANCE.

REALLY?

GEH RAUS!

HIER IST NICHT EIN NUTTEN HAUS!*

* THIS ISN'T A BORDELLO.

WHAT DO YOU THINK? YOU THINK I DON'T KNOW ANYTHING ABOUT YOUR "SECRET PROSTITUTION"?

HAVE YOU NO SHAME? HE'S MY BOYFRIEND!

OF COURSE! IT'S OBVIOUS.

WHAT? TO YOU, TRUE AUSTRIANS DON'T GO OUT WITH GIRLS LIKE ME? IS THAT IT?

YOU WOULD HAVE MADE FREUD AN EXCELLENT PATIENT!*

FRAU DOCTOR HELLER WAS A CRACKPOT. SHE WAS A REAL PSYCHO-PATH, A CRAZY WOMAN. I REALLY WANTED TO INSULT HER, BUT I HAD PROMISED MY MOTHER THAT I WOULDN'T.

* I HAD JUST READ HIS THREE ESSAYS ON THE THEORY OF SEXUALITY.

SO I INSULTED HER VERY STRONGLY IN PERSIAN.

دکتر هیلر، درت سگتو!!

SHE DIDN'T UNDERSTAND ANYTHING AND I GOT TO LET OFF STEAM.

MARKUS AND I DIDN'T KNOW WHERE TO GO. WE OFTEN ENDED UP IN HIS CAR, WHERE WE SMOKED JOINTS TO DISTRACT OURSELVES.

LISTEN, I HEARD OF A CAFÉ WHERE WE CAN BUY CHEAP HASH. DO YOU WANT TO GO SEE? I CAN'T FIND ANYWHERE TO PARK.

OF COURSE!

HERE'S 200 SHILLINGS.

NO, IT'S OKAY, I'VE GOT MONEY.

I WENT IN. I WAS VERY, VERY SCARED. IT WAS THE FIRST TIME THAT I'D SET FOOT IN SUCH A SORDID PLACE.

CAFÉ CAMERA →

BUT IT WASN'T A BIG DEAL. AFTER ALL, I WAS DOING IT FOR LOVE.

EXCUSE ME, I WANT TWO BAGS FOR 200 BUCKS.

FOLLOW ME.

HERE.

THANKS.

MARKUS WAS PROUD OF ME. SO PROUD THAT HE TOLD THE WHOLE SCHOOL THAT HIS GIRLFRIEND HAD CONTACTS AT CAFÉ CAMERA.

THIS IS HOW, FOR LOVE, I BEGAN MY CAREER AS A DRUG DEALER. HADN'T I FOLLOWED MY MOTHER'S ADVICE? TO GIVE THE BEST OF MYSELF? I WAS NO LONGER A SIMPLE JUNKIE, BUT MY SCHOOL'S OFFICIAL DEALER.

THE CROISSANT

LUCKILY, I HAD BENEFITED ENOUGH FROM A SOLID EDUCATION TO NEVER DRIFT TOO FAR. IT WAS THE END OF MY LAST YEAR. I WAS GOING TO TAKE THE FRENCH BACCALAUREATE.

WHEN I STUDIED WITH THE OTHERS, I REALIZED THAT I HAD MANY GAPS. I NEEDED A MIRACLE TO PASS.

AND THIS MIRACLE HAPPENED ONE NIGHT IN JUNE, DURING MY SLEEP.

"HEY, MARJI, THE SUBJECT ON THE BAC, IT WILL BE MONTESQUIEU'S "SLAVERY OF THE NEGROES.""

THE NEXT MORNING I CALLED MY MOTHER,

WHO CALLED GOD, WHO IN TURN SENT HIS MESSAGE TO THE EXAMINER.

EACH TIME THAT I ASKED MY MOTHER TO PRAY FOR ME, MY WISH WAS GRANTED.

DO YOU LIKE THE 18TH CENTURY?

YES.

DO YOU LIKE MONTESQUIEU?

YES.

YOU HAVE THIRTY MINUTES TO PREPARE "SLAVERY OF THE NEGROES."

I GOT A 17, THE BEST GRADE IN SCHOOL.

THEN CAME SUMMER. TO BE TRUTHFUL, I WASN'T MAKING ANYTHING BY DEALING BECAUSE I WAS DOING IT AS A FAVOR. SO I SET OUT TO FIND SOME ODD JOBS.

IT WAS SOMETIMES BORING.

SOMETIMES FUN.

ONE DAY I SAW AN AD IN A NEWSPAPER: "CAFÉ SOLE IS LOOKING FOR A WAITRESS, THREE EUROPEAN LANGUAGES REQUIRED."

YOU SPEAK GERMAN, ENGLISH AND FRENCH. THAT'S GOOD. HAVE YOU EVER WORKED IN A BAR?

YES*

GOOD! YOU START TOMORROW. BUT WATCH OUT! THE CUSTOMER IS ALWAYS RIGHT!!

* I LIED.

CAFÉ SOLE WAS LOCATED IN THE BEST NEIGHBORHOOD IN VIENNA, I WAS PAID DECENTLY, BUT IT WASN'T ALWAYS EASY WITH THE CUSTOMERS. SOMETIMES, I REALLY WANTED TO SLAP THEM.

"THE CUSTOMER IS ALWAYS RIGHT." "THE CUSTOMER IS ALWAYS RIGHT"...

NONETHELESS, I HAD AN ALLY. IT WAS SVETLANA, THE YUGOSLAVIAN CHEF.

WHAT'S THE MATTER, SWEETIE?

SOME MORON PINCHED MY BUTT.

TELL ME, WHAT DID HE ORDER, THIS SON-OF-A-BITCH?

A WIENER SCHNITZEL.

GOD FORGIVE ME!

RAAK PTOUH!

THERE! JUSTICE IS DONE.

SHE REALLY MADE ME LAUGH. THANKS TO HER, I WAS ABLE TO WORK THERE WITHOUT HAVING TO INJURE A FEW MEN WHERE IT COUNTS.

WAS SO BUSY I DIDN'T NOTICE WHEN THE TART OF THE SCHOOL YEAR ARRIVED.

MARJANE SATRAPI! THE PRINCIPAL WANTS TO SEE YOU.

I SAW THAT YOU HAD THE BEST SCORE FOR THE FRENCH BAC. ALL MY CONGRATULATIONS.

THANK YOU, SIR.

HAVE A SEAT.

IF YOU WILL, THE USAGE OF CERTAIN SUBSTANCES DOES NOT HAVE THE SAME EFFECT ON EVERYONE. IN CERTAIN INDIVIDUALS, IT CAN LEAD TO DEPLORABLE CONSEQUENCES.

LET ME EXPLAIN MYSELF. WE HAVE A REAL PROBLEM WITH THE CONSUMPTION OF CANNABIS IN THIS SCHOOL.

WHOEVER PROCURES IT FOR THE STUDENTS OF THIS ESTABLISHMENT COULD BE SEVERELY PUNISHED.

YOU ARE INTELLIGENT AND I TRUST I WON'T HAVE TO SPEAK TO YOU ABOUT THIS A SECOND TIME.

NO, YOU WON'T HAVE TO.

REMEMBER YOUR-SELF, SATRAPI, I'M COUNTING ON YOU!

YES, YES.

I WAS VERY SCARED. IT WAS THE END OF MY CAREER.

ADMITTEDLY, I WASN'T SELLING DRUGS ANYMORE, BUT I HAD STARTED TAKING MORE AND MORE. AT FIRST, MARKUS WAS VERY IMPRESSED,

ANOTHER ONE?? YOU'RE TOO STRONG!

THEN, HE STARTED TO LECTURE ME,

IN THE NAME OF GOD! LOOK AT WHAT YOU'RE BECOMING.

AND FINALLY, HE DISTANCED HIMSELF.

THIS DECADENT SIDE, WHICH HAD SO PLEASED HIM AT FIRST, ENDED UP PROFOUNDLY ANNOYING HIM.

I SHOULD SAY THAT I WAS SMOKING TOO MANY JOINTS. I WAS CONSTANTLY TIRED AND I OFTEN FELL ASLEEP.

THE DEFINITE INTEGRAL OF FUNCTION F ON . . .

MARJANE, ARE YOU OKAY?

WHAT?

DO YOU FEEL WELL?

WHAT DO YOU WANT ME TO SAY, SIR? THAT I'M THE VEGETABLE THAT I REFUSED TO BECOME?

THAT I'M SO DISAPPOINTED IN MYSELF THAT I CAN NO LONGER LOOK AT MYSELF IN THE MIRROR? THAT I HATE MYSELF?...

EVERYTHING'S FINE, SIR. I'M A LITTLE SICK, I FEEL VERY TIRED.

I REMAINED IN THIS STATE FOR THE REST OF THE SCHOOL YEAR, BUT THANKS TO THE REGISTERED LETTERS, SENT TO GOD EVERY DAY BY MY MOTHER, I GRADUATED BY THE SKIN OF MY TEETH. I WAS RELIEVED.

IT WAS 1988. MARKUS HAD STARTED STUDYING THEATER. I HAD REGISTERED AT THE FACULTY OF TECHNOLOGY, BUT I NEVER WENT.

YOU DON'T WANT TO GO OUT?

I DON'T HAVE TIME, MY EXAMS ARE NEXT WEEK.

THIS SAME YEAR, I BECAME AWARE THAT THE PRESIDENT OF AUSTRIA WAS NAMED KURT WALDHEIM.

THROUGH MARKUS, I HAD GOTTEN TO KNOW SOME OTHER STUDENTS. WE WOULD OFTEN GET TOGETHER AT THE CAFÉ HAWELKA, WHERE WE DISCUSSED POLITICS.

IT'S THE RETURN OF NAZISM, IT'S SERIOUS.

WE SHOULDN'T EXAGGERATE. WALDHEIM WAS ELECTED A YEAR AND A HALF AGO. IF THERE HAD BEEN ANY RADICAL CHANGES, WE WOULD HAVE KNOWN.

HOW CAN YOU SAY THAT? WE'VE GONE FROM SOCIALISM TO NAZISM.

PERSONALLY, I DIDN'T UNDERSTAND THIS DIFFERENCE. THE FIRST TIME I SAW SKINHEADS WAS IN 1984. AT THE TIME, I DIDN'T EVEN KNOW WHAT IT MEANT. AND I DIDN'T SPEAK MUCH GERMAN. SO I DIDN'T UNDERSTAND WHAT THEY WANTED WITH ME. I SENSED THAT THEY WERE HOSTILE, BUT HAVING GROWN UP WITH THE GUARDIANS OF THE REVOLUTION, I KNEW WHAT TO DO IN THIS KIND OF SITUATION...

I KEPT A LOW PROFILE.

SINCE THEN, I HADN'T NOTICED THEIR NUMBERS GROWING.

ASSHOLES, THEY'RE EVERYWHERE. YOU THINK THAT THERE AREN'T ANY WHERE I COME FROM? THEY'RE TEN TIMES MORE FEARSOME THAN YOURS. IN IRAN, THEY KILL THE PEOPLE WHO DON'T THINK LIKE THE LEADERS!

IT'S INTERESTING TO HAVE AN OUTSIDE OPINION.

YES, IT'S TRUE.

DURING THIS PERIOD, THE STUDENTS IN QUESTION, LIKE MOST YOUNG VIENNESE, WERE VERY POLITICIZED. THEY DEMONSTRATED EVERY SO OFTEN AGAINST THE GOVERNMENT IN POWER. SOMETIMES I JOINED THEM.

THEY SAID THAT THE OLD NAZIS HAD BEEN TEACHING "MEIN KAMPF" IN THEIR HOMES TO NEW NAZIS SINCE THE BEGINNING OF THE 80S, THAT SOON THERE WOULD BE A RISE IN THE EXTREME RIGHT THROUGHOUT EUROPE.

IT'S CRAZY HOW PEOPLE ARE ALL COWARDS. AND HERE WE ARE IN VIENNA. CAN YOU IMAGINE HOW IT MUST BE IN THE TYROL!!

BUT I'VE BEEN TO THE TYROL, I THOUGHT THEY WERE VERY NICE.

MY FRIEND'S FATHER EVEN MADE ME A FRAME ...

IT'S BECAUSE YOU'RE A GIRL. IF YOU WERE A BOY WITH FRIZZY HAIR AND YOUR SKIN WAS A LITTLE DARKER, IT WOULDN'T HAVE BEEN LIKE THAT.

I ASKED MYSELF IF THEY WOULD HAVE SAT BESIDE ME IF I HAD BEEN A FRIZZY-HAIRED AND DARK-SKINNED BOY?

AS FOR MARKUS, HE NEVER PARTICIPATED IN ANYTHING. HE WAS WRITING HIS PLAY.

YOU'RE NOT COMING WITH US?

UHH, NO! I'M WORKING, I DON'T HAVE TIME.

AND ANYWAY, IT'S A WASTE OF TIME. WALDHEIM WAS DEMOCRATICALLY ELECTED. IT WAS THE WILL OF THE PEOPLE.

CLICK CLICK

AND YOUR CONSCIENCE? WHAT HAVE YOU DONE WITH YOUR CONSCIENCE?

I WRITE. CULTURE AND EDUCATION ARE THE LETHAL WEAPONS AGAINST ALL KINDS OF FUNDAMENTALISM. WE HAVE TO EDUCATE THE PEOPLE SO THAT THEY DON'T VOTE FOR NAZIS.

YEAH, THE INTELLECTUALS ARE TOO PRECIOUS TO WASTE THEIR TIME SHOUTING!

WHATEVER..

IN ANY CASE, IT'S THE COWARDICE OF PEOPLE LIKE YOU WHO GIVE DICTATORS THE CHANCE TO INSTALL THEMSELVES!

THESE ARGUMENTS MARKED THE BEGINNING OF THE END OF OUR STORY.

NEVERTHELESS HE, LIKE I, TRIED TO SAVE OUR RELATIONSHIP. WE HAD BEEN TOGETHER ALMOST TWO YEARS. THE NIGHT BEFORE MY BIRTHDAY,

I'VE BEEN INVITED TO GRAZ BY A FRIEND.

THAT'S GOOD.

IT DOESN'T BOTHER YOU THAT I WON'T BE CELEBRATING MY BIRTHDAY WITH YOU?

NO, NOT AT ALL.

IT'LL BE GOOD FOR YOU.

IT WAS GOOD TIMING AFTER ALL. MAYBE THIS VACATION WAS GOING TO SAVE OUR RELATIONSHIP.

YOU'RE GOING TO MISS ME, YOU'LL SEE. . .

GOOD, I'M GOING TO SLEEP AT YOUR HOUSE TONIGHT. MY TRAIN IS AT 7:30 TOMORROW.

WAIT, YOU'RE CLOSER TO THE STATION THAN I AM. IF YOU COME OVER, YOU'LL MISS YOUR TRAIN.

YES, YOU'RE RIGHT!

WHEN YOU GET BACK, WE'LL CELEBRATE TOGETHER.

SO I SLEPT AT MY HOUSE AND THE NEXT MORNING . . .

...I MISSED MY TRAIN.

THIS MUST BE DESTINY'S SIGN THAT I SHOULD CELEBRATE TURNING EIGHTEEN WITH HIM.

I HAD AN INGENIOUS IDEA: "I AM GOING TO SURPRISE HIM BY BRINGING HIM HOT CROISSANTS."

OH YEAH, I'M JUST TOO COOL!

I TURNED THE KEY IN THE LOCK DELICATELY, NOT TO WAKE HIM, TO BETTER SURPRISE HIM.

HELLOOO!

IT WAS LIKE A BAD AMERICAN MOVIE. ONE OF THOSE FILMS WHERE THE SURPRISED MAN WRAPS HIMSELF IN A SHEET OUT OF MODESTY AND SAYS:

WAIT, I CAN EXPLAIN EVERYTHING!

...IT'S NOT WHAT YOU THINK...

...I LOVE YOU, MARJANE, YOU MUST BELIEVE ME, I LOVE YOU...

BASTARD, ASSHOLE, SHITFACE

IF THAT'S HOW IT IS, GET OUT! GO ON, BEAT IT!!

SO, BY ORDER OF THE TRAITOROUS MARKUS, I BEAT IT. I NEVER SAW HIM AGAIN.

THE VEIL

MY BREAKUP WITH MARKUS REPRESENTED MORE THAN A SIMPLE SEPARATION. I HAD JUST LOST MY ONE EMOTIONAL SUPPORT, THE ONLY PERSON WHO CARED FOR ME, AND TO WHOM I WAS ALSO WHOLLY ATTACHED.

I HAD NO FAMILY OR FRIENDS. I HAD COUNTED ON THIS RELATIONSHIP FOR EVERYTHING. THE WORLD HAD JUST CRUMBLED IN FRONT OF MY EYES.

AH, THERE YOU ARE! I LOST MY BROOCH. I'M SURE THAT YOU'RE THE ONE WHO TOOK IT.

LEAVE ME ALONE, PLEASE!

OH NO, YOU CAN'T GET AWAY WITH THIS.

GO TO HELL, LEAVE! I DETEST YOU, I HATE YOU!

EVERYTHING REMINDED ME OF MARKUS. THIS BEDSPREAD, IT WAS HIS BIRTHDAY PRESENT TO ME.

THIS POSTER, HE BOUGHT IT FOR ME AT THE PICASSO SHOW AT THE MUSEUM OF MODERN ART.

HIS T-SHIRT. OH, HIS T-SHIRT!

ASIDE FROM HIM, WHO ELSE WAS SINCERELY INTERESTED IN ME DURING THESE FOUR YEARS IN VIENNA?

WHERE WAS MY MOTHER TO STROKE MY HAIR?

WHERE WAS MY GRANDMOTHER TO TELL ME THAT LOVERS, I WOULD HAVE THEM BY THE DOZEN?

WHERE WAS MY FATHER TO PUNISH THIS BOY WHO DARED HURT HIS DAUGHTER? WHERE?

IN THIS ROOM, EVERYTHING EVOKED MARKUS. I COULDN'T STAND IT ANYMORE.

SO I GOT DRESSED,

I TOOK MY BAG,

MY PASSPORT, THE PLANE TICKET MY PARENTS HAD GIVEN ME TO VISIT THEM AT CHRISTMAS, AND A LITTLE MONEY.

WHERE ARE YOU GOING LIKE THAT?

ADIEU!

YOU'RE NOT GOING TO GET OUT OF THIS SO EASILY!

GO FUCK YOURSELF.

THIEF! I'M GOING TO CALL THE POLICE! I AM GOING TO DO THIS AND THAT . . .

CLACK

236

IT WAS NOVEMBER 22. MY BIRTHDAY. IT WAS BITTERLY COLD. I STAYED ON A BENCH, IMMOBILE ...
I WATCHED THE PEOPLE GOING TO WORK ...

... THEN COMING BACK ...

NIGHT FELL ...

"NIGHT BRINGS GOOD COUNSEL," MY GRANDMOTHER ALWAYS TOLD ME.

IN EFFECT, SHE CLEARED UP A LOT OF POINTS. SUDDENLY, I HAD A REVELATION.

MARKUS IS A REAL BASTARD.

ALL THOSE TIMES WHEN, ON THE PRETEXT OF NOT FINDING A PARKING PLACE, HE MADE ME GO DOWN INTO CAFÉ CAMERA...

...HE KNEW THAT COPS CAME BY FROM TIME TO TIME ON RAIDS.

IT WOULDN'T HAVE BOTHERED HIM IF I HAD BEEN ARRESTED.

AND THE TIME WHEN HIS MOTHER MEANLY TOLD ME OFF...

...HE COULD HAVE TAKEN MY DEFENSE INSTEAD OF SENDING ME HOME!...

...NOT TO MENTION THE FIRST TIME WE WENT OUT TO A NIGHTCLUB TOGETHER, WHEN HE ASKED ME TO PAY FOR GAS AND ONCE THE GAS WAS PAID FOR HE TOLD ME:

WHAT I LOVE ABOUT YOU, IT'S YOUR REBELLIOUS SIDE AND YOUR NATURAL NONCHALANCE.

REPRESSED AS HE WAS, HE MUST HAVE IDENTIFIED WITH MY REBELLIOUS SIDE.

HOW COULD I HAVE BEEN SO BLIND? WHAT RELATIONSHIP? WHAT LOVE? WHAT SUPPORT? WHAT AN ASSHOLE!!!

HE TOLD ME THAT HIS MOTHER CUT OFF HIS ALLOWANCE.

I DON'T KNOW WHAT TO DO. I'M STARTING UNIVERSITY IN A MONTH. IF I START WORKING AT THE SAME TIME, IT'S GOING TO TAKE ME TEN YEARS TO FINISH MY STUDIES.

DON'T WORRY, I HAVE SOME SAVINGS.

IN THIS WAY, ALL THE MONEY THAT MY PARENTS HAD SENT ME, WHICH I WAS SUPPOSED TO LIVE ON FOR A YEAR, WAS SPENT IN THREE MONTHS.

THE CHECK?

IT'S FOR ME.

IT'S NOT POSSIBLE: HIS MOTHER LOVED HIM TOO MUCH TO CUT OFF HIS ALLOWANCE. I'M SURE SHE WAS GIVING HIM MONEY. HE MUST HAVE BLOWN IT ALL ON HER.

THAT BITCH ↑↑

I WAS GOING COMPLETELY CRAZY.

TODAY, IN RETROSPECT, I NO LONGER CONDEMN HIM. MARKUS HAD A HISTORY, A FAMILY, FRIENDS. I HAD NO ONE BUT HIM. I WANTED HIM TO BE AT ONCE MY BOYFRIEND, MY FATHER, MY MOTHER, MY TWIN.

I HAD PROJECTED EVERYTHING ONTO HIM. IT WAS SURELY NOT EASY FOR A BOY OF NINETEEN.

WHAT MISERY.

I SPENT MY FIRST NIGHT ON THE STREET. THERE WERE PLENTY OF OTHERS ...

IN THE MORNING, I TOOK THE TRAM.

INSIDE, THERE WERE TWO SPOTS THAT WERE VERY WARM, BECAUSE THEY WERE ABOVE THE MOTOR. I FELL ASLEEP ON ONE OF THESE SEATS. IT WAS PEACEFUL.

FOR ALMOST A MONTH, I LIVED AT THIS RHYTHM: THE NIGHT PROSTRATE AND THE DAY LETTING MYSELF BE CARRIED ACROSS VIENNA BY SLEEP AND THE TRAMWAY.

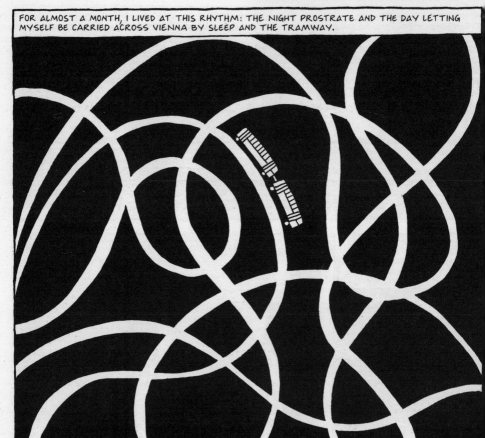

VERY QUICKLY, MY SAVINGS VANISHED. I WAS BROKE.

IT'S INCREDIBLE HOW QUICKLY YOU CAN LOSE YOUR DIGNITY. I FOUND MYSELF SMOKING BUTTS,

LOOKING FOR FOOD IN TRASH CANS,

I, WHO BEFORE COULDN'T EVEN TASTE FROM OTHERS' PLATES.

SOON, I WAS RECOGNIZED AND THROWN OUT OF ALL THE TRAMS.

SO I HAD TO FIND A WELL-HIDDEN PLACE TO SLEEP AT NIGHT. NIGHTS ON THE STREET COULD END VERY BADLY FOR A YOUNG GIRL LIKE ME.

I DIDN'T HAVE ANYONE. MY ENTIRE EXISTENCE HAD BEEN PLANNED AROUND MARKUS. IT'S SURELY FOR THIS REASON THAT I FOUND MYSELF WANDERING LIKE THIS.

IT WAS UNTHINKABLE THAT I GO BACK TO SEE ZOZO.

I DON'T CARE. OUR APARTMENT IS TOO SMALL.

NOR INGRID.

YOU DROPPED US FOR A GUY WHO WASN'T EVEN WORTH IT.

AS FOR FRAU DOCTOR HELLER, LET'S NOT EVEN TALK ABOUT HER. SHE REPRESENTED ABSOLUTE EVIL IN MY EYES.

I SPENT MORE THAN TWO MONTHS ON THE STREET IN THE MIDDLE OF WINTER.

KOUMF KOUMF

IT WAS VERY COLD.

ROUFH KOF KOF

I GOT SICK.

KEUH KEUH

I STARTED TO COUGH A LITTLE,

RRRM KREUH KOF

THEN A LITTLE MORE,

MPF KKOF KOF

THEN A LITTLE MORE STRONGLY,

KROUMPF KROUF

MY COUGH BECAME CONTINUOUS,

KRA KRA

UNTIL I SPIT BLOOD,

KOF REUH

AND ENDED UP...

I WOKE UP IN A HOSPITAL. IT WAS A MIRACLE. IF I HAD FAINTED DURING THE NIGHT, NO ONE WOULD HAVE NOTICED AND THE GLACIAL COLD WOULD SURELY HAVE PREVENTED ME FROM FULFILLING MY DESTINY.

HAD KNOWN A REVOLUTION THAT HAD MADE ME LOSE PART OF MY FAMILY.

BREATHE, BREATHE

I HAD SURVIVED A WAR THAT HAD DISTANCED ME FROM MY COUNTRY AND MY PARENTS . . .

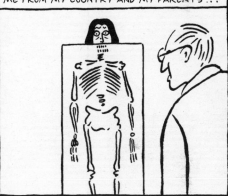

PEDAL AS FAST AS YOU CAN.

. . . AND IT'S A BANAL STORY OF LOVE THAT ALMOST CARRIED ME AWAY.

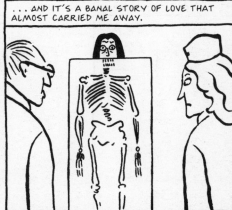

YOU HAVE A CLEAN BILL OF HEALTH. WE HAVE CONDUCTED A COMPLETE CHECK-UP.

SO, YOU HAD SEVERE BRONCHITIS WITHOUT GETTING TREATMENT. I FORBID YOU TO SMOKE. ONE SINGLE CIGARETTE AND YOU WILL PUT YOURSELF IN SERIOUS DANGER.

WHERE DO YOU LIVE?

IN IRAN.

IN IRAN?

YES, WELL, I DON'T REALLY HAVE AN ADDRESS IN VIENNA.

TAKE CARE OF YOURSELF.

CAN I MAKE A TELEPHONE CALL?

I SUDDENLY REMEMBERED THIS CONVERSATION WITH MY MOTHER.

YOU KNOW, ZOZO OWES ME 3000 SHILLINGS. IF YOU HAVE THE COURAGE YOU CAN GO RECLAIM THEM.

I'LL SEE.

EVEN IF IT COST ME TO CALL ZOZO, I DIDN'T HAVE A CHOICE. I DIDN'T EVEN HAVE A GROSCHEN.

OK, I'M COMING THIS AFTERNOON.

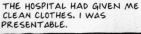
THE HOSPITAL HAD GIVEN ME CLEAN CLOTHES. I WAS PRESENTABLE.

HELLO.

HELLO.

SAY, YOU'VE GROWN. WHERE DID YOU DISAPPEAR TO? YOUR UNCLE MASSOUD CAME FROM GERMANY TO LOOK FOR YOU.

MY UNCLE?

YES, YOUR UNCLE! HE MOVED HEAVEN AND EARTH TO FIND YOU.

YOUR PARENTS, TOO. THEY'VE ALREADY CALLED ME TEN TIMES.

MY PARENTS?

WELL, WHAT DO YOU THINK? THAT YOU CAN DISAPPEAR FOR THREE MONTHS WITHOUT THEM WORRYING?

IF THEY DIDN'T HAVE TO WAIT FOUR MONTHS TO GET A VISA, THEY WOULD ALREADY BE HERE.

DRING! DRING!

LOOK, HERE ARE THE 3000 SHILLINGS, I'M GOING TO ANSWER THE PHONE.

IT'S FOR YOU, IT'S YOUR PARENTS.

MY PARENTS?

ANOTHER MIRACLE HAD JUST OCCURRED.

MY FATHER'S VOICE WAS SOFT AND SOOTHING:

- DAD, IT'S YOU?

- MY DARLING, WE LOOKED FOR YOU EVERYWHERE.

- CAN I COME BACK?

- OF COURSE, WHAT A QUESTION.

- DAD, PROMISE ME TO NEVER ASK ME ANYTHING ABOUT THESE THREE MONTHS.

- I PROMISE YOU... HERE'S YOUR MOTHER.

MY MOTHER'S VOICE WAS TENDER, TOO.

- I AM VERY HAPPY...

- MOM, PLEASE, DON'T CRY.

- THESE ARE TEARS OF JOY.

- MOM...

- COME HOME, DARLING, WE ARE WAITING FOR YOU...

- MOM...

- NO ONE WILL ASK YOU ANY QUESTIONS. IT'S A PROMISE.

BEFORE MY DEPARTURE, I WENT BY FRAU DOCTOR HELLER'S.

I CAME TO GET MY THINGS.

HERE THEY ARE!

WHERE IS THE REST?

THERE IS NO REST. THE REST WILL COMPENSATE THE BROOCH THAT YOU STOLE FROM ME.

I DIDN'T SAY ANYTHING. IN ANY CASE, I COULDN'T TAKE FOUR YEARS OF MY LIFE BACK WITH ME.

I FOUND AN INEXPENSIVE HOTEL. I HAD FIVE DAYS AHEAD OF ME, BEFORE THE NEXT FLIGHT TO TEHRAN.

I FINALLY FOUND A PLACE OF MY OWN, SOME PRIVACY.

DESPITE THE DOCTOR'S ORDERS, I BOUGHT MYSELF SEVERAL CARTONS OF CIGARETTES.

YOU ARE PUTTING YOURSELF IN SERIOUS DANGER...

I THINK THAT I PREFERRED TO PUT MYSELF IN SERIOUS DANGER RATHER THAN CONFRONT MY SHAME. MY SHAME AT NOT HAVING BECOME SOMEONE, THE SHAME OF NOT HAVING MADE MY PARENTS PROUD AFTER ALL THE SACRIFICES THEY HAD MADE FOR ME. THE SHAME OF HAVING BECOME A MEDIOCRE NIHILIST.

246

THE FIVE DAYS PASSED LIKE THE WIND AND THE CIGA-RETTES DIDN'T GET THE BET-TER OF ME. I GOT DRESSED,

I PACKED MY BAG...

...I AGAIN PUT ON MY VEIL...

...AND SO MUCH FOR MY INDIVIDUAL AND SOCIAL LIBERTIES...

...I NEEDED SO BADLY TO GO HOME.

THE RETURN

AFTER FOUR YEARS LIVING IN VIENNA, HERE I AM BACK IN TEHRAN. FROM THE MOMENT I ARRIVED AT MEHRABAD AIRPORT AND CAUGHT SIGHT OF THE FIRST CUSTOMS AGENT, I IMMEDIATELY FELT THE REPRESSIVE AIR OF MY COUNTRY.

DO YOU HAVE ANYTHING FORBIDDEN? FASHION MAGAZINES, TAPES, ALCOHOL, PORK ...

NO, SIR!

PLEASE FIX YOUR VEIL, MY SISTER!

YES, MY BROTHER.

NEXT! COME ON, SPEED IT UP!

BROTHER AND SISTER ARE THE TERMS USED IN IRAN BY THE REPRESENTATIVES OF THE LAW TO GIVE ORDERS TO PEOPLE, WITHOUT OFFENDING THEM.

THERE WERE PEOPLE EVERYWHERE. EACH PASSENGER WAS BEING MET BY A DOZEN PEOPLE. SUDDENLY, AMONGST THE CROWD, I SPOTTED MY PARENTS ...

...BUT IT WASN'T RECIPROCAL. OF COURSE IT MADE SENSE. ONE CHANGES MORE BETWEEN THE AGES OF FOURTEEN AND EIGHTEEN THAN BETWEEN THIRTY AND FORTY.

DAD!

EBI! LOOK! IT'S MARJI!

MARJ..?

MY DARLING, MY DAUGHTER, OH MY! I DIDN'T RECOGNIZE YOU!

I KNEW THAT I HAD GROWN, BUT IT WAS ONLY ONCE I WAS IN THE ARMS OF MY FATHER THAT I REALLY FELT IT. HE, WHO HAD ALWAYS BEFORE APPEARED SO IMPOSING, WAS ABOUT THE SAME SIZE AS ME.

I CAN'T BELIEVE MY EYES! TELL US, ARE YOU HUNGRY?

DAD, YOU KNOW WHAT IT'S LIKE ON IRAN AIR. THEY FEED YOU AT LEAST FIFTY TIMES.

THEN WE GOT IN THE CAR.

MY FATHER DIDN'T HAVE HIS CADILLAC ANYMORE, BUT DROVE A RENAULT 5 INSTEAD. THAT SAME CADILLAC IN WHICH I WAS ASHAMED TO SIT BECAUSE IT WAS SO DIFFICULT TO ACCEPT BEING MORE COMFORTABLE THAN OTHERS. NOW THAT I MYSELF HAD UNDERSTOOD DISTRESS, I NO LONGER ASKED THESE KINDS OF QUESTIONS. I WOULD EVEN HAVE PREFERRED THAT HE COME GET ME WITH A BETTER CAR, AS A WAY TO REMIND ME OF A MORE GLORIOUS TIME.

I DIDN'T FEEL LIKE TALKING. I PRETENDED TO LOOK AT THE CITY, EVEN THOUGH IT WAS TOO DARK TO SEE ANYTHING.

WELCOME HOME!

THEY WERE THE MOST COMFORTING WORDS THAT I HAD HEARD IN A LONG TIME.

I WENT STRAIGHT TO THE LIVING ROOM. THERE WAS STILL THAT SOFA ON WHICH MY PARENTS HAD ANNOUNCED THAT THEY WERE SENDING ME TO AUSTRIA.

ENTERING INTO A CONVERSATION ABOUT THIS SUBJECT SCARED ME SO MUCH THAT I HEADED FOR MY ROOM LIKE A BOOR WITHOUT SAYING GOOD NIGHT OR GOODBYE.

MY ROOM ...
MY ROOM!!

I WAS OVERJOYED TO FINALLY HAVE A PLACE OF MY OWN AND THIS REASSURED ME.

I DIDN'T WANT TO TURN ON THE LIGHT. I COULDN'T BEAR TO SEE EVERYTHING AGAIN SO QUICKLY.

I SPENT A GOOD PART OF THE NIGHT IN THE EMPTINESS, JUST HAPPY TO BE THERE.

AND THE NEXT MORNING.

YAY! IT SNOWED!

IN VIENNA, I HATED SNOW. ESPECIALLY WHEN I FOUND MYSELF ON THE STREET. YOU APPRECIATE SNOW MUCH BETTER WHEN YOU SEE IT FROM THE WINDOW OF A WARM ROOM.

I TOOK STOCK OF MY SURROUNDINGS.

BEFORE LEAVING IRAN, I WORSHIPPED PUNKS, TO THE POINT OF HAVING DRAWN ONE ON MY WALL.

PFFF! WHAT SHIT!

THEN, I TOOK STOCK OF MY PROPERTY. I OWNED AN EMPTY ARMOIRE...

...A TOO-SMALL DESK...

...A BED, A RUG, AND A CASSETTE-RADIO.

I WOULDN'T MIND LISTENING TO SOME KIM WILDE.

I LOOKED IN THE DRAWER, WHERE I USUALLY KEPT MY TAPES.

I DIDN'T FIND THEM.

SO I WENT TO SEE MY MOTHER. SHE WOULD SURELY KNOW WHERE THEY WERE. MAYBE SHE EVEN LISTENED TO THEM TO REMEMBER ME.

GOOD MORNING, MOM!

GOOD MORNING! ALREADY DRESSED!

DO YOU WANT SOME TEA? AN OMELET, SOME TOAST..?

I'M NOT HUNGRY. TEA IS FINE.

DO YOU REMEMBER FRAU DOCTOR KELLER'S DISGUSTING TEA?

HER NAME WAS HELLER! OF COURSE! HOW COULD I POSSIBLY FORGET THAT HORSE PISS?

AH, THERE'S NOTHING LIKE IRANIAN TEA!

OH YES, ESPECIALLY WITH A CIGARETTE. DO YOU WANT ONE?

MOM!!

WHAT? YOU KNOW THE PROVERB: "PROSPERITY CONSISTS OF TWO THINGS: TEA AFTER A MEAL, AND A CIGARETTE AFTER TEA."

IT WAS THE FIRST TIME THAT MY MOTHER HAD SPOKEN TO ME IN THIS TONE: IN HER EYES NOW, I HAD BECOME AN ADULT.

MOM, I CAN'T FIND MY TAPES. I LOOKED EVERYWHERE FOR THEM! DO YOU KNOW WHERE THEY ARE?

WELL, HMM, YOU SEE... SINCE I DIDN'T THINK THAT... THAT YOU WOULD COME BACK ONE DAY, I GAVE...I GAVE THEM TO HOMA.

HOMA WAS THE DAUGHTER OF ONE OF HER FRIENDS. SHE WAS FIVE YEARS YOUNGER THAN ME. A CHILD!

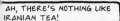

AFTER ALL, MOM HADN'T BEEN WRONG. IN ANY CASE, I NO LONGER LIKED THE IDOLS OF MY ADOLESCENCE.

YOU'RE RIGHT! I'M GOING TO BUY MYSELF SOME NEW ONES!

CAN YOU GIVE ME A SPONGE?

A SPONGE? OF COURSE, DARLING.

I DECIDED TO TAKE THIS LITTLE PROBLEM AS A SIGN. IT WAS TIME TO FINISH WITH THE PAST...

...AND TO LOOK TOWARD THE FUTURE.

A FEW HOURS LATER...

AH, POUNEH! HOW ARE YOU? MARJI IS...

NO! TELL HER THAT I'VE GONE OUT!

SHE'S GONE OUT! SHE'LL CALL YOU BACK!

WHO TOLD HER THAT I WAS HERE?

I DID. SHE IS YOUR BEST FRIEND.

PLEASE, DON'T TELL ANYONE THAT I'M BACK. I DON'T WANT TO SEE PEOPLE!

OKAY, I'LL BE HOME IN A COUPLE OF HOURS.

DON'T FORGET YOUR VEIL.

OH SHIT! I'LL HAVE TO PUT IT BACK ON!

IT WASN'T JUST THE VEIL TO WHICH I HAD TO READJUST, THERE WERE ALSO ALL THE IMAGES: THE SIXTY-FIVE-FOOT-HIGH MURALS PRESENTING MARTYRS, ADORNED WITH SLOGANS HONORING THEM, SLOGANS LIKE "THE MARTYR IS THE HEART OF HISTORY" OR "I HOPE TO BE A MARTYR MYSELF" OR "A MARTYR LIVES FOREVER."

ESPECIALLY AFTER FOUR YEARS SPENT IN AUSTRIA, WHERE YOU WERE MORE LIKELY TO SEE ON THE WALLS "BEST SAUSAGES FOR 20 SHILLINGS," THE ROAD TO READJUSTMENT SEEMED VERY LONG TO ME.

There were also the streets...

...many had changed names. they were now called martyr what's-his-name avenue or martyr something-or-other street.

It was very unsettling.

I felt as though I were walking through a cemetery.

... surrounded by the victims of a war I had fled.

It was unbearable. I hurried home.

THAT NIGHT.

HI! I'M HOME!

DO YOU ALWAYS GET HOME SO LATE?

AH YES, I HAVE A LOT OF WORK THESE DAYS.

NOW THAT THE WAR WAS OVER, MY FATHER, AN ENGINEER, DIDN'T KNOW WHERE TO BEGIN.

EVERYTHING HAS TO BE REBUILT NOW.

WHILE WE WAIT FOR THE NEXT WAR WHICH WILL DESTROY EVERYTHING AGAIN.

WHAT NEXT WAR?

ONE HAS TO BE REALISTIC. FOR OVER A CENTURY OUR REGION HAS BEEN UNSTABLE. ONE DAY THEY NATIONALIZE THE OIL, THE NEXT THEY INSTALL A DICTATOR . . .

. . .THEN IT'S THE SIX-DAY WAR, THEN IT'S AFGHANISTAN'S TURN AND THE RETURN OF THE ISRAELI-PALESTINIAN CONFLICT. WE'LL SEE WHAT COMES NEXT.

I WOULD NEVER HAVE THOUGHT THAT I WOULD ONE DAY HEAR MY MOTHER SOUND SO DISILLUSIONED.

THERE WAS AN UNCOMFORTABLE SILENCE. EVEN MY MOTHER WAS ILL AT EASE.

HAPPILY, MY FATHER INTERVENED.

SO, DID YOU GET SOME REST? DID YOU SEE HOW IT SNOWED? I HAD TO PUT CHAINS ON MY TIRES TO BE ABLE TO DRIVE. INCREDIBLE! SIXTEEN INCHES OF SNOW!!

I KNOW, IT'S MAGNIFICENT.

DID YOU WALK AROUND A LITTLE? WHAT DID YOU THINK OF TEHRAN?

SORDID.

I WAS SHOCKED. AT LEAST ONE STREET IN THREE IS NAMED AFTER A MARTYR.

AND WE ARE IN THE NORTH OF THE CITY. IF YOU GO INTO THE POOR QUARTERS IN THE SOUTH OF TEHRAN, ALMOST ALL THE STREETS ARE CALLED MARTYR SO-AND-SO.

PEOPLE DON'T KNOW ANYMORE WHY WE'VE HAD EIGHT YEARS OF WAR. WHY THEIR CHILDREN HAVE DIED...

THIS ENTIRE WAR WAS JUST A BIG SETUP TO DESTROY BOTH THE IRANIAN AND THE IRAQI ARMIES. THE FORMER WAS THE MOST POWERFUL IN THE MIDDLE EAST IN 1980, AND THE LATTER REPRESENTED A REAL DANGER TO ISRAEL.

THE WEST SOLD WEAPONS TO BOTH CAMPS AND WE, WE WERE STUPID ENOUGH TO ENTER INTO THIS CYNICAL GAME... EIGHT YEARS OF WAR FOR NOTHING!

SO NOW THE STATE NAMES STREETS AFTER MARTYRS TO FLATTER THE FAMILIES OF THE VICTIMS. IN THIS WAY, PERHAPS, THEY'LL FIND SOME MEANING IN ALL THIS ABSURDITY.

YES, BUT THERE IS ALSO SOMETHING ELSE. THIS AFTERNOON ON TV, I SAW MOTHERS WHO WERE CLAIMING TO BE OVERJOYED AND GRATIFIED BY THE DEATHS OF THEIR CHILDREN. I CAN'T FIGURE OUT IF IT'S FAITH OR COMPLETE STUPIDITY...

IT'S A BIT OF BOTH... FOR TEN YEARS THEY'VE BEEN MADE TO BELIEVE THAT THE MARTYRS ARE LIVING IN A FIVE-STAR HOTEL IN PARADISE!

IN THE MEANTIME, THE WAR FEELS MORE LIKE HELL! IF YOU KNEW... THE FEW MONTHS THAT LED UP TO THE CEASE-FIRE WERE PARTICULARLY HORRIBLE.

TELL ME, DAD. I'M ALL EARS.

ONE MONTH BEFORE THE ARMISTICE, IRAQ BEGAN BOMBING TEHRAN EVERY DAY, AS IF IT WERE NECESSARY TO DESTROY AS MUCH AS POSSIBLE BEFORE IT WAS OVER...

...THE PEACE HADN'T YET BEEN ANNOUNCED WHEN THE ARMED GROUPS OPPOSED TO THE ISLAMIC REGIME, THE IRANIAN MUJAHIDEEN,* ENTERED THE COUNTRY FROM THE IRAQI BORDER WITH THE SUPPORT OF SADDAM HUSSEIN TO LIBERATE IRAN FROM THE HANDS OF ITS FUNDAMENTALIST LEADERS.

*THE TERM "MUJAHIDEEN" ISN'T SPECIFIC TO AFGHANISTAN. IT MEANS A COMBATANT.

YOU SURELY HEARD ABOUT IT.

NO, DAD, I DIDN'T KNOW.

WHAT DO YOU MEAN?

EBI!! REALLY! SHE JUST SPENT FOUR YEARS IN EUROPE!

YES, OF COURSE.

WHAT WAS I SAYING?... RIGHT, THE MUJAHIDEEN THOUGHT THAT SINCE IT WAS THE END OF THE WAR, OUR ARMY WOULDN'T HAVE THE STRENGTH TO FIGHT ANYMORE.

ARE YOU SURE THAT THIS IS A GOOD TIME TO TELL ALL THIS?

• • •

MOM! LEAVE HIM ALONE! I'M INTERESTED.

...SO, THE MUJAHIDEEN ALSO KNEW THAT THE MAJORITY OF IRANIANS WERE AGAINST THE REGIME, AND THEY WERE THERE-FORE COUNTING ON POPULAR SUPPORT. BUT THERE WAS ONE THING THAT WASN'T IN THEIR CALCULATIONS: THEY ENTERED FROM IRAQ. THE SAME IRAQ THAT HAD ATTACKED US AND AGAINST. WHICH WE HAD BEEN FIGHTING FOR EIGHT YEARS.

WITH THE RESULT THAT, WHEN THEY ARRIVED IN IRAN, NO ONE WELCOMED THEM. FOR THE MOST PART, THEY WERE KILLED BY THE GUARDIANS OF THE REVOLUTION AND THE ARMY.

I'M GOING TO BED.

BUT THE REGIME GOT SCARED BECAUSE IF THESE OPPONENTS HAD REACHED TEHRAN, THEY WOULD HAVE FREED THOSE WHO REPRESENT-ED A REAL THREAT TO THE GOVERNMENT...

GOOD NIGHT.

...THAT IS TO SAY THE POLITICAL PRISONERS WHO WERE THE LEGITIMATE HEIRS OF THE REVOLUTION AND WHO CONSTITUTED OUR COUNTRY'S INTELLIGENTSIA...

...SO THE STATE DECIDED TO ELIMINATE THE PROBLEM. THEY PROPOSED THE FOLLOWING CHOICE TO THE DETAINEES: EITHER THEY COULD RENOUNCE THEIR REVOLUTIONARY IDEAS, AND PROMISE FIDELITY AND LOYALTY TO THE ISLAMIC REPUBLIC, IN WHICH CASE THEY WERE DONE SERVING THEIR TIME ...

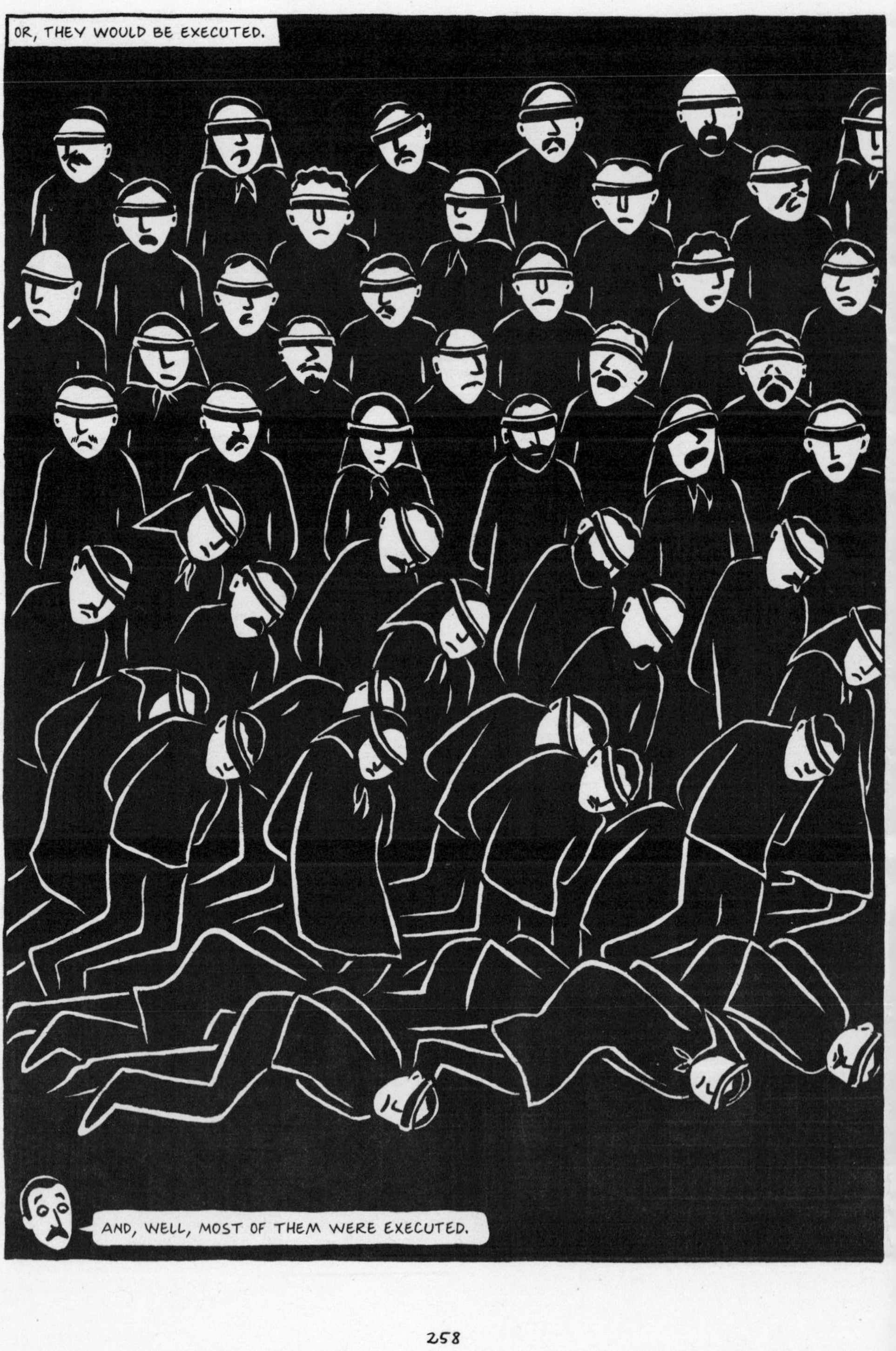
OR, THEY WOULD BE EXECUTED.
AND, WELL, MOST OF THEM WERE EXECUTED.

HOW MANY DID THEY KILL?

NO ONE KNOWS EXACTLY. MANY THOUSANDS, OR RATHER, MANY TENS OF THOUSANDS OF PEOPLE.

AND THE VICTIMS OF THE WAR?

BETWEEN 500,000 AND 1,000,000.

NOT COUNTING THOSE DISABLED BY THE WAR, THE POPULATIONS RAVAGED BY CHEMICAL WEAPONS...

...THOSE WHO LOST THEIR MINDS FROM THE EXPLOSIONS...

...THE ORPHANS, THE WIDOWS, THE REFUGEES, THE MATERIAL DESTRUCTION...

BUT ALL THAT IS BEHIND US. WE MUST GO FORWARD NOW. WE MUST REBUILD EVERYTHING!

DESPITE MY FATHER'S SOUNDING MOTIVATED, I DIDN'T FEEL ANY REAL CONVICTION IN HIS VOICE. HE SEEMED TO ME AS BLASÉ AS MY MOTHER.

LET'S TURN IN. TOMORROW I HAVE A LONG DAY AT WORK. DO YOU HAVE ANY PLANS?

NO, NOT YET.

NEXT TO MY FATHER'S DISTRESSING REPORT, MY VIENNESE MISAD-VENTURES SEEMED LIKE LITTLE ANECDOTES OF NO IMPORTANCE.

SO I DECIDED THAT I WOULD NEVER TELL THEM ANYTHING ABOUT MY AUSTRIAN LIFE. THEY HAD SUFFERED ENOUGH AS IT WAS.

THE JOKE

I HAD BEEN IN TEHRAN FOR TEN DAYS. DESPITE MY RELUCTANCE, IN THE END MY ENTIRE FAMILY CAME TO SEE ME. I DIDN'T KNOW WHETHER OR NOT THEY KNEW ABOUT MY EUROPEAN FAILURE. I WAS SCARED THAT THEY WOULD BE DISAPPOINTED.

YOU MUST SPEAK GOOD GERMAN NOW.

I KNOW HOW TO SAY "ICH LIEBE DICH" HEE HEE HEE!

YES, I SPEAK A LITTLE.

THANK YOU FOR THE FLOWERS.

THIS IS UNCLE ARDESHIR, MY MOTHER'S UNCLE. HE'S RETIRED FROM THE NATIONAL EDUCATION SYSTEM.

WHEN I THINK OF VIENNA, I IMMEDIATELY THINK OF SISSI. YOU MUST HAVE SEEN THE FILM STARRING ROMY!

YES.

THAT'S MINA, MY FIRST COUSIN. SHE'S AN IMBECILE. SHE TALKS ABOUT ROMY SCHNEIDER AS IF SHE WERE HER BEST FRIEND.

MARJANE, THE STARS SHINE IN THE SKY AND YOU IN MY HEART ...

THESE ARE OUR NEIGHBORS. THEY'RE THE INCARNATION OF THE PERFECT FAMILY.

EVEN THOUGH I KNEW THAT THEY WERE COMING TO SEE ME OUT OF FRIENDSHIP AND KINDNESS, I'D QUICKLY HAD ENOUGH OF RECEIVING THEM EVERY DAY.

BUT THERE WAS NOTHING TO BE DONE, THE VISITS CONTINUED ...

ASIDE FROM MY PARENTS, THE ONLY PERSON TO WHOM I REALLY WANTED TO TALK WAS MY GRANDMOTHER. BUT SHE CAME AFTER EVERYONE ELSE.

GRANDMA, WHERE WERE YOU?

I WAS WAITING FOR THE TRIBE TO GO FIRST! OH MY!! HOW YOU'VE GROWN. SOON YOU'LL BE CATCHING THE LORD'S BALLS.

SHE WAS STILL HER OLD SELF.

AFTER MY FAMILY, IT WAS MY FRIENDS' TURN. I HAD FEWER APPREHENSIONS ABOUT THEM: WE WERE THE SAME AGE, WHICH SHOULD MAKE IT EASIER TO CONNECT.

HI!

HOW ARE YOU?

UHHH...

I WAS WRONG. THEY ALL LOOKED LIKE THE HEROINES OF AMERICAN TV SERIES, READY TO GET MARRIED AT THE DROP OF A HAT, IF THE OPPORTUNITY PRESENTED ITSELF.

WHY DO YOU LOOK LIKE A NUN? NO ONE WOULD EVER GUESS THAT YOU'D LIVED IN EUROPE.

OH, REALLY?

COMPARED TO HER FASHIONABLE MAKEUP, I REALLY DID EXUDE ALL THE ALLURE OF A NUN.

COME ON, TALK TO US! YOU MUST HAVE A MILLION THINGS TO TELL US ABOUT.

I DON'T KNOW...

WELL, WHY DON'T YOU TELL US WHAT THE NIGHTCLUBS IN VIENNA WERE LIKE?

IT'S JUST THAT... I DIDN'T GO THAT OFTEN... I DON'T REALLY LIKE THEM MUCH.

WHAT?

OH STOP PRETENDING TO BE SO SHOCKED! DON'T YOU REMEMBER HOW SHE WAS? ALWAYS GIVING LESSONS!! SHE'S A "REBEL," THIS ONE!

IF THERE WERE STILL NIGHTCLUBS IN TEHRAN, I'D BE THERE EVERY NIGHT!

HEE! HEE! HEE! HEE! ME TOO!

I HAD A HARD TIME REMEMBERING WHAT HAD BROUGHT US TOGETHER BEFORE.

A PART OF ME UNDERSTOOD THEM. WHEN SOMETHING IS FORBIDDEN, IT TAKES ON A DISPROPORTIONATE IMPORTANCE. MUCH LATER, I LEARNED THAT MAKING THEMSELVES UP AND WANTING TO FOLLOW WESTERN WAYS WAS AN ACT OF RESISTANCE ON THEIR PART.

NEVERTHELESS, I FELT TERRIBLY ALONE.

SOME DAYS LATER.

LALEH CALLED FOR YOU.

PFFF . . .

OH! . . . MY FRIENDS . . . MY FRIENDS, I FIND THEM ALL SO UNBEARABLY INANE!

YOU KNOW, IT'S NOT ENTIRELY THEIR FAULT. NO ONE IS ASKING THEM TO BE INTELLIGENT! COMPLETELY THE OPPOSITE, IN FACT!

GIVE IT SOME THOUGHT, MY CHILD. THERE MUST BE SOME PEOPLE THAT YOU'D LIKE TO SPEND TIME WITH!

GRANDMA WAS RIGHT. I WOULD HAVE BEEN VERY HAPPY TO SEE THE KIDS I USED TO PLAY WITH IN THE STREET.

I'D LIKE TO SEE ARASH AND KIA AGAIN . . .

. . . YES! ARASH AND KIA! KIA ESPECIALLY. WE HAD SO MUCH FUN TOGETHER. AND, HE'S A GUY. HE MUST HAVE SOMETHING OTHER THAN MAKEUP ON HIS MIND.

UHH . . .

MY MOTHER'S RESPONSE SEEMED NORMAL. SHE NEVER REALLY LIKED HIM. SHE THOUGHT THAT HE WAS BADLY BROUGHT UP AND ENCOUR- AGED ME TO DO STUPID THINGS.

MOM, DON'T WORRY. WE'RE ALL GROWN UP NOW. IF I SEE HIM, WE'RE NOT GOING TO BREAK WINDOWS, OR ATTACK PEOPLE WITH NAILS.

IT'S JUST THAT KIA . . .

KIA WHAT?

WELL, HE WAS CALLED UP FOR SERVICE BUT HE PREFERRED TO LEAVE THE COUNTRY ILLEGALLY.

AND WHERE DID HE GO?

NOWHERE . . . THEY ARRESTED HIM. THEN, LIKE EVERYONE ELSE, HE WAS REQUIRED TO DO HIS MILITARY SERVICE . . . THEY SENT HIM TO THE FRONT AND . . .

AND THEN WHAT? IS HE DEAD?

ALMOST.

ALMOST DEAD???

YES, WELL HOW DO YOU SAY . . . HE IS DISABLED.

I DECIDED TO GO SEE HIM. I LEARNED THAT HIS FAMILY HAD MOVED. MY MOTHER SET UP AN INQUIRY IN THE NEIGHBORHOOD AND FINALLY FOUND THEIR TELEPHONE NUMBER.

HELLO? COULD I PLEASE SPEAK TO KIA?

LET ME GET HIM... KIA!! TELEPHONE!

KIA! HI-DO YOU REMEMBER ME?

UHH...NO.

AND "MASSA-CRE RAMIN WITH NAILS!" DOES THAT RING A BELL?

MARJI!! IS IT YOU?

NO, THIS IS HER MOTHER!

HA!HA!HA!

OH IT'S SO GOOD TO HEAR YOUR VOICE!! WHEN CAN WE SEE EACH OTHER?

TOMORROW IF YOU WANT. DO YOU HAVE OUR ADDRESS?

I WAS RELIEVED. HE DIDN'T SEEM "ALMOST DEAD" AT ALL.

THE NEXT DAY, I PUT ON MY BEST CLOTHES. IT HAD SNOWED AGAIN. I SPENT TWO HOURS IN TRAFFIC JAMS, ENOUGH TIME TO ASK MYSELF ALL KINDS OF QUESTIONS: "WHAT IF HE LOST AN EYE?," "WHAT IF HE LOST A LEG?," "WHAT IF HE IS HORRIBLY DISFIGURED?"...

WHEN I FINALLY GOT TO HIS HOUSE, I WASN'T AT ALL SURE IF I WANTED TO GO IN.

MISS, YOU HAVE TO GET OUT. WE'RE THERE.

WHATEVER HIS STATE, I WAS CONVINCED OF THE JUSTICE OF MY MISSION.

WHAT FLOOR ARE YOU GOING TO?

THE THIRD. I'VE COME TO VISIT MY CHILDHOOD FRIEND, KIA ABADI.

OH! THAT'S GREAT!

THE NEIGHBOR'S "THAT'S GREAT" CALMED ME DOWN EVEN MORE. IF SOMETHING REALLY SERIOUS HAD HAPPENED, HE CERTAINLY WOULDN'T HAVE SAID THAT.

I WAS CONFIDENT.

DING DONG

OH KIA!...

...HELLO.

...IT'S CRAZY HOW YOU'VE CHANGED!... COME IN, PLEASE, COME IN!

LOOK AT THAT! YOU'VE BECOME A REAL WOMAN.

AH WELL! WE ALL END UP HAVING TO ACCEPT OURSELVES!

YES... I KNOW THAT BETTER THAN ANYONE!

WHAT AN IDIOT, REALLY, WHAT AN IDIOT I AM!

I QUICKLY CHANGED THE SUBJECT.

DO YOU REMEMBER OUR FRIEND RAMIN?

I ESPECIALLY REMEMBER US AND OUR IRON KNUCKLES! THE POOR BOY! HE MUST HAVE BEEN SCARED SHITLESS!

BLAH BLAH BLAH BLAH BLAH

YES, BLAH BLAH BLAH BLAH

DO YOU WANT SOMETHING TO DRINK?

NO, I'M FINE, THANKS.

I'M THIRSTY, I'M GOING TO GET A COKE.

IN THAT CASE, I'LL HAVE ONE TOO.

I DIDN'T DARE LOOK AT HIM ANYWHERE BUT IN THE EYES.

IT WASN'T UNTIL HE WAS ON HIS WAY TO THE KITCHEN THAT I NOTICED HE ONLY HAD THE USE OF HIS RIGHT ARM.

HERE, CAN YOU HELP ME PLEASE?

OF COURSE! GIVE ME THAT!

GLUG, GLUG GLUG

SHIT

THIS TIME, HE'S THE ONE WHO SAVED THE SITUATION.

SO, YOU'RE BACK FROM AUSTRIA? HOW WAS IT THERE?

IT WAS FINE. BUT TELL ME MORE ABOUT YOU. HOW ARE YOU DOING?

I'M DOING AS WELL AS I CAN... I WANT TO GO TO THE UNITED STATES, I HAVE AN UNCLE WHO'S A DOCTOR IN BOSTON. THEY'RE GOING TO MAKE ME TWO BEAUTIFUL PROSTHESES, ONE FOR MY LEG AND ONE FOR MY ARM. BUT WE HAVE TO SEE WHETHER OR NOT THE AMERICANS WILL GIVE ME A VISA.

...   ...

ONE OF MY FRIENDS TOLD ME A GREAT STORY. DO YOU WANT TO HEAR IT?

SURE, GO AHEAD.

HERE GOES. IT'S THE STORY OF A GUY WHO FINDS HIMSELF AT THE FRONT DURING THE WAR. A GRENADE LANDS DIRECTLY ON HIS HEAD...

... HE'S BLOWN INTO A THOUSAND PIECES...

...THE STRETCHER-BEARERS ARRIVE, COLLECT THE PIECES, PUT THEM IN A LARGE BAG...

...AND RUSH HIM BACK TO TEHRAN AT TOP SPEED.

EMERGENCY

HE ENDED UP LANDING IN A GOOD HOSPITAL. THERE, THE DOCTORS SET THEMSELVES TO STICKING THE PIECES BACK TOGETHER. THEY STITCHED AND STITCHED.

...AND FINALLY, AFTER ONE HUNDRED FIFTY OPERATIONS AND A YEAR AND A HALF OF BANDAGES...

HE BECAME, ONCE AGAIN, A WHOLE MAN.

OH, DOCTOR. I'VE NEVER FELT SO GOOD. THANKS TO YOU, I CAN BEGIN A NEW LIFE.

TO HELP HIM LEAD HIS NEW LIFE, HIS FAMILY DECIDED TO FIND HIM A WIFE. HIS MOTHER DID THE ROUNDS OF THEIR FRIENDS AND THEIR NEIGHBORS AND FOUND A RARE PEARL. AND AS TRADITION REQUIRES, THE MAN, ACCOMPANIED BY HIS FAMILY, WENT TO ASK FOR THE YOUNG GIRL'S HAND.

OUR SON IS EXCEPTIONAL!

OUR DAUGHTER IS MAGNIFICENT!

AFTER LONG NEGOTIATIONS OVER THE AMOUNT OF THE DOWRY,* THE WEDDING RINGS, THE DRESS, THE FLOWERS, THE HAIRDRESSER, THE MAKEUP ARTIST, THE WEDDING VIDEO CREW, THE CATERERS, THE WAITERS, THE MUSICIANS, THE NUMBER OF GUESTS, THE TWO FAMILIES REACHED AN AGREEMENT.

IT'S THE MOST BEAUTIFUL DAY OF MY LIFE.

I'LL LOVE YOU FOREVER.

*IN IRAN, IT'S THE HUSBAND WHO MUST PAY HIS WIFE A DOWRY.

AND WHAT COMES AFTER THE WEDDING?

UHH... I DON'T KNOW...

AFTER THE WEDDING COMES "THE HONEYMOON NIGHT"!

MY DEAR, I CAN'T WAIT ANY LONGER!

I'M COMING, MY DOE, I'M COMING.

OH, YOUR MOTHER WAS RIGHT TO SAY YOU WERE EXCEPTIONAL, YOU ARE SO...

IN THE NAME OF GOD! WHAT IN THE WORLD IS THAT?

WHY ISN'T IT IN THE RIGHT PLACE?

OH WELL, IT'S NO BIG DEAL. IT STILL WORKS!

WHAT DO YOU MEAN IT'S NO BIG DEAL???!!!

YOUR THING IS ON YOUR HIP, INSTEAD OF BEING BETWEEN YOUR LEGS AND YOU DARE TO TELL ME THAT "IT'S NO BIG DEAL" ???!!

YES, BUT IT WORKS...

...LOOK!

I DON'T WANT TO SEE ANYTHING! I WAS SOLD DAMAGED GOODS!!

I WANT A DIVORCE AS OF TOMORROW!!!

THAT DAY, I LEARNED SOMETHING ESSENTIAL: WE CAN ONLY FEEL SORRY FOR OURSELVES WHEN OUR MISFORTUNES ARE STILL SUPPORTABLE...

...ONCE THIS LIMIT IS CROSSED, THE ONLY WAY TO BEAR THE UNBEARABLE IS TO LAUGH AT IT.

SKIING

I WASN'T ABLE TO TAKE A STEP BACK EVEN THOUGH I KNEW THAT IT WAS THE ONLY WAY TO GET OUT OF MY FUNK.

AFTER SEVERAL WEEKS, MY FAMILY AND THOSE CLOSE TO ME DECIDED THAT IT WAS TIME I BENEFITED FROM THEIR GOOD ADVICE:

YOU SHOULD JOIN A GYM. I KNOW A GOOD CLUB.

YOU SHOULD FIND YOURSELF A GOOD HUSBAND.

YOU SHOULD REGISTER FOR SOME PREP COURSES. YOU MUST GO TO UNIVERSITY.

YOU SHOULD...

BUT I DIDN'T WANT TO EXERCISE, OR GET MARRIED, OR STUDY...

...I JUST WANTED THEM TO KNOW THAT I TOO HAD SUFFERED...

MY LIFE IN VIENNA WAS FAR FROM EASY...

I LIVED IN THE STREET.

I WAS ALONE.

OH!

I SPIT UP BLOOD.

NO ONE LOVED ME.

OH!

OH! POOR YOU!

...FOR THEM TO FEEL SOME COMPASSION FOR ME...

OH MY DEAR, YOU HAVE SUFFERED TOO MUCH... DRINK THIS HERB TEA.

IT'S FRESH-SQUEEZED ORANGE JUICE, I MADE IT MYSELF.

DO YOU WANT ME TO DO A LITTLE DANCE FOR YOU?

FOR THEM TO UNDERSTAND ME.

I UNDERSTAND YOU.

CERTAINLY, THEY'D HAD TO ENDURE THE WAR, BUT THEY HAD EACH OTHER CLOSE BY. THEY HAD NEVER KNOWN THE CONFUSION OF BEING A THIRD-WORLDER, THEY HAD ALWAYS HAD A HOME!

AT THE SAME TIME, HOW COULD THEY HAVE PITIED ME? I WAS SO SHUT OFF.

I KEPT REPEATING TO MYSELF THAT I MUSN'T CRACK UP.

| I THOUGHT THAT BY COMING BACK TO IRAN, EVERYTHING WOULD BE FINE. | THAT I WOULD FORGET THE OLD DAYS. | BUT MY PAST CAUGHT UP WITH ME. | MY SECRETS WEIGHED ME DOWN. |

I BECAME DEPRESSED.

MARJI, I'M GOING GROCERY SHOPPING. DO YOU NEED ANYTHING?

CIGARETTES, PLEASE.

I RENTED "LA DOLCE VITA." DON'T YOU WANT TO WATCH IT TOGETHER?

NO ...

EVEN MY GRANDMA COULD NO LONGER GET ME TO LAUGH.

...HE FARTED! IT SMELLED LIKE A DEAD RAT ...

I WAS ALWAYS IN FRONT OF THE TV. THERE WAS A JAPANESE SERIES, CALLED "OSHIN," THAT I WATCHED OFTEN. IT WAS THE STORY OF A POOR GIRL WHO CAME TO WORK IN TOKYO.

AT FIRST, SHE CLEANED HOUSES, THEN SHE BECAME A HAIRDRESSER AND MET A GUY WHOSE MOTHER WAS OPPOSED TO THEIR MARRIAGE.

YOU ARE NOTHING BUT A HAIRDRESSER, YOU AREN'T WORTHY OF MY SON! GET OUT, YOU ROTTEN GIRL!

NO! I LOVE HIM!

I DIDN'T UNDERSTAND WHY THE MOTHER-IN-LAW HATED HAIRDRESSERS SO MUCH.

MUCH LATER, I GOT TO KNOW A GIRL WHO DUBBED TELEVISION SHOWS. SHE TOLD ME THAT OSHIN WAS IN FACT A GEISHA AND SINCE HER PROFESSION DIDN'T SUIT ISLAMIC MORALS, THE DIRECTOR OF THE CHANNEL HAD DECIDED THAT SHE'D BE A HAIRDRESSER.

IT WAS BELIEVABLE BECAUSE OSHIN AND HER COURTESAN FRIENDS SPENT THEIR TIME MAKING CHIGNONS.

TO LIFT ME OUT OF MY DEPRESSION, MY FRIENDS SUGGESTED TAKING ME SKIING. ONE OF THEIR PARENTS HAD A CHALET AT DIZIN.* I DIDN'T WANT TO GO, BUT MY MOTHER INSISTED SO MUCH THAT I ENDED UP ACCEPTING.

* A SKI RESORT ABOUT THIRTY MILES FROM TEHRAN.

YOU KNOW, YOU CAN RENT EQUIPMENT. IF YOU WANT, WE CAN TEACH YOU HOW TO SKI.

NO, THANKS, I AM VERY HAPPY LIKE THIS.

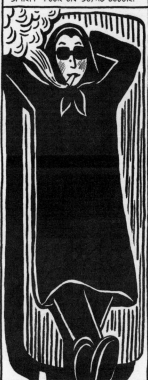

ACTUALLY, I FELT ON TOP OF THE WORLD. THE MOUNTAIN, THE BLUE SKY, THE SUN, ... ALL OF IT SUITED ME. LITTLE BY LITTLE MY HEAD AND MY SPIRIT TOOK ON SOME COLOR.

EVENING.

OH MY! I'M EXHAUSTED!

I SAW LOTS OF CUTE GUYS, TALL, MUSCLED ...

OH YES!!! HEE HEE HEE!

TELL US, HAVE YOU HAD SEX?

OF COURSE, I'M NINETEEN!

SO, DO TELL, HOW WAS IT?

SUPPOSEDLY, IT HURTS A LOT THE FIRST TIME.

IT MUST BE GREAT ...

IT DEPENDS WITH WHO. IT'S NOT ALWAYS PLEASURABLE.

WHAT DO YOU MEAN? YOU'VE DONE THE DEED WITH MANY PEOPLE?

WELL, I MEAN ... I'VE HAD A FEW EXPERIENCES.

SO, WHAT'S THE DIFFERENCE BETWEEN YOU AND A WHORE???

UNDERNEATH THEIR OUTWARD APPEARANCE OF BEING MODERN WOMEN, MY FRIENDS WERE REAL TRADITIONALISTS.

THEY WERE OVERRUN BY HORMONES AND FRUSTRATION, WHICH EXPLAINED THEIR AGGRESSIVENESS TOWARD ME. TO THEM, I HAD BECOME A DECADENT WESTERN WOMAN.

I RETURNED HOME EVEN MORE DEPRESSED.

OH! YOU'RE SO TAN. IT LOOKS GREAT ON YOU!

LIAR!

MARJI, TALK TO ME. WHAT'S WRONG? IS THERE ANYTHING I CAN DO?

NO, MOM!

MAYBE YOU SHOULD SEE SOMEONE ... A SHRINK, PERHAPS?

I FOLLOWED MY MOTHER'S ADVICE. FIRST I SAW A LEADING PSYCHOTHERAPIST ...

I'M ASHAMED OF HAVING DONE NOTHING WITH MY LIFE ... HAPPILY, NO ONE KNOWS THE DETAILS, FOR GOOD REASON. I DON'T TELL THEM ANYTHING. I FEEL LIKE I'M CONSTANTLY WEARING A MASK.

YOUR STORY IS AS MUDDLED AS YOU ARE.

... THEN ANOTHER ...

WHEN I WAS IN VIENNA, MY LIFE DIDN'T MATTER TO ANYONE AND THAT OBVIOUSLY HAD AN EFFECT ON MY OWN SELF-ESTEEM. I WAS REDUCED TO NOTHING. I THOUGHT THAT IN COMING BACK TO IRAN, THIS WOULD CHANGE.

...

... AND STILL ANOTHER AND ANOTHER ...

DOCTOR, I'M NOT WELL. I HAVE NO DRIVE. NOTHING GIVES ME PLEASURE.

YOUR PROBLEM COMES UNDER THE DOMAIN OF PSYCHIATRY. YOU SHOULD BE ON MEDICATION.

THANK YOU, DOCTOR, THANK YOU!

FINALLY SOMEONE HAD FOUND A CURE FOR MY MALAISE.

THE TABLETS THAT HE PRE-SCRIBED ME WERE EFFECTIVE...

... I FELT "WELL."

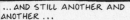

I WAS OFTEN IN A TRANCE.

marjane, do you want to come

the Caspian Sea

yes

BUT AS SOON AS THE EFFECT OF THE PILLS WORE OFF, I ONCE AGAIN BECAME CONSCIOUS. MY CALAMITY COULD BE SUMMARIZED IN ONE SENTENCE: I WAS NOTHING.

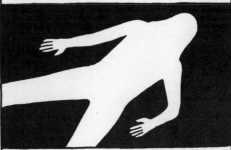

I WAS A WESTERNER IN IRAN, AN IRANIAN IN THE WEST. I HAD NO IDENTITY. I DIDN'T EVEN KNOW ANYMORE WHY I WAS LIVING.

SO I DECIDED TO DIE. A FEW WEEKS AFTER MY RESOLUTION...

YOU SAID THAT YOU WOULD COME WITH US, TO SEE THE CASPIAN SEA... IF YOU WANT, WE CAN CANCEL THE TRIP. WE DON'T WANT TO LEAVE YOU...

REALLY, DAD! DIDN'T I MANAGE IN VIENNA? NO, IT'S OKAY, YOU SHOULD GO! IN ANY CASE, I NEED TO BE ALONE.

AND SO THEY WENT FOR TEN DAYS.

THE DAY AFTER THEIR DEPARTURE, I MADE MY ARRANGEMENTS. I HAD SEEN, IN A FILM, A WOMAN WHO DRANK WINE BEFORE SLITTING HER WRISTS. NOT HAVING ANY WINE, I DRANK A HALF BOTTLE OF VODKA.

YUCK

I COULDN'T BRING MYSELF TO PUSH THE BLADE INTO MY FLESH. I HAD ALWAYS BEEN VERY AFRAID OF BLOOD. NEVERTHELESS, SINCE I WAS DRUNK, I MANAGED TO GRAZE MYSELF.

AS FOR THE REST, I FOLLOWED THE FILM. I STRETCHED OUT IN A HOT BATH, WAITING FOR MY BLOOD TO EMPTY OUT. BUT IT KEPT COAGULATING.

IT MUST BE SAID THAT IT'S A LITTLE DIFFICULT TO KILL YOURSELF WITH A FRUIT KNIFE. WEAPONS WITH BLADES WERE NOT MADE FOR ME. I NEEDED TO FIND SOMETHING ELSE.

SO I WAITED UNTIL MY WRIST HEALED TO SWALLOW ALL MY ANTI-DEPRESSANTS.

I TOLD MYSELF THAT IT WAS THE LAST TIME I WOULD SEE THE SUN. I ALSO SPARED A THOUGHT FOR MY PARENTS.

IT WAS THE END ...

..THREE DAYS LATER ...

IT'S MY HAND! SHIT! I'M STILL ALIVE!

WHEN I WOKE UP, THE DRUGS THAT I HAD TAKEN GAVE ME SEVERAL HOURS' WORTH OF HALLUCINATIONS.

SO I WENT TO SEE MY THERAPIST.

YOU SWALLOWED THEM ALL? ARE YOU SURE?

YES ...

THAT DOSE SHOULD HAVE BEEN ENOUGH TO FINISH OFF AN ELEPHANT! ... EVEN THOUGH I'M NOT A BELIEVER, ASIDE FROM DIVINE INTERVENTION, I CAN'T FIND ANY OTHER EXPLANATION FOR YOUR SURVIVAL.

I INFERRED FROM THIS THAT I WAS NOT MADE TO DIE.

FROM NOW ON, I'M TAKING MYSELF IN HAND.

BODY HAIR BEING AN OB-SESSION OF THE ORIENTAL WOMAN, I BEGAN WITH HAIR REMOVAL.

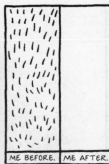

ME BEFORE. ME AFTER.

THEN I GOT RID OF MY OLD CLOTHES.

AND HAD SOME NEW CLOTHES MADE.

A MODERN WARDROBE.

ORIGINAL SHOES.

A FASHIONABLE HAIRCUT.

A PERMANENT.

I BECAME A SOPHISTICATED WOMAN ...

SHOPPING.

MAKEUP.

AND AS A HEALTHY MIND IS FOUND IN A HEALTHY BODY, I TOOK UP EXERCISE.

MORE AND MORE,

AND MORE AND MORE,

TO THE POINT WHERE I BECAME AN AEROBICS INSTRUCTOR.

AND FIVE AND SIX... AND ONE AND TWO...

♪♫ EYE OF THE TIGER ♪♫

STRONG AND INVINCIBLE LIKE THIS, I WAS GOING TO MEET MY NEW DESTINY.

MY PARENTS OBVIOUSLY NEVER KNEW THE REASONS FOR MY METAMORPHOSIS. MY NEW APPROACH TO LIFE DELIGHTED THEM TO THE POINT OF THEIR BUYING ME A CAR, BY WAY OF ENCOURAGEMENT.

I HAD NEW FRIENDS, I WENT TO PARTIES ... IN SHORT, MY LIFE HAD TAKEN A COMPLETELY NEW TURN. ONE EVENING IN APRIL 1989, I WAS INVITED TO MY FRIEND ROXANA'S HOUSE.

WELCOME, PLEASE MAKE YOURSELF AT HOME.

ASIDE FROM THE LADY OF THE HOUSE, I DIDN'T KNOW ANYONE.

I'M REZA. HOW ARE YOU?

AND YOURSELF?

CAN I SIT DOWN?

PLEASE DO.

WHAT DO YOU DO?

I'M AN AEROBICS INSTRUC- TOR, I ALSO TEACH FRENCH.

HAVE YOU LIVED IN FRANCE?

NO, IN AUSTRIA, BUT I STUDIED AT THE LYCÉE FRANÇAIS IN TEHRAN AND IN VIENNA.

WERE YOU AT THE LYCÉE RAZI?*

YES, WERE YOU TOO?

NO, NOT ME, MY FRIENDS.

AND YOU? WHAT DO YOU DO?

PAINTING.

NO WAY! I PAINT TOO!!

*THE NAME OF THE LYCÉE FRANÇAIS IN TEHRAN.

OH YOU! EITHER YOU TALK OR YOU SMOKE! COME ON, COME DANCE A LITTLE!

WHO'S THAT GUY?

REZA? HE'S ONE OF OUR NEIGHBORS. BE CAREFUL! HE'S A LADIES' MAN...

...A MERCILESS SEDUCER!

OH REALLY? HE SEEMS VERY NICE.

OH YES, HE HIDES HIS GAME WELL!

OH, WHERE IS HE?

OUF!

ROXANA WAS WRONG.

HI AGAIN!

HI!

SORRY TO HAVE LEFT YOU BUT I HADN'T SEEN HAMID IN A WHILE.

WHO'S HAMID?

THAT GUY I WAS TALKING TO. WE WERE AT THE FRONT TOGETHER.

YOU WERE IN THE WAR?

YES, LIKE EVERYONE ELSE! BY THE WAY, HAVE YOU HEARD THE STORY OF THE SOLDIER WHO EX- PLODED INTO A THOUSAND PIECES?

HE'S THE GUY WHO GETS MARRIED AND HAS HIS THING ON HIS HIP?

UHH... YEAH!

HEE, HEE, HEE ..HEE, HEE, HEE ...

IT'S TRUE THAT IT'S VERY FUNNY ...IT'S THE JOKE OF FORMER SOLDIERS.

SO, YOU FOUGHT IN THE WAR AGAINST IRAQ?

YES, I WAS A TANK GUNNER.

WHAT? YOU KILLED PEOPLE?

OH, I DON'T KNOW. WHEN YOU FIRE, YOU DON'T KNOW EXACTLY WHERE IT HITS ...

AT THE SAME TIME, DURING COMBAT, YOU DON'T HAVE TIME FOR QUALMS. EVERYTHING IS A QUESTION OF SURVIVAL ...

... WHEN THE IRAQIS ATTACKED US WITH CHEMICAL WEAPONS, I KNEW I HAD TO CLIMB THE MOUNTAIN, AS FAST AS POSSIBLE.

THE MOUNTAIN? WHY?

BECAUSE, WHEN THE BOMB EXPLODES, THERE'S A CLOUD OF TOXIC CHEMICALS THAT'S RELEASED. IF YOU ARE HIGH ENOUGH, IT CAN'T REACH YOU.

IT'S TIME FOR DINNER!

... SO HAMID AND I, WE RAN TOWARD THE SUMMITS OF THE ZAGROS* ...

WHAT A MAN!

PFF...

*A MOUNTAIN CHAIN IN THE WEST OF IRAN

THEN, WE SPENT A WEEK IN THE MOUNTAINS, WITHOUT FOOD. WE ATE SNOW SO AS NOT TO DIE FROM DEHYDRATION.

WHAT HEROES!

THAT MUST HAVE BEEN TERRIBLY HARD!

HARD ... YES, BUT HUMAN BEINGS ARE MUCH MORE RESILIENT THAN WE THINK.

I KNOW.

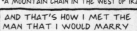

AND THAT'S HOW I MET THE MAN THAT I WOULD MARRY TWO YEARS LATER.

AFTER THIS PARTY, ROXANA NEVER SPOKE TO ME AGAIN. APPARENTLY, HER BEST FRIEND WANTED TO GO OUT WITH REZA ... UNFORTUNATELY, WE DON'T ALWAYS GET WHAT WE WANT.

EVERYTHING ABOUT US WAS OPPOSITE

HIS ROOM | MY ROOM

HIS CHILDHOOD FRIENDS | MY CHILDHOOD FRIENDS

HIS FAVORITE ACTIVITY | MY FAVORITE ACTIVITY

HIS IDEAL LIFE | MY IDEAL LIFE

HIS RELATIONSHIP WITH HIS MOTHER | MY RELATIONSHIP WITH MY MOTHER

YES MOM, I'M COMING HOME IN AN HOUR AND A HALF. DON'T WORRY!

DON'T YOU WANT TO LET YOUR PARENTS KNOW?

NO, WHY?

HIS SOCIAL LIFE | MY SOCIAL LIFE

THE IMAGE I HAD OF HIM | THE IMAGE HE HAD OF ME

HE SOUGHT IN ME A LOST LIGHTHEARTEDNESS. | AND I SOUGHT IN HIM A WAR WHICH I HAD ESCAPED.

IN SHORT, WE COMPLEMENTED EACH OTHER.

WE NEEDED EACH OTHER SO MUCH THAT WE VERY QUICKLY STARTED TO TALK ABOUT OUR SHARED FUTURE.

WHAT DO YOU HAVE PLANNED FOR THE FUTURE?

I WANT TO LEAVE HERE. EITHER I'LL GO TO EUROPE, OR TO THE UNITED STATES, BUT I WON'T STAY HERE.

WHERE WILL YOU GO IN EUROPE?

ITALY, FRANCE, SWEDEN, SPAIN, ENGLAND... IT DOESN'T REALLY MATTER. I JUST DON'T WANT TO LIVE IN IRAN ANYMORE.

AND US?

YOU'LL COME WITH ME!

I DON'T WANT TO LEAVE THE COUNTRY RIGHT AWAY.

IT'S BECAUSE YOU ARE STILL NOSTALGIC. YOU'LL SEE, A YEAR FROM NOW PEOPLE WILL DISGUST YOU. ALWAYS INTERFERING IN THINGS THAT DON'T CONCERN THEM.

MAYBE SO, BUT IN THE WEST YOU CAN COLLAPSE IN THE STREET AND NO ONE WILL GIVE YOU A HAND.

DON'T WORRY! WE'LL FIND A SOLUTION!

HAPPILY, GETTING A VISA PROVED TO BE EXCEEDINGLY DIFFICULT. SO WE DECIDED TO STUDY FOR THE NATIONAL EXAM* SO AS NOT TO WASTE YEARS OF OUR LIVES DOING NOTHING. IT WAS VERY HARD! IT HAD BEEN SIX YEARS SINCE REZA HAD GRADUATED HIGH SCHOOL. HE WAS OUT OF PRACTICE FOR STUDYING. AS FOR ME, I HADN'T READ OR WRITTEN IN PERSIAN SINCE I WAS FOURTEEN.

* IN IRAN, YOU CAN'T ENTER UNIVERSITY WITHOUT HAVING PASSED THE NATIONAL EXAM.

JUNE 1989. AFTER TWO MONTHS OF HARD WORK, THE BIG DAY FINALLY ARRIVED.

THE CANDIDATES TOOK THE EXAMS IN DIFFERENT PLACES, ACCORDING TO THEIR SEX.

THERE WERE QUESTIONNAIRES SPECIFIC TO EACH SECTION.

TO GET INTO THE COLLEGE OF ART, IN ADDITION TO THE OTHER TESTS, THERE WAS A DRAWING QUALIFICATION. I WAS SURE THAT ONE OF ITS SUBJECTS WOULD BE "THE MARTYRS," AND FOR GOOD REASON! SO I PRACTICED BY COPYING A PHOTO OF MICHELANGELO'S "LA PIETÀ" ABOUT TWENTY TIMES. ON THAT DAY, I REPRODUCED IT BY PUTTING A BLACK CHADOR ON MARY'S HEAD, AN ARMY UNIFORM ON JESUS, AND THEN I ADDED TWO TULIPS, SYMBOLS OF THE MARTYRS,* ON EITHER SIDE SO THERE WOULD BE NO CONFUSION.

I WAS VERY PLEASED WITH MY DRAWING.

*IT'S SAID THAT RED TULIPS GROW FROM THE BLOOD OF MARTYRS.

... WE HAD TO WAIT SEVERAL WEEKS BEFORE GETTING THE RESULTS IN THE "ETELAAT,"* WHICH DIDN'T COME OUT UNTIL 3 P.M. WE WERE IN FRONT OF THE KIOSKS AT 1.

LOOK, THERE'S MY NAME!

* NAME OF A NEWSPAPER.

SHIT! HERE'S YOURS TOO!

KNOWING THAT 40% OF THE PLACES WERE RESERVED FOR CHILDREN OF MARTYRS AND THOSE DISABLED BY THE WAR, THE SEATS WERE LIMITED. IT WAS AN UNEXPECTED STROKE OF LUCK THAT WE BOTH PASSED THE NATIONAL EXAM.

SINCE WE WEREN'T MARRIED, WE COULDN'T KISS EACH OTHER IN PUBLIC, OR EVEN GIVE ONE ANOTHER A FRIENDLY HUG TO EXPRESS OUR EXTREME JOY. WE RISKED IMPRISONMENT AND BEING WHIPPED. SO WE GOT INTO THE CAR QUICKLY ...

... WHERE HE PUT HIS HAND ON MINE.

IT WAS EXTRAORDINARY.

AFTER DROPPING REZA OFF AT HIS HOUSE, I WENT HOME.

MOM! DAD! I GOT IN! I WAS ADMITTED FOR GRAPHIC ARTS!

BRAVO! WE KNOW. WE SAW YOUR AND REZA'S NAMES IN THE PAPER.

OH DAD! IT'S SO GREAT!

YES, YES, IT'S WONDERFUL!

NOW, ALL THAT'S LEFT IS THE IDEOLOGICAL TEST, BUT THAT'S JUST A DETAIL.

SHIT!

MY DEAR, UNFORTUNATELY, IT'S NOT JUST A DETAIL.

REALLY?

YES, MY COUSIN BAHMAN'S DAUGHTER WASN'T ADMITTED TO UNIVERSITY BECAUSE HER MOTHER BELONGED TO THE REGIME'S OPPOSITION AND HAD SPENT TWO YEARS IN PRISON.

YOU MUST LEARN TO PRAY IN ARABIC, THE NAMES OF ALL THE IMAMS, THEIR HISTORIES, THE PHILOSOPHY OF SHIISM, ETC., ETC., ... IF YOU WANT, I'LL HELP YOU.

NO, THAT'S OKAY ...

I TRIED TO LEARN EVERYTHING BY HEART. I HAD THE BEST OF INTENTIONS ...

... BUT THE WORDS WERE SO OBSCURE THAT I WASN'T ABLE TO RETAIN ANYTHING ...

AFTER MANY DAYS OF RELIGIOUS STUDY, I ENDED UP CONVINCED THAT THE ONLY WAY TO GET OVER THIS LAST HURDLE WAS TO PRAY.

God, help me!

THE DAY OF THE IDEOLOGICAL TEST.

NEXT!

IS IT DIFFICULT?

PFFF...

MISS SATRAPI, I SEE FROM YOUR FILE THAT YOU HAVE LIVED IN AUSTRIA ... DID YOU WEAR THE VEIL THERE?

NO, I HAVE ALWAYS THOUGHT THAT IF WOMEN'S HAIR POSED SO MANY PROBLEMS, GOD WOULD CERTAINLY HAVE MADE US BALD.

DO YOU KNOW HOW TO PRAY?

AND MAY I KNOW WHY?

NO

LIKE ALL IRANIANS, I DON'T UNDERSTAND ARABIC. IF PRAYING IS TALKING TO GOD, I PREFER TO DO IT IN A LANGUAGE THAT I KNOW. I BELIEVE IN GOD, BUT I SPEAK TO HIM IN PERSIAN.

THE PROPHET MOHAMMED SAID: "GOD IS CLOSER TO US THAN OUR JUGULAR VEINS." GOD IS ALWAYS WITH US, HE IS IN US! RIGHT?

THANK YOU, MISS SATRAPI, YOU CAN GO NOW.

I SHOULD HAVE SHUT MY MOUTH, STUDIED HARDER, I SHOULD HAVE ..., IT'S ALL OVER ...

LOOK WHERE YOU'RE GOING, YOU IDIOT!

TWO WEEKS LATER ...

HERE'S YOUR LETTER OF ADMISSION!

NO WAY!

YES, MY DEAR. NOW, YOU ARE A STUDENT!

A FEW MONTHS LATER, I LEARNED VIA THE DIRECTOR OF THE DEPARTMENT OF ART THAT THE MULLAH WHO HAD INTERVIEWED ME HAD REALLY APPRECIATED MY HONESTY. APPARENTLY, HE'D EVEN SAID THAT I WAS THE ONLY ONE WHO DIDN'T LIE. I WAS LUCKY. I HAD STUMBLED ON A TRUE RELIGIOUS MAN.

THE MAKEUP

OUR SUCCESS ON THE EXAM MADE REZA AND ME MORE CALM ABOUT OUR SHARED FUTURE. NOW WE WERE ABLE TO STAY TOGETHER, BECAUSE NEITHER OF US WAS GOING TO LEAVE IRAN WITHOUT THE OTHER. FROM THEN ON, WE BECAME A REAL COUPLE, WHICH NATURALLY MEANT THAT WE BEGAN TO PICK ON EACH OTHER. I REPROACHED HIM FOR NOT BEING ACTIVE ENOUGH. HE CHOSE TO CRITICIZE MY PHYSICAL CHARACTERISTICS: NOT ELEGANT ENOUGH, NOT MADE-UP ENOUGH, ETC., ETC., ...

AT THE TIME, I THOUGHT I SHOULD MAKE SOME EFFORTS... ONE DAY, WHEN WE HAD A RENDEZVOUS IN FRONT OF THE SAVAFIEH BAZAAR,* I ARRIVED VERY MADE-UP TO GIVE HIM A SURPRISE.

LATE, AS USUAL!

* NAME OF A SHOPPING CENTER

SUDDENLY, FROM THE OTHER SIDE OF THE STREET, I SAW A CAR FULL OF GUARDIANS OF THE REVOLUTION ARRIVE, FOLLOWED BY A BUS. WHEN THEY CAME WITH THE BUS, IT MEANT A RAID.

IF THEY SEE ME WITH THIS LIPSTICK, THEY'LL TAKE ME AWAY.

THIS CALLED FOR ACTION.

WHAT AM I GOING TO DO?

THAT'S IT!! I'VE GOT IT!

I HAD TO DISTRACT THEM. I HAD TO GO SEE THEM BEFORE THEY SAW ME.

MY BROTHER! MY BROTHER!

YES MY SISTER!

THERE'S A GUY WHO SAID SOMETHING INDECENT TO ME.

OH!

WHERE'S THE BASTARD, I'LL SHUT HIM UP ONCE AND FOR ALL!

OVER THERE! ON THE STEPS! THAT'S HIM!!!

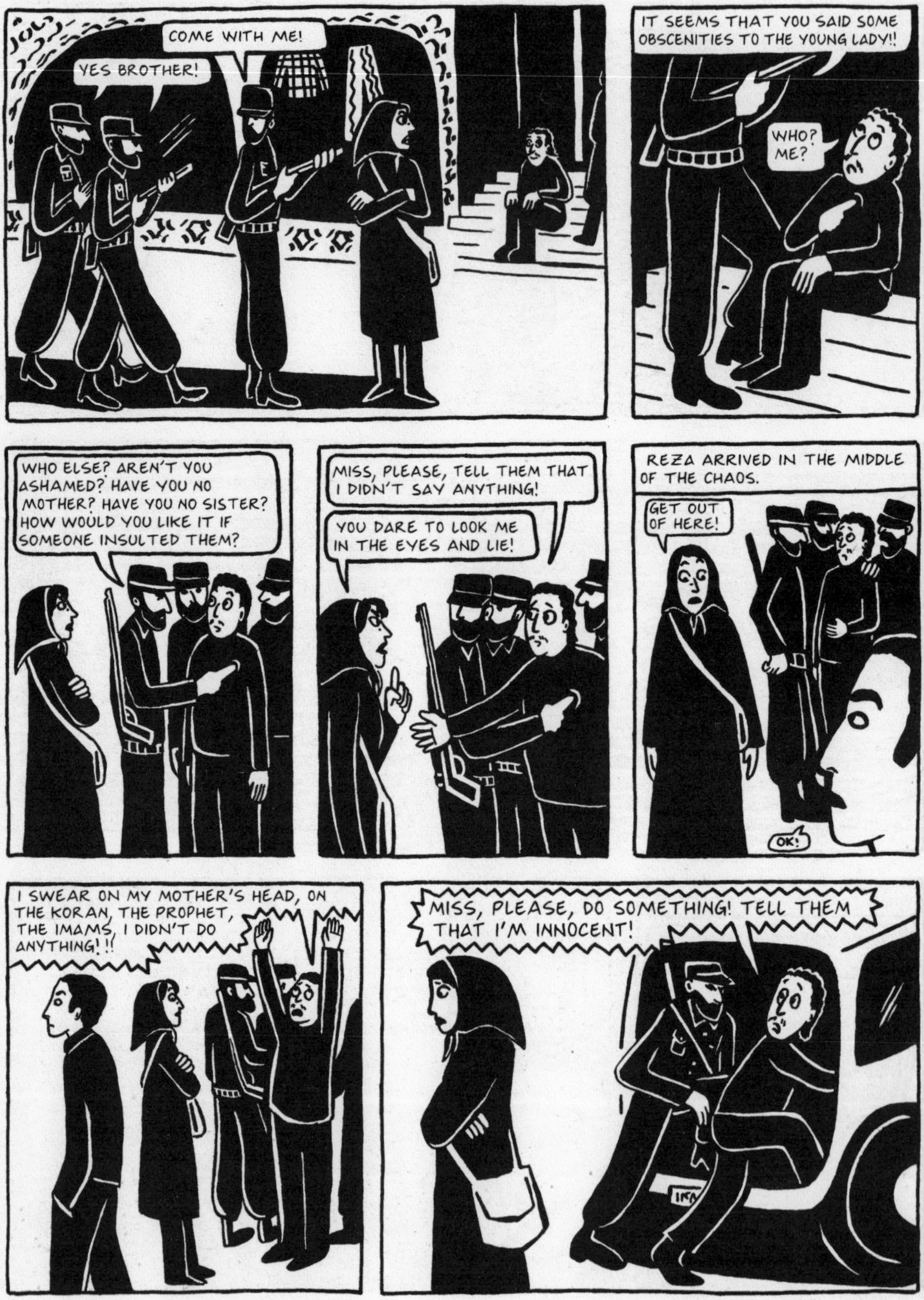
YES BROTHER!
COME WITH ME!
IT SEEMS THAT YOU SAID SOME OBSCENITIES TO THE YOUNG LADY!!
WHO? ME?
WHO ELSE? AREN'T YOU ASHAMED? HAVE YOU NO MOTHER? HAVE YOU NO SISTER? HOW WOULD YOU LIKE IT IF SOMEONE INSULTED THEM?
MISS, PLEASE, TELL THEM THAT I DIDN'T SAY ANYTHING!
YOU DARE TO LOOK ME IN THE EYES AND LIE!
REZA ARRIVED IN THE MIDDLE OF THE CHAOS.
GET OUT OF HERE!
OK!
I SWEAR ON MY MOTHER'S HEAD, ON THE KORAN, THE PROPHET, THE IMAMS, I DIDN'T DO ANYTHING! !!
MISS, PLEASE, DO SOMETHING! TELL THEM THAT I'M INNOCENT!

WHEW!!

I WAS SAVED...

I JUST HAD TO FIND REZA.

HE WASN'T FAR.

WHAT ARE YOU DOING OUT WEARING THAT FLASHY LIPSTICK THAT DOESN'T EVEN SUIT YOU?

IT DOESN'T SUIT ME?

NO!

WHO'S THAT GUY THEY PICKED UP?

I DON'T KNOW. SOME POOR GUY WHO JUST HAPPENED TO BE THERE. WHEN I SAW THEM ARRIVE, I FIGURED THAT THE ONLY WAY TO GET AWAY WAS TO PLAY "THE POOR WOMAN WHO NEEDS PROTECTION." SO I TOLD THEM THAT THAT GUY HAD SPOKEN INDECENTLY TO ME AND THEY ARRESTED HIM.

YOU DID THAT??!!

HA! HA! HA! HA! THAT'S TOO COOL! WHAT AN INSTINCT FOR SURVIVAL!

YOU THINK?

ABSOLUTELY! HA! HA! HA!

COME ON, LET'S GO SOMEWHERE ELSE! IT'S DANGEROUS HERE!

BUT THEY'RE GONE!

WHEN THEY CARRY OUT RAIDS, THERE'S NEVER ONLY ONE PATROL. THERE WILL BE OTHERS.

IT MUST BE SAID THAT DURING THIS PERIOD, YOUNG COUPLES WHO SHOWED THEMSELVES IN PUBLIC WERE RUNNING A RISK.

IF THEY WERE MARRIED, THERE OBVIOUSLY WOULDN'T HAVE BEEN A PROBLEM ...

MY BROTHER, WHAT IS YOUR RELATIONSHIP TO THIS WOMAN?

SHE'S MY WIFE.

BUT IT WAS PREFERABLE TO HAVE A PHOTOCOPY OF YOUR MARRIAGE CERTIFICATE ON YOU.

OKAY, IT'S FINE!

THE TROUBLES BEGAN IF THE TWO YOUNG PEOPLE WERE NOT UNITED BY SACRED TIES.

WHAT IS YOUR RELATIONSHIP TO THIS MAN?

HE'S MY COUSIN.

ESPECIALLY IF THEY HAD JUST MET.

WHAT'S YOUR MOTHER'S NAME?

AZAM KOLAHDOUZ

WHAT'S HIS MOTHER'S NAME?

I FORGOT.

WHAT'S THAT? HE'S YOUR COUSIN, RIGHT? YOU MUST KNOW THE NAME OF YOUR AUNT!

COME ON, GET IN THE CAR!

THEY TOOK THEM TO THE COMMITTEE.* THEN THEY CALLED THEIR PARENTS WHO CAME TO FREE THEIR CHILDREN, BY PAYING A FINE.

SIR, YOUR DAUGHTER IS AT THE COMMITTEE OF SAAD ABAD, ACCOMPANIED BY A YOUNG MAN...A CERTAIN SAID! THEY WERE WALKING TOGETHER IN THE PARK. IT'S AN ACT AGAINST THE RELIGIOUS MORAL CODE AND THE VALUES OF OUR REPUBLIC. YOU CAN COME GET HER IN EXCHANGE FOR 20,000 TUMANS** IN CASH, OTHERWISE SHE WILL BE WHIPPED.

SORRY! SORRY!

SORRY

*THE COMMISSARIAT OF THE GUARDIANS OF THE REVOLUTION.
**AT THE TIME, THE MONTHLY SALARY OF A GOVERNMENT WORKER.

WE ARE LUCKY TO HAVE PARENTS WHO ACCEPT OUR RELATIONSHIP. WE DON'T HAVE TO SEE EACH OTHER IN THE STREET LIKE OTHERS! MOST FAMILIES ARE TRADITIONALISTS. THEY ARE AS TYRANNICAL AS THE STATE.

IN ANY CASE, IF THEY ARREST US, ALL WE HAVE TO SAY IS THAT WE'RE ENGAGED. IT DOESN'T MATTER. IN THE WORST CASE, WE PAY AND IT'S FINE!

EXCEPT WE SHOULDN'T GIVE A CENT TO THOSE ASSHOLES!

WHAT INGRATITUDE! THOSE ASSHOLES JUST PROTECTED YOU FROM A PERVERT.

STOP... ACTUALLY, WHAT ARE THEY GOING TO DO TO HIM?

TO WHO?

TO THE POOR GUY THEY JUST ARRESTED INSTEAD OF ME!

NOTHING! HE'LL GET A FEW SLAPS! THAT'S ALL!

THOUGH, THEY'RE SO SICK THAT IT'S POSSIBLE THEY'LL HANG HIM. YOU REMEMBER MY FRIENDS DARIUS AND NADER?

YES?

WELL, THEY WERE COMING HOME FROM A PARTY LATE ONE NIGHT, WHEN THE GUARDIANS OF THE REVOLUTION STOPPED THEM,

AT FIRST, THEY THOUGHT THAT IT WAS SIMPLY A ROUTINE CHECK, BUT AFTER HAVING INSPECTED THEIR PAPERS, THE BEARDED GUY ASKED THEM:

WHAT'S YOUR RELA- TIONSHIP TO THIS MAN?

HE'S MY FRIEND.

...THEY THOUGHT THEY'D HAVE A LITTLE FUN.

WHAT DO YOU MEAN BY "FRIEND"?

THAT WE GO OUT TOGETHER!

DIRTY FAG!

DARIUS HAD HIS NOSE BROKEN. NADER GOT A FEW KICKS. HE LIMPS... BUT THEY CAME OUT OF IT WELL, CONSIDERING. HERE, IF YOU ARE HOMOSEXUAL, ACCORDING TO THE LAW, IT'S CAPITAL PUNISHMENT!

I KNOW.

COME ON, LET'S GO HOME.

RIGHT NOW?

YES!

ARE YOU COMING OVER?

IF YOU LIKE.

THE OUTSIDE BEING DANGEROUS, WE OFTEN FOUND OURSELVES INSIDE, AT HIS HOUSE OR AT MY HOUSE. THIS SITUATION WAS SUFFOCATING ME.

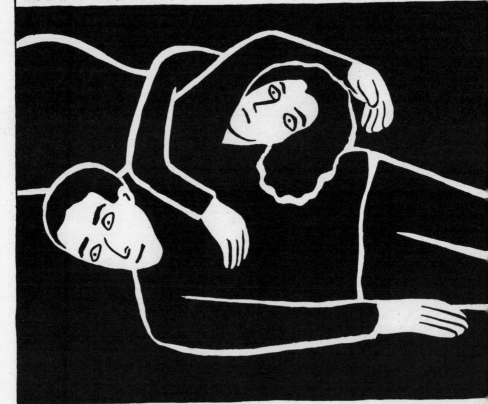

WE COULDN'T DO ANYTHING ELSE BUT CLOSE IN ON EACH OTHER.

I GOT HOME QUITE EARLY.

GRANDMA! WHAT A WONDERFUL SURPRISE! WHERE ARE MOM AND DAD?

THEY WENT TO THE MOVIES. I STAYED HOME TO SEE YOU.

I HAVE SOMETHING TO TELL YOU!

...SO I LOOKED AROUND ME AND I FOUND A GUY WHO LOOKED A LITTLE SCRUFFY. I WENT OVER TO THE BEARDED MEN...

...THEY ARRESTED HIM! HA! HA! HA!... THEY TOOK THE GUY AWAY! HA! HA! HA!

HA! HA! HA! HA! HA!

AND YOU FIND THAT FUNNY?

YOU DON'T?

NO! I THINK THAT YOU'RE A SELFISH BITCH! THAT'S WHAT I THINK!!!

HAVE YOU FORGOTTEN WHO YOUR GRANDFATHER WAS? HE SPENT A THIRD OF HIS LIFE IN PRISON FOR HAVING DEFENDED SOME INNOCENTS! AND YOUR UNCLE ANOOSH? HAVE YOU FORGOTTEN HIM TOO???! HE GAVE HIS LIFE FOR HIS IDEAS! WHAT HAVE I TAUGHT YOU? HUNH???

"INTEGRITY"!! DOES THIS WORD MEAN ANYTHING TO YOU?

I'M LEAVING. TAKE SOME TIME TO THINK ABOUT THIS! IT'S THE BLOOD OF YOUR GRANDPA AND OF YOUR UNCLE THAT RUNS IN YOUR VEINS! SHAME ON YOU!

MY GRANDMA HAD JUST YELLED AT ME FOR THE FIRST TIME IN MY LIFE.

I DECIDED THAT IT WOULD ALSO BE THE LAST.

293

THE CONVOCATION

SEPTEMBER 1989. I WAS FINALLY A STUDENT.

THE BREAKFAST THAT MY MOTHER HAD PREPARED JUST LIKE SHE USED TO, THE MELANCHOLY ATMOSPHERE OF THE BEGINNING OF AUTUMN, MY UNIFORM ... EVERYTHING REMINDED ME OF THE BEGINNING OF SCHOOL.

I'M REALLY EXCITED!

REZA FOUND ME ON THE WAY.

TUUUUT! TUUUTUUUUT!

DO YOU THINK THAT WE CAN TELL PEOPLE WE'RE TOGETHER?

ARE YOU CRAZY? NOT ON YOUR LIFE. IF THE ADMINISTRATION DISCOVERS OUR RELATIONSHIP, WE'LL BE KICKED OUT! TO THEM, WE'RE BREAKING THE LAW!

HE WAS EXAGGERATING A LITTLE. FROM THE MOMENT WE ARRIVED AT UNIVERSITY, ALTHOUGH BOYS AND GIRLS DIDN'T MIX, THIS DIDN'T STOP THEM FROM THROWING EACH OTHER FLIRTATIOUS LOOKS.

NATURALLY! AFTER ALL, LAW OR NO LAW, THESE WERE HUMAN BEINGS.

MANY OF THE STUDENTS KNEW ONE ANOTHER ALREADY. IN LISTENING TO THEM, I UNDERSTOOD THAT THEY'D TAKEN THE PREPARATORY CLASSES TOGETHER. OUR FIRST LESSON WAS "ART HISTORY."

WHAT IS GENERALLY KNOWN AS ARAB ART AND ARCHITECTURE SHOULD IN FACT BE CALLED THE ART OF THE ISLAMIC EMPIRE, WHICH STRETCHED FROM CHINA TO SPAIN. THIS ART IS A CROSS BETWEEN INDIAN, PERSIAN, AND MESOPOTAMIAN ART. THOSE WHOM WE CONSIDER, LIKE AVICENNA, TO BE "ARAB SCHOLARS" ARE FOR THE MOST PART ANYTHING BUT ARABS. EVEN THE FIRST BOOK OF ARABIC GRAMMAR WAS WRITTEN BY AN IRANIAN.

IT WAS FUNNY TO SEE TO WHAT EXTENT THE ISLAMIC REPUBLIC WAS NOT ABLE TO PUT AN END TO OUR CHAUVINISM. TO THE CONTRARY! PEOPLE OFTEN COMPARED THE OBSCURANTISM OF THE NEW REGIME TO THE ARAB INVASION. ACCORDING TO THIS LOGIC, "BEING PERSIAN" MEANT "NOT BEING A FANATIC." BUT THIS PARALLEL WENT ONLY SO FAR CONSIDERING THE FACT THAT OUR GOVERNMENT WASN'T COMPOSED OF ARAB INVADERS BUT PERSIAN FUNDAMENTALISTS.

AT LUNCH TIME.

THE PROFESSOR IS VERY INTERESTING, BUT OH MY! DOES HIS MOUTH SMELL. EVEN THIRTY FEET AWAY YOU CAN SMELL HIS JACKAL'S BREATH!

AMONG THE GUYS, A FEW EVEN HAVE HAIR CUTS!!! MY GOD!

HA! HA! HA!

DESPITE THEIR UPTIGHT APPEARANCE, THE GIRLS IN MY CLASS SEEMED TO BE QUITE THE COMEDIANS.

HEY! LOOK, THE GUY IN THE BLUE SHIRT... HE'S REALLY NOT BAD!

THEY WERE TALKING ABOUT REZA. I SUDDENLY FOUND THEM A LOT LESS FUNNY.

HI, I'M SHOUKA.

AND I'M NIYOOSHA.

NICE TO MEET YOU. I'M MARJANE.

NIYOOSHA HAD VERY GREEN EYES WHICH MADE HER THE MOST SOUGHT AFTER GIRL AT THE COLLEGE. (THE MAJORITY OF IRANIANS HAVE BLACK EYES.)

YOU'VE LIVED ABROAD?

YES, HOW DID YOU KNOW?

BECAUSE OF YOUR MAGHNAEH.* YOU WEAR IT LIKE A BEGINNER.

SHOUKA WAS VERY FUNNY. UNFORTUNATELY, WHEN SHE GOT MARRIED TWO YEARS LATER, HER HUSBAND FORBADE HER FROM ASSOCIATING WITH ME. TO HIM, I WAS AN AMORAL PERSON.

*HOODED HEAD-SCARF

IT'S TRUE THAT WEARING THE VEIL WAS A REAL SCIENCE. YOU HAD TO MAKE A SPECIAL FOLD, LIKE THIS:

NOT A HAIR SHOWS IN PROFILE.

BUT YOU SEE TUFTS FROM THE FRONT.

NEVERTHELESS, THINGS WERE EVOLVING... YEAR BY YEAR, WOMEN WERE WINNING AN EIGHTH OF AN INCH OF HAIR AND LOSING AN EIGHTH OF AN INCH OF VEIL.

WITH PRACTICE, EVEN THOUGH THEY WERE COVERED FROM HEAD TO FOOT, YOU GOT TO THE POINT WHERE YOU COULD GUESS THEIR SHAPE, THE WAY THEY WORE THEIR HAIR AND EVEN THEIR POLITICAL OPINIONS. OBVIOUSLY, THE MORE A WOMAN SHOWED, THE MORE PROGRESSIVE AND MODERN SHE WAS.

COMING HOME THAT EVENING.

HI EVERYONE!

HI.

SO, HOW WAS YOUR FIRST DAY?

LOOK WHAT GRANDMA BROUGHT FOR YOU.

GRANDMA?

EVER SINCE MY COWARDLY ACT MY GRANDMA HADN'T BEEN SPEAKING TO ME.

WHAT'S THIS?

IT'S A COTTON HEAD-SCARF!

THIS WAY YOUR HEAD CAN BREATHE. OTHERWISE YOU'LL BE BALD IN NO TIME.

SHE HAD GIVEN ME A GIFT, SHE HAD THOUGHT OF MY HAIR, SHE WAS TALKING TO ME ...

... WHEW! SHE HAD FORGIVEN ME.

OH, GRANDMA! THANK YOU!!

FINE, FINE, IT'S OKAY!

I HAD FORGOTTEN HER EXTREME INTRANSIGENCE.

ONE WEEK LATER.

THE CLEAN-SHAVEN GUY, RIGHT OVER THERE, WHAT'S HIS NAME...? REZA, YES, REZA, DO YOU KNOW HIM?

NO, WHY?

WELL, HE CAN'T STOP OGLING YOU, HEE! HEE! HEE! HEE!

NO, NO, I HADN'T EVEN NOTICED HIM!

YOU'RE RIGHT, HE'S NOT THAT GREAT.

OH, HE'S NOT SO BAD.

SEE, YOU DO KNOW HIM!

FACED WITH THE PERSPICACITY OF MY GIRLFRIENDS, I HAD NO CHOICE BUT TO ADMIT THE TRUTH.

STUDENTS, STUDENTS.

SUCH DISCERNMENT!

I CONFESS! I SAW HIM LAST NIGHT IN YOUR CAR.

DIRTY LIAR! YOU REALLY GOT ME!

SHHH! LISTEN TO WHAT THE DIRECTOR IS SAYING!

YOUR PRESENCE IS REQUIRED AT 3 O'CLOCK AT THE MAIN CAMPUS! ALL THOSE WHO ARE ABSENT WILL BE BARRED FROM ATTENDING CLASSES FOR TWO WEEKS!

IT WAS AT THE MAIN CAMPUS THAT THE SUBJECTS COMMON TO ALL THE COLLEGES WERE TAUGHT. IT WAS MUCH MORE REPRESSIVE THAN OUR COLLEGE. AS ARTISTS, WE BENEFITED FROM A LITTLE MORE LIBERTY. FOR EXAMPLE, THERE GIRLS AND BOYS HAD TO TAKE DIFFERENT STAIRCASES, WHILE WHERE WE WERE, EVERYONE USED THE SAME STAIRCASE.

I DIDN'T GET THE STAIRCASE THING, BECAUSE IN ANY CASE, WE FOUND OURSELVES TOGETHER UPSTAIRS. BUT SHOUKA SAID THAT IT WAS TO KEEP THE BOYS FROM WATCHING OUR BUTTS WHILE WE CLIMBED.

I THINK SHE WAS RIGHT.

ONCE IN THE AMPHITHEATER, WE DISCOVERED THE REASON FOR OUR CONVOCATION: THE ADMINISTRATION HAD ORGANIZED A LECTURE WITH THE THEME OF "MORAL AND RELIGIOUS CONDUCT," TO SHOW US THE RIGHT PATH.

WE CAN'T ALLOW OURSELVES TO BEHAVE LOOSELY! IT'S THE BLOOD OF OUR MARTYRS WHICH HAS NOURISHED THE FLOWERS OF OUR REPUBLIC. TO ALLOW ONESELF TO BEHAVE INDECENTLY IS TO TRAMPLE ON THE BLOOD OF THOSE WHO GAVE THEIR LIVES FOR OUR FREEDOM. ALSO, I AM ASKING THE YOUNG LADIES PRESENT HERE TO WEAR LESS-WIDE TROUSERS AND LONGER HEAD-SCARVES. YOU SHOULD COVER YOUR HAIR WELL, YOU SHOULD NOT WEAR MAKEUP, YOU SHOULD...

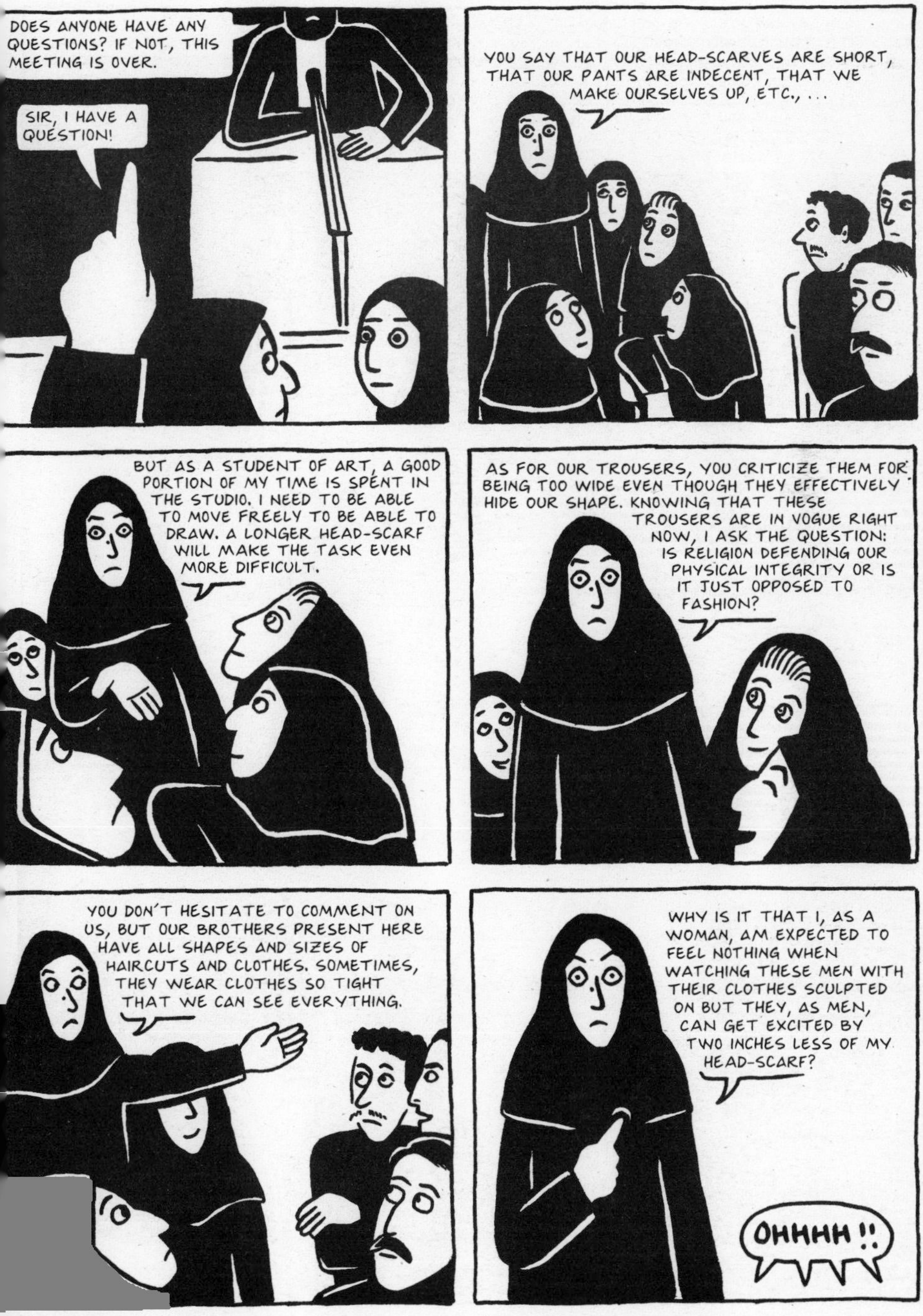
DOES ANYONE HAVE ANY QUESTIONS? IF NOT, THIS MEETING IS OVER.
SIR, I HAVE A QUESTION!
YOU SAY THAT OUR HEAD-SCARVES ARE SHORT, THAT OUR PANTS ARE INDECENT, THAT WE MAKE OURSELVES UP, ETC., ...
BUT AS A STUDENT OF ART, A GOOD PORTION OF MY TIME IS SPENT IN THE STUDIO. I NEED TO BE ABLE TO MOVE FREELY TO BE ABLE TO DRAW. A LONGER HEAD-SCARF WILL MAKE THE TASK EVEN MORE DIFFICULT.
AS FOR OUR TROUSERS, YOU CRITICIZE THEM FOR BEING TOO WIDE EVEN THOUGH THEY EFFECTIVELY HIDE OUR SHAPE. KNOWING THAT THESE TROUSERS ARE IN VOGUE RIGHT NOW, I ASK THE QUESTION: IS RELIGION DEFENDING OUR PHYSICAL INTEGRITY OR IS IT JUST OPPOSED TO FASHION?
YOU DON'T HESITATE TO COMMENT ON US, BUT OUR BROTHERS PRESENT HERE HAVE ALL SHAPES AND SIZES OF HAIRCUTS AND CLOTHES. SOMETIMES, THEY WEAR CLOTHES SO TIGHT THAT WE CAN SEE EVERYTHING.
WHY IS IT THAT I, AS A WOMAN, AM EXPECTED TO FEEL NOTHING WHEN WATCHING THESE MEN WITH THEIR CLOTHES SCULPTED ON BUT THEY, AS MEN, CAN GET EXCITED BY TWO INCHES LESS OF MY HEAD-SCARF?
OHHHH!!

AFTER THE LECTURE.

YOU'RE REALLY COURAGEOUS.

BRAVO! WHAT FRANK SPEAKING!

THANKS.

SATRAPI!

YOU'VE BEEN SUMMONED BY THE ISLAMIC COMMISSION... GOOD LUCK!

IS IT SERIOUS?

I REALLY DON'T KNOW.

THE DIRECTOR OF OUR COLLEGE HAD STUDIED IN THE UNITED STATES AND REMAINED QUITE SECULAR.

WHAT IS IT?

I'VE BEEN SUMMONED BY THE ISLAMIC COMMISSION!

OH SHIT!

WISH ME LUCK!

IT WAS AS IF I WERE GOING TO MEET MY EXECUTIONER.

... BUT TO MY PLEASANT SUR-PRISE, MY EXECUTIONER PROVED TO BE THE "TRUE RELIGIOUS" MAN, THE ONE WHO HAD PASSED ME ON THE IDEOLOGICAL TEST.

SO MISS SATRAPI... ALWAYS SAYING WHAT YOU THINK... IT'S GOOD! YOU'RE HONEST, BUT YOU ARE LOST.

YES.

READ THE SACRED TEXT. YOU'LL SEE THAT WEARING THE VEIL IS SYNONYMOUS WITH EMANCIPATION.

IF YOU SAY SO.

IT IS NOT I WHO SAYS IT, IT'S GOD... I'M GOING TO GIVE YOU A SECOND CHANCE. THIS TIME, YOU'RE NOT EXPELLED. IN EXCHANGE, I AM ASKING YOU TO IMAGINE THE UNIFORM ADAPTED TO THE NEEDS OF THE STUDENTS IN YOUR COLLEGE. NOTHING EXTRAVAGANT, YOU UNDERSTAND.

OF COURSE.

I APPLIED MYSELF. DESIGNING THE "MODEL" THAT WOULD PLEASE BOTH THE ADMINISTRA-TION AND THE INTERESTED PARTIES WASN'T EASY. I MADE DOZENS OF SKETCHES.

THIS WAS THE RESULT OF MY RESEARCH.

SHORT HEAD-SCARF

WIDE TROUSERS

THOUGH SUBTLE, THESE DIFFER-ENCES MEANT A LOT TO US.

THIS LITTLE REBELLION RECON-CILED MY GRANDMOTHER AND ME.

IT'S FEAR THAT MAKES US LOSE OUR CONSCIENCE. IT'S ALSO WHAT TRANSFORMS US INTO COWARDS. YOU HAD GUTS! I'M PROUD OF YOU!

AND THIS IS HOW I RECOVERED MY SELF-ESTEEM AND MY DIGNITY. FOR THE FIRST TIME IN A LONG TIME, I WAS HAPPY WITH MYSELF.

THE SOCKS

To keep us from straying off the straight path, our studios were separated from those of the boys.

I'm your anatomy professor. In the past, we drew nudes, but things have changed. Your model will be covered. Try to make the best of it.

We tried,

We looked...

...from every direction...

...and from every angle...

But not a single part of her body was visible.

We nevertheless learned to draw drapes.

AFTER A FEW WEEKS, WE DISCOVERED, ALONG WITH OUR PROFESSOR, THAT IT WAS PREFERABLE TO HAVE A MODEL ON WHOM YOU COULD AT LEAST DISTINGUISH THE LIMBS. OUR DIRECTOR APPROVED.

ONE EVENING, BEFORE THE COLLEGE CLOSED, ONE OF THE SUPERVISORS PAID ME A VISIT.

WHAT ARE YOU DOING HERE SO LATE?

I'M DRAWING.

WHY ARE YOU LOOKING AT THIS MAN?

WELL, BECAUSE I'M DRAWING HIM.

YES, BUT YOU'RE NOT ALLOWED TO LOOK AT HIM. IT'S AGAINST THE MORAL CODE.

WHAT WOULD YOU HAVE ME DO? SHOULD I DRAW THIS MAN WHILE LOOKING AT THE DOOR???!!

YES.

THESE ABSURD SITUATIONS WERE QUITE FREQUENT. ONE DAY, FOR EXAMPLE, I WAS SUPPOSED TO GO SEE MY DENTIST, BUT CLASSES FINISHED LATER THAN EXPECTED.

SUDDENLY, I HEARD A VOICE OVER THE LOUDSPEAKER:

THE LADY IN THE BLUE COAT! DON'T RUN!

THE LADY IN THE BLUE COAT!!! STOP RUNNING!

??

HEY—BLUE COAT! STOP RUNNING!

???

ME?

MADAM, WHY WERE YOU RUNNING?

I'M VERY LATE! I WAS RUNNING TO CATCH MY BUS.

YES... BUT... WHEN YOU RUN, YOUR BEHIND MAKES MOVEMENTS THAT ARE... HOW DO YOU SAY... OBSCENE!

WELL THEN DON'T LOOK AT MY ASS!

I YELLED SO LOUDLY THAT THEY DIDN'T EVEN ARREST ME.

WE CONFRONTED THE REGIME AS BEST WE COULD.

IN 1990, THE ERA OF GRAND REVOLUTIONARY IDEAS AND DEMONSTRATIONS WAS OVER. BETWEEN 1980 AND 1983, THE GOVERNMENT HAD IMPRISONED AND EXECUTED SO MANY HIGH-SCHOOL AND COLLEGE STUDENTS THAT WE NO LONGER DARED TO TALK POLITICS.

OUR STRUGGLE WAS MORE DISCREET.

IT HINGED ON THE LITTLE DETAILS. TO OUR LEADERS, THE SMALLEST THING COULD BE A SUBJECT OF SUBVERSION.

SHOWING YOUR WRIST.

A LOUD LAUGH.

HAVING A WALKMAN.

IN SHORT . . . EVERYTHING WAS A PRETEXT TO ARREST US.

I EVEN REMEMBER SPENDING AN ENTIRE DAY AT THE COMMITTEE BECAUSE OF A PAIR OF RED SOCKS.

THE REGIME HAD UNDERSTOOD THAT ONE PERSON LEAVING HER HOUSE WHILE ASKING HERSELF:

ARE MY TROUSERS LONG ENOUGH?

IS MY VEIL IN PLACE?

CAN MY MAKE-UP BE SEEN?

ARE THEY GOING TO WHIP ME?

NO LONGER ASKS HERSELF:

WHERE IS MY FREEDOM OF THOUGHT?

WHERE IS MY FREEDOM OF SPEECH?

MY LIFE, IS IT LIVABLE?

WHAT'S GOING ON IN THE POLITICAL PRISONS?

IT'S ONLY NATURAL! WHEN WE'RE AFRAID, WE LOSE ALL SENSE OF ANALYSIS AND REFLECTION. OUR FEAR PARALYZES US. BESIDES, FEAR HAS ALWAYS BEEN THE DRIVING FORCE BEHIND ALL DICTATORS' REPRESSION.

SHOWING YOUR HAIR OR PUTTING ON MAKEUP LOGICALLY BECAME ACTS OF REBELLION.

UNFORTUNATELY, MANY OF US WERE REBELS ONLY IN APPEARANCE. ONE DAY, IN CLASS...

MARJANE! YOUR PENCIL CASE!

THANKS DORNA, THANKS!

YOU'RE WELCOME.

YOU TAKE THE PILL?

YES.

ME TOO, I'M IRREGULAR. ARE YOU IRREGULAR, TOO?

NO, NOT AT ALL. I TAKE IT BECAUSE I SLEEP WITH MY BOYFRIEND!

OOOOH!!!!

A LITTLE DECENCY, PLEASE!

CAN YOU EXPLAIN TO ME WHAT'S INDECENT ABOUT MAKING LOVE WITH YOUR BOYFRIEND?

SHUT UP!

SHUT UP YOURSELF! MY BODY IS MY OWN! I GIVE IT TO WHOMEVER I WANT! IT'S NOBODY ELSE'S BUSINESS!

I DIDN'T SAY EVERYTHING I COULD HAVE: THAT SHE WAS FRUSTRATED BECAUSE SHE WAS STILL A VIRGIN AT TWENTY-SEVEN! THAT SHE WAS FORBIDDING ME WHAT WAS FORBIDDEN TO HER! THAT TO MARRY SOMEONE THAT YOU DON'T KNOW, FOR HIS MONEY, IS PROSTITUTION. THAT DESPITE HER LOCKS OF HAIR AND HER LIPSTICK, SHE WAS ACTING LIKE THE STATE. THAT... ETC.... THAT DAY, HALF THE CLASS TURNED ITS BACK ON ME.

HAPPILY, THERE WAS STILL THE OTHER HALF. LITTLE BY LITTLE, I GOT TO KNOW THE STUDENTS WHO THOUGHT LIKE ME.

WE WOULD GO TO ONE ANOTHER'S HOUSES, WHERE WE POSED FOR EACH OTHER ... WE HAD AT LAST FOUND A PLACE OF FREEDOM.

AT FIRST THERE WERE ONLY FIVE OF US.

THEN ...

AND FINALLY ...

WE WERE MUCH MORE NUMEROUS THAN I WOULD HAVE BELIEVED.

OUR PROFESSOR WAS SO HAPPY TO SEE THE SKETCHES WE DID AT HOME.

BRAVO! AN ARTIST SHOULD DEFY THE LAW! I CON- GRATULATE YOU!

THE MORE TIME PASSED, THE MORE I BECAME CONSCIOUS OF THE CONTRAST BETWEEN THE OFFICIAL REPRESENTATION OF MY COUNTRY AND THE REAL LIFE OF THE PEOPLE, THE ONE THAT WENT ON BEHIND THE WALLS.

OUR BEHAVIOR IN PUBLIC AND OUR BEHAVIOR IN PRIVATE WERE POLAR OPPOSITES.

... THIS DISPARITY MADE US SCHIZOPHRENIC.

TO FIND A SEMBLANCE OF EQUILIBRIUM, WE PARTIED ALMOST EVERY NIGHT...

... BUT EVEN IN OUR HOMES, THEY DIDN'T LEAVE US ALONE.

I SAW A PATROL OF GUARDIANS OF THE REVOLUTION OUT THE WINDOW! I THINK THEY'RE COMING TO ARREST US!

COME ALONG YOU LITTLE BASTARD! YOU'RE ORGANIZING PARTIES! I'LL CURE YOU OF YOUR TASTE FOR PLEASURE!

THEY CARTED EVERYONE OFF TO PRISON. OBVIOUSLY, WE WERE VERY SCARED THE FIRST TIME.

... BUT WE QUICKLY GOT USED TO IT. WE WOULD EVEN ARRIVE LAUGHING.

OH BEARDED ONE, YOUR BEARD STINKS!

THEN CAME THE USUAL SPIEL...

..AGAINST THE MORAL CODE... THE BLOOD OF MARTYRS... TWENTY THOUSAND TUMANS...

OUR PARENTS PAID AND WE WERE RELEASED.

...UNTIL THE NEXT TIME. TO BE ABLE TO PARTY, YOU HAD TO HAVE MEANS.

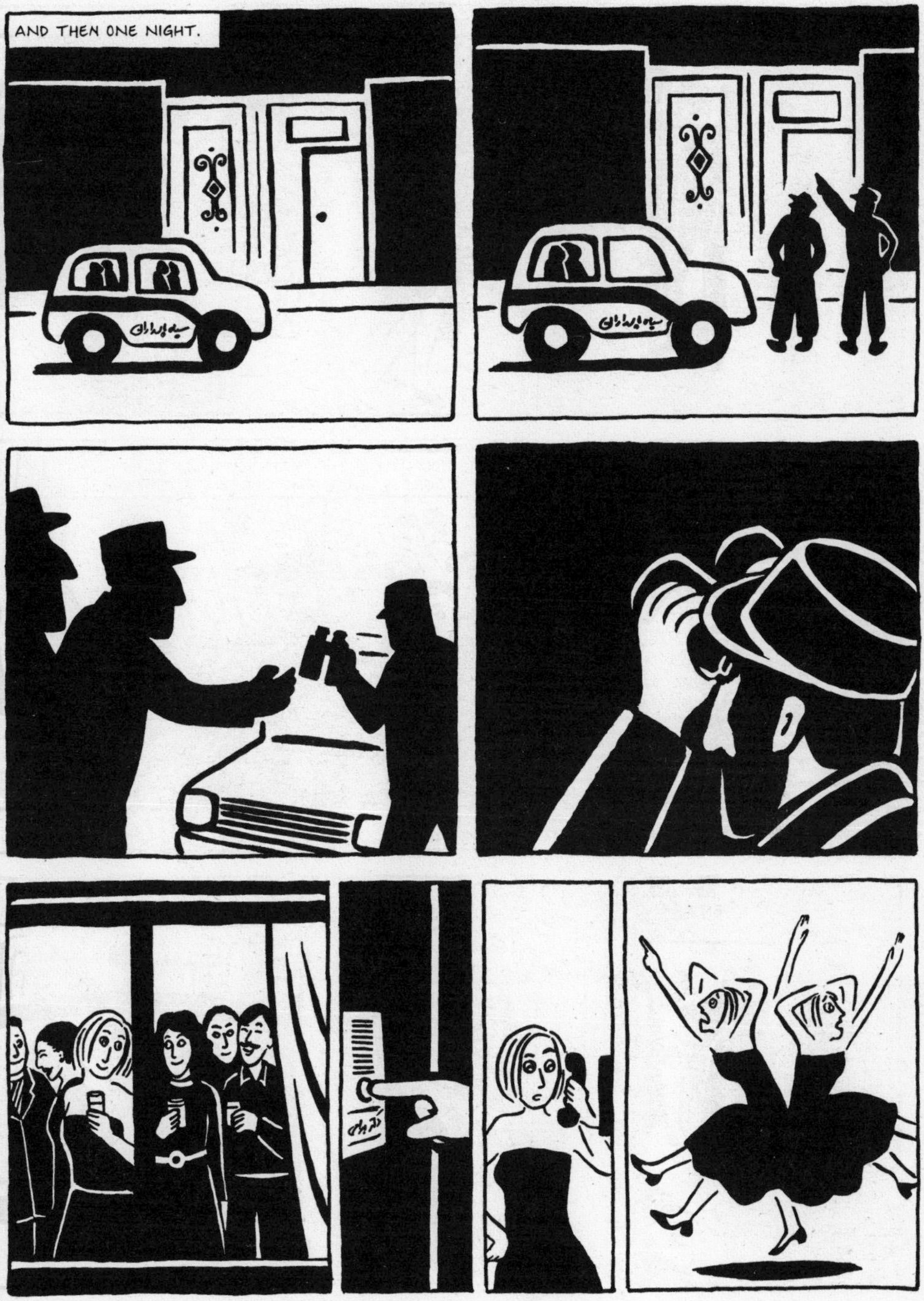
AND THEN ONE NIGHT.

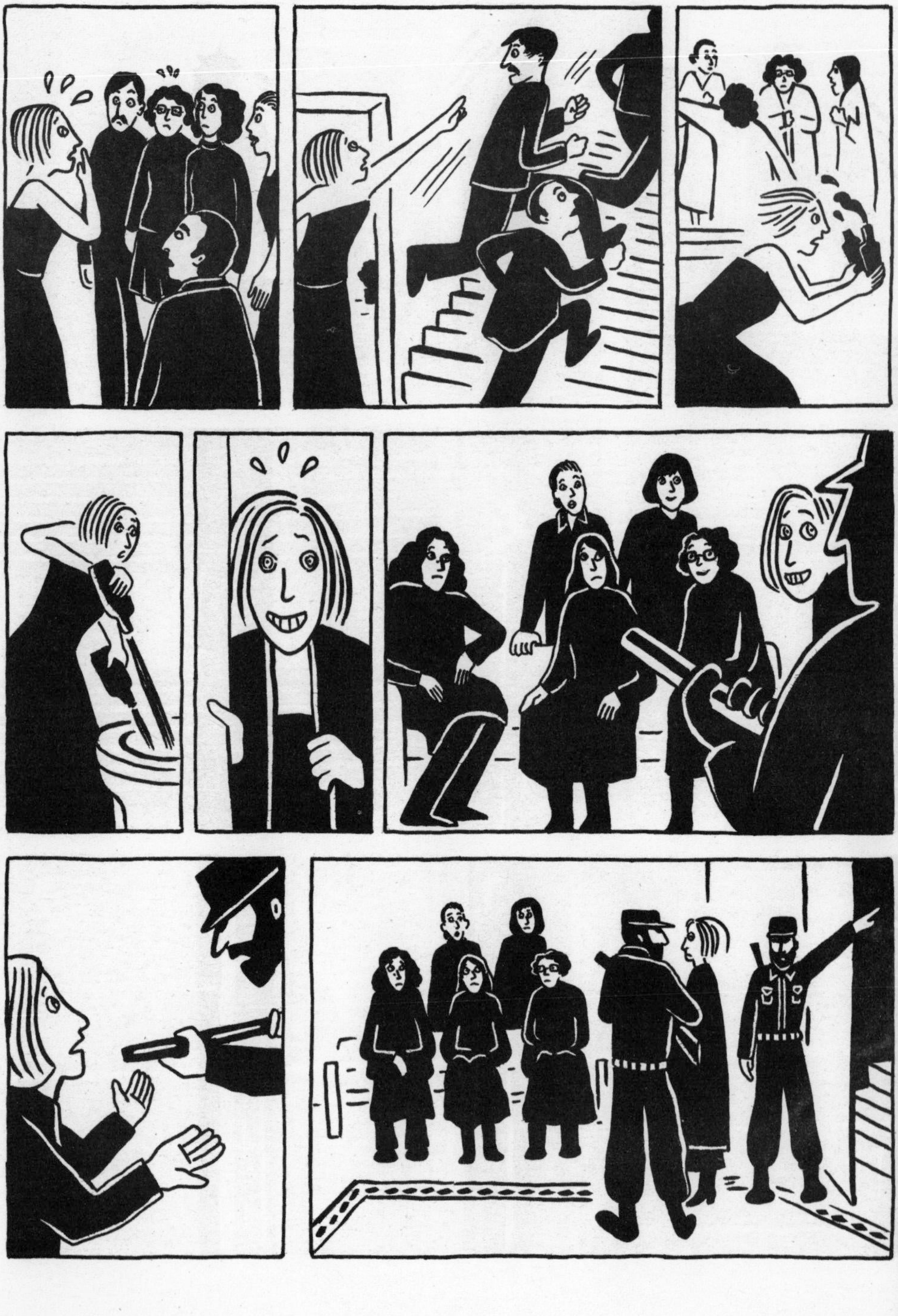

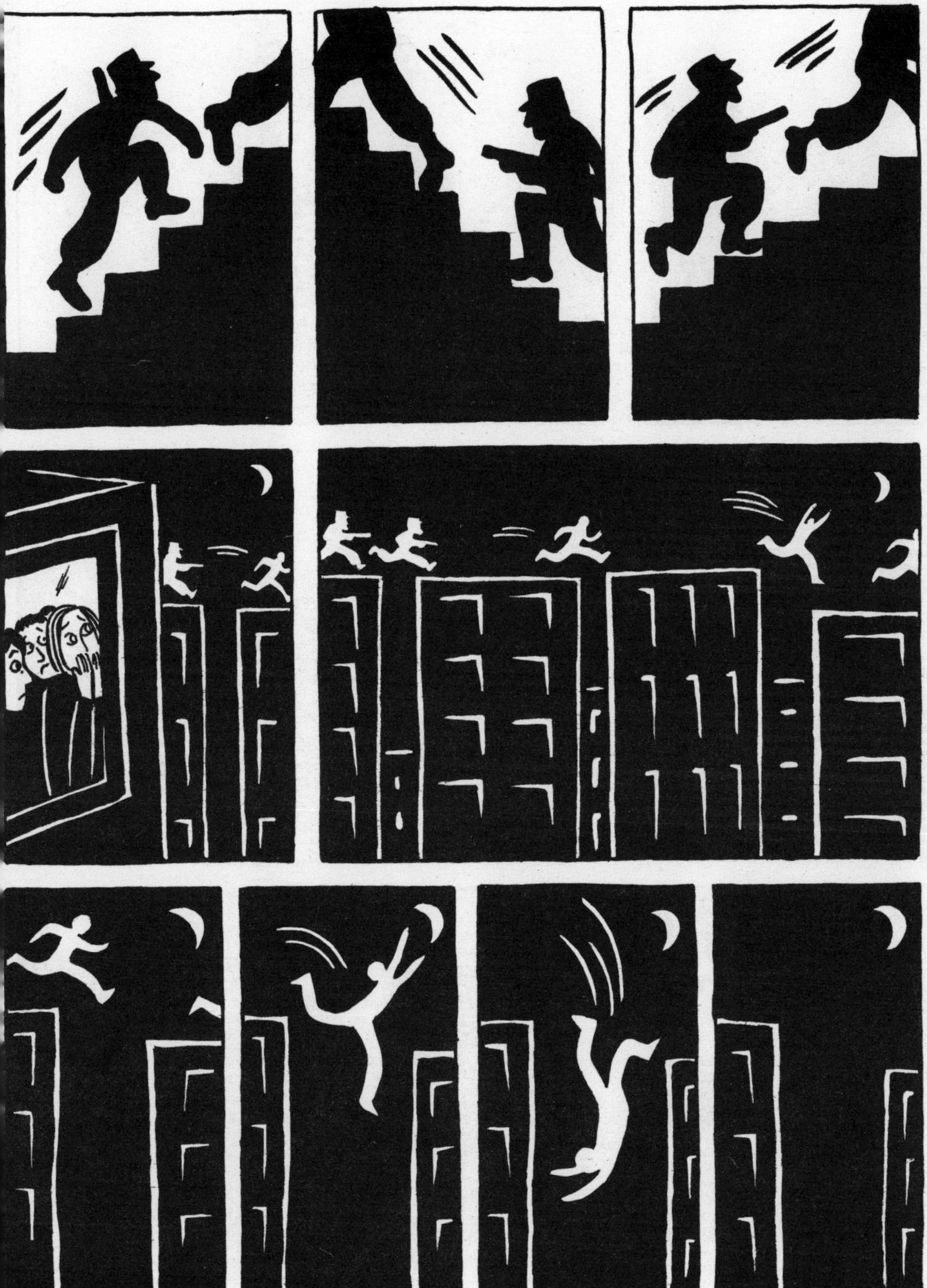

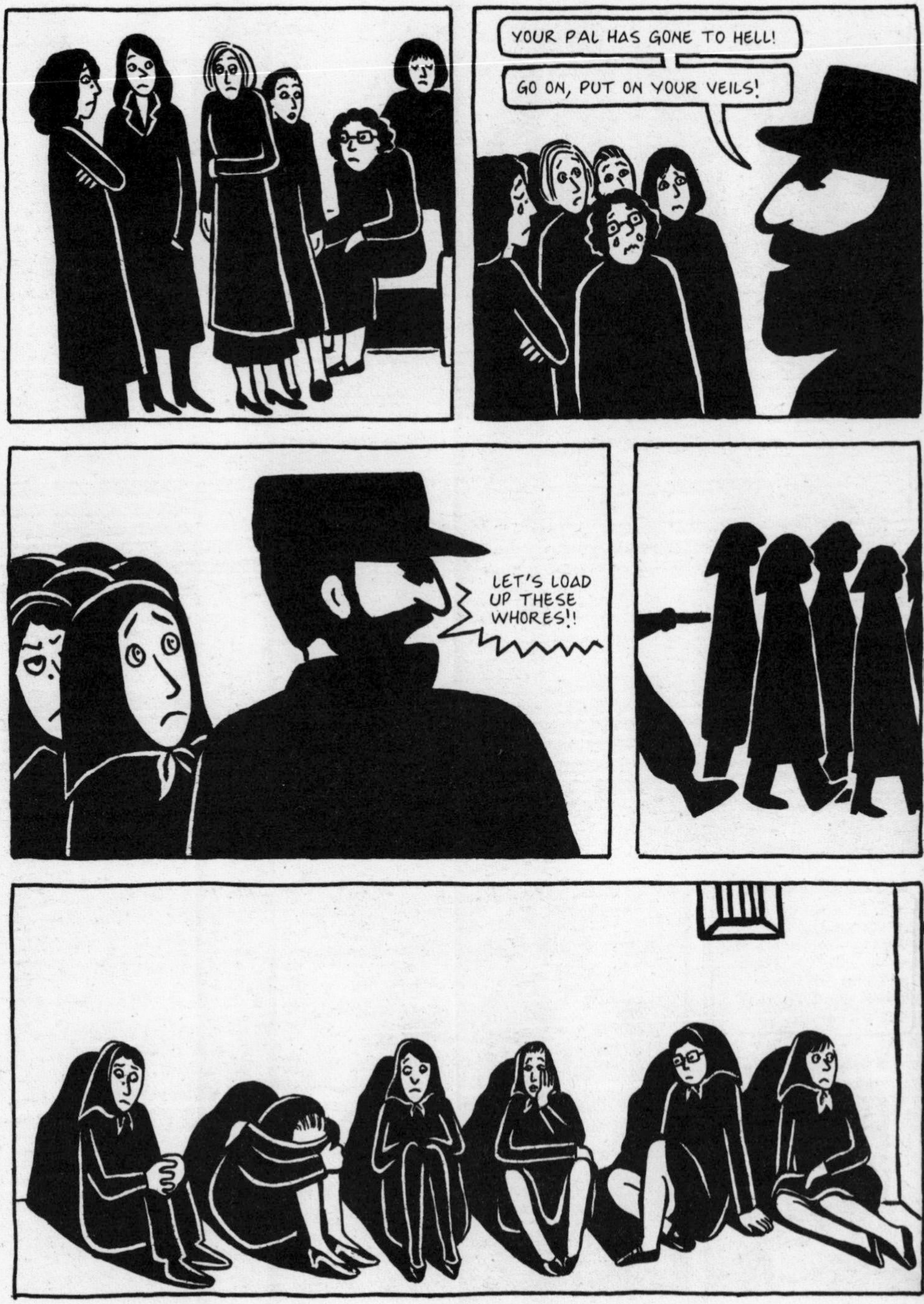
YOUR PAL HAS GONE TO HELL!
GO ON, PUT ON YOUR VEILS!
LET'S LOAD UP THESE WHORES!!

DAD, FARZAD IS... I KNOW. I WAS SCARED... MAYBE YOU SHOULD...

BUT HE DIDN'T FINISH HIS SENTENCE. DESPITE THE DANGER, MY FATHER ALWAYS LET ME LIVE THE WAY I FELT WAS RIGHT.

THE NEXT DAY, WE GATHERED AT MY HOUSE.

POOR FARZAD. HE WAS SO HANDSOME. I CAN'T BELIEVE HE'S DEAD!

I COULD KILL THOSE BEARDED MEN WITH MY OWN HANDS.

I'M NOT COMING TO ANY MORE PARTIES. IT'S TOO FRIGHTENING!

YOU'RE WRONG. THAT'S EXACTLY WHAT THEY WANT! TO STOP US FROM LIVING! NOTHING BOTHERS THEM MORE THAN TO SEE US HAPPY!

ALI IS RIGHT!

THAT SAME NIGHT, ALI HAD A BIG PARTY AT HIS HOUSE.

I NEVER DRANK SO MUCH IN MY LIFE.

313

THE WEDDING

IN 1991, I WAS IN MY SECOND YEAR OF GRAPHIC ARTS.

EVERYTHING WAS GOING WELL: MY STUDIES INTERESTED ME, I LOVED MY BOYFRIEND, I WAS SURROUNDED BY FRIENDS.

MY FRIENDS AND I HAD EVOLVED. I HAD TEMPERED MY WESTERN VISION OF LIFE AND THEY, FOR THEIR PART, HAD MOVED AWAY FROM TRADITION. AS A RESULT, MANY UNMARRIED COUPLES HAD FORMED.

IT MUST BE SAID THAT IT WAS DIFFICULT TO BE TOGETHER OUTSIDE OF MARRIAGE. IF WE WENT ON A TRIP:

SIR, WE WOULD LIKE A ROOM FOR TWO NIGHTS.

YOUR MARRIAGE CERTIFICATE, PLEASE.

...IF WE WANTED TO RENT AN APARTMENT:

I'M A REAL ESTATE AGENT. MY AIM IS TO SIGN A MAXIMUM NUMBER OF CONTRACTS. YOUR FAMILY SITUATION DOESN'T MATTER TO ME, BUT THE OWNER REFUSES. TO BE FAIR, HE'S RIGHT. HE'LL HAVE PROBLEMS WITH THE AUTHORITIES ... AND THEN FROM A MORAL STANDPOINT, WHAT YOU'RE DOING IS NOT RIGHT. YOU SHOULD GET MARRIED.

DEEP DOWN, NEITHER REZA NOR I WAS READY TO GET ENGAGED. IN TWO YEARS, WE HAD ONLY SEEN EACH OTHER AT HIS HOUSE OR AT MY HOUSE (I MEAN, AT OUR PARENTS' HOUSES).

I LOVE YOU. DO YOU WANT TO GET MARRIED?

?

I'M ONLY TWENTY-ONE! I HAVEN'T SEEN ANYTHING YET! BUT I LOVE HIM! HOW CAN I KNOW IF HE'S THE MAN OF MY LIFE WITHOUT HAVING LIVED WITH HIM? ..

SO?

GIVE ME A LITTLE TIME.

TAKE AS MUCH TIME AS YOU NEED.

I NEEDED TO TALK IT OVER WITH MY PARENTS BUT MY MOTHER WAS ON A TRIP ABROAD.

HAPPILY, MY FATHER WAS HOME.

DAD! REZA ASKED ME TO MARRY HIM. I DON'T KNOW WHAT TO DO.

YOU'RE THE ONLY ONE WHO CAN KNOW. AT THE SAME TIME, IF YOU WANT TO KNOW HIM, YOU MUST LIVE WITH HIM, AND FOR THAT, YOU MUST MARRY.

WORST CASE, WE DIVORCE.

WELL, YES.

A FEW DAYS LATER, MY DECISION WAS MADE: I WAS GOING TO GET MARRIED. I ANNOUNCED IT TO MY FATHER. HE INVITED US, ME AND REZA, TO A RESTAURANT TO TALK ABOUT IT.

WELCOME!

AFTER DINNER.

AS YOUR FUTURE FATHER-IN-LAW, I'M TAKING THE LIBERTY OF ASKING YOU THREE THINGS.

FIRST: YOU ARE SURELY AWARE THAT IN THIS COUNTRY A WOMAN'S "RIGHT TO DIVORCE" IS NOT GUARANTEED. SHE ONLY HAS IT IF HER HUSBAND ALLOWS THIS OPTION DURING THE SIGNING OF THE MARRIAGE CERTIFICATE. MY DAUGHTER MUST ENJOY THIS RIGHT.

SECOND: MY WIFE AND I HAVE RAISED OUR DAUGHTER WITH COMPLETE FREEDOM. IF SHE SPENDS HER WHOLE LIFE IN IRAN, SHE'LL WITHER. I'M THEREFORE ASKING THE BOTH OF YOU TO LEAVE TO CONTINUE YOUR STUDIES IN EUROPE AFTER YOUR DIPLOMA. YOU WILL HAVE MY FINANCIAL SUPPORT.

THIRD: LIVE TOGETHER AS LONG AS YOU FEEL TRULY HAPPY. LIFE IS TOO SHORT TO BE LIVED BADLY.

WAITER, THE CHECK, PLEASE!

YES, SIR.

LONG AFTERWARD MY FATHER ADMITTED TO ME THAT HE HAD ALWAYS KNOWN THAT I WOULD GET DIVORCED. HE WANTED ME TO REALIZE BY MYSELF THAT REZA AND I WERE NOT MADE FOR EACH OTHER. HE WAS RIGHT.

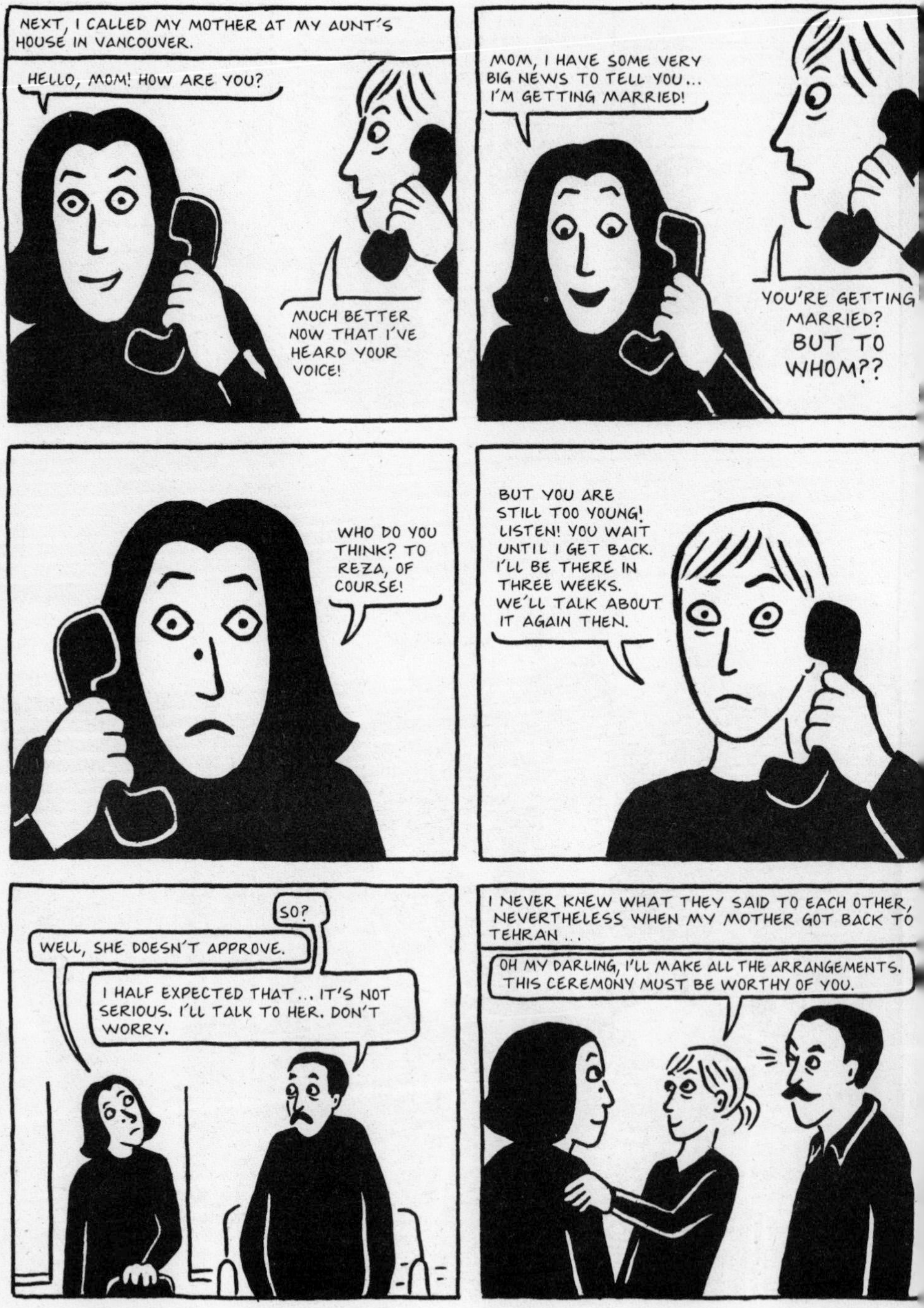
NEXT, I CALLED MY MOTHER AT MY AUNT'S HOUSE IN VANCOUVER.
HELLO, MOM! HOW ARE YOU?
MUCH BETTER NOW THAT I'VE HEARD YOUR VOICE!
MOM, I HAVE SOME VERY BIG NEWS TO TELL YOU... I'M GETTING MARRIED!
YOU'RE GETTING MARRIED? BUT TO WHOM??
WHO DO YOU THINK? TO REZA, OF COURSE!
BUT YOU ARE STILL TOO YOUNG! LISTEN! YOU WAIT UNTIL I GET BACK. I'LL BE THERE IN THREE WEEKS. WE'LL TALK ABOUT IT AGAIN THEN.
SO?
WELL, SHE DOESN'T APPROVE.
I HALF EXPECTED THAT... IT'S NOT SERIOUS. I'LL TALK TO HER. DON'T WORRY.
I NEVER KNEW WHAT THEY SAID TO EACH OTHER, NEVERTHELESS WHEN MY MOTHER GOT BACK TO TEHRAN...
OH MY DARLING, I'LL MAKE ALL THE ARRANGEMENTS. THIS CEREMONY MUST BE WORTHY OF YOU.

AND STARTING THE NEXT DAY.

WHAT DO YOU THINK OF THIS?

UHH ... IT'S A PRETTY DRESS, BUT I CAN'T WEAR SOMETHING LIKE THAT.

NEXT, SHE TOOK ME TO A PLACE KNOWN FOR ITS "WEDDING HAIRDOS," TO TRY SOME OUT.

DO YOU LIKE IT, BABY?

...

I WAS THE SUBJECT OF DOZENS OF EXPERIMENTS, OF ALL KINDS: MAKEUP, FLOWER BOUQUETS, SHOES, ...

I KNOW THAT YOU WANT TO DO YOUR BEST FOR ME, BUT I DETEST WEDDING DRESSES, FASHIONABLE HAIRSTYLES AND ALL THE REST. COULDN'T WE HAVE JUST A SMALL LITTLE PARTY...

LISTEN, WE HAVE ONLY ONE CHILD: YOU! IT'S POSSIBLE THAT THIS WILL BE YOUR ONE AND ONLY WEDDING. YOU DRESS AND WEAR YOUR HAIR THE WAY YOU WANT, BUT LET US AT LEAST CELEBRATE THIS EVENT IN OUR OWN WAY.

I GAVE IN, AND MY PARENTS TOOK ADVANTAGE BY INVITING FOUR HUNDRED PEOPLE, HAVING TWO BANDS, A VIDEO CREW, FLOWERS ...

THE BRIDE IS HERE!

MY DARLING!

FIRST, WE WENT BEFORE THE MULLAH.

MR. REZA... DO YOU TAKE MISS MARJANE ...
MISS MARJANE ... DO YOU TAKE MR. REZA ...

YES!

YES!

THEN IT WAS FOLKLORE'S TURN. TRADITION REQUIRED THAT A HAPPILY MARRIED WOMAN RUB TWO SUGAR LOAVES ABOVE OUR HEADS TO PASS ON HER JOY AND PROSPERITY.

TRADITION ALSO REQUIRED THAT WE PLUNGE OUR FINGERS IN HONEY ...

AND THAT WE SUCK ONE ANOTHER'S FINGERS TO BEGIN OUR MARRIED LIFE ON A SWEET NOTE.

THEN CAME THE GIFTS.

HERE, IT'S FOR YOU!

MOM!

SO, WHEN CAN WE EXPECT KIDS?

SOON.

YOU LOOK RADIANT!

THANK YOU!

ARE YOU THE BRIDE?

HEE! HEE! HEE! NO, SHE IS!

?

MOM, ARE YOU IN THERE?

NO!

HAVE YOU BEEN CRYING?

NO.

I HAD ONLY TO PUT MY HAND ON HER SHOULDER FOR HER TO START AGAIN.

I HAVE ALWAYS WANTED FOR YOU TO BECOME INDEPENDENT, EDUCATED, CULTURED ... AND HERE YOU ARE GETTING MARRIED AT TWENTY-ONE. I WANT YOU TO LEAVE IRAN, FOR YOU TO BE FREE AND EMANCIPATED ...

MY SWEET LITTLE MOM! TRUST ME. I KNOW WHAT I'M DOING.

THE REST OF THE EVENING ALTERNATED BETWEEN LAUGHTER AND TEARS BUT ESPECIALLY LOTS OF WEARINESS. FINALLY, AT TWO IN THE MORNING ...

GOODBYE!

BE HAPPY!

GOOD LUCK!

WE WENT HOME ...

... WHEN THE APARTMENT DOOR CLOSED, I HAD A BIZARRE FEELING.

... I WAS ALREADY SORRY! I HAD SUDDENLY BECOME "A MARRIED WOMAN." I HAD CONFORMED TO SOCIETY, WHILE I HAD ALWAYS WANTED TO REMAIN IN THE MARGINS. IN MY MIND, "A MARRIED WOMAN" WASN'T LIKE ME. IT REQUIRED TOO MANY COMPROMISES. I COULDN'T ACCEPT IT, BUT IT WAS TOO LATE.

DESPITE EVERYTHING I TRIED, MY EXISTENTIALIST AND IDENTITY CRISIS WAS ONLY ONE PART OF THE PROBLEM. THE OTHER PART WAS REZA.

I'D LIKE TO HANG THE PAINTING THERE!

NO, I PREFER IT HERE!

I'M GOING TO HAVE LUNCH AT MY PARENTS' HOUSE. ARE YOU COMING?

NO, I DON'T FEEL LIKE IT.

DON'T YOU WANT TO COME TO KIANA'S BIRTHDAY PARTY?

NO. I'LL BE BACK LATE.

WHATEVER YOU WANT.

IN RETROSPECT, I CAN SEE THAT I HAD ALWAYS KNOWN THAT IT WOULDN'T WORK BETWEEN US. BUT AFTER MY PITIFUL LOVE STORY IN VIENNA, I NEEDED TO BELIEVE IN SOMEONE AGAIN...

...SO MUCH SO THAT I CONTINUALLY LIED TO HIM.

I LOVE GIRLS IN SUITS.

THAT'S JUST MY STYLE!

I DON'T LIKE RUDE GIRLS.

OH! I HATE THEM!

I LIKE LIGHT EYES.

...AND I BOUGHT MYSELF BLUE CONTACTS.

BLAH BLAH BLAH BLAH BLAH BLAH BLAH BLAH BLAH BLAH

I AGREE WITH EVERYTHING YOU SAY!

HE MARRIED:

Her

AND FOUND HIMSELF WITH:

HER

320

AFTER ONE MONTH OF MARRIAGE, WE SET UP SEPARATE BEDROOMS.

HE HAD HIS LIFE ...

WHERE'S YOUR WIFE?

ON VACATION, WITH HER COUSIN.

...AND I HAD MINE.

AND REZA'S WELL?

YEAH, HE'S WITH HIS BROTHER.

WE HAD BEEN CONSIDERED THE MODEL COUPLE FOR SO LONG AND BY SO MANY PEOPLE THAT WE WEREN'T ABLE TO ACCEPT OUR FAILURE ...

... WE WERE KEEPING UP APPEARANCES IN PUBLIC.

IS SHE GOING TO SHUT HER BIG MOUTH?

WHAT AN ASS!

BUT AS SOON AS WE WERE ALONE.

YOU NEVER WANT TO GO OUT! IF I HAVE TO GO EVERYWHERE ALONE, WHAT'S THE POINT OF LIVING TOGETHER?

I LET YOU DO WHATEVER YOU WANT! I'M NOT ONE OF THOSE MACHO MEN WHO EXPECTS YOU TO REPORT BACK! SO LEAVE ME ALONE!

IN THE SPACE OF TWO MONTHS, WE WENT FROM WEEKLY FIGHTS TO DAILY INSULTS.

THE SATELLITE

IN 1991, THE YEAR OF MY MARRIAGE, IRAQ ATTACKED KUWAIT.

SERVES THEM RIGHT! THEY SUPPORTED THAT BASTARD SADDAM HUSSEIN FOR EIGHT YEARS AGAINST US! THEY SHOULD REAP WHAT THEY SOWED!

SADDAM IS OVERARMED AND THE KUWAITIS CONTINUE TO SURPASS THEIR OIL PRODUCTION QUOTA! LET THEM EXTERMINATE EACH OTHER!

NOW THAT IRAN HAS DECLARED ITSELF NEUTRAL IN THIS AFFAIR, THE KUWAITIS ARE APOLOGIZING FOR HAVING SUPPORTED OUR ENEMY! SOON THEY'LL EVEN COME EXILE THEMSELVES HERE!

THAT'S WHAT THEY DID.

THE KUWAITI IMMIGRANTS WERE EASY TO IDENTIFY. THEY HAD VERY MODERN CARS, IN CONTRAST TO IRANIANS, ECONOMICALLY DESTROYED AFTER THE LONG YEARS OF WAR. MY ONLY CONTACT WITH THEM WAS ONE SUMMER DAY IN THE STREET.

HOW MUCH? HOW MUCH?

FUCK YOU! SON OF A BITCH!!

WHEN I RECOUNTED THIS MISADVENTURE TO AN UNCLE WHO KNEW KUWAIT WELL, HE TOLD ME: "THERE, AS IN ALL THE ARAB COUNTRIES, WOMEN ARE SO LACKING IN RIGHTS THAT FOR A KUWAITI, A GIRL WHO WALKS OUTSIDE WHILE DRINKING A COKE CAN'T BE ANYTHING BUT A PROSTITUTE."

ASIDE FROM THESE LITTLE DISAPPOINTMENTS, WE DIDN'T FEEL AT ALL CONCERNED ABOUT THE EVENTS, EVEN IF THEY WERE TAKING PLACE IN THE PERSIAN GULF, WHICH IS TO SAY, IN OUR BACKYARD!

MARJI, COME SEE!

THIS WAR HAS UNLEASHED A PANIC IN EUROPEAN COUNTRIES...

PEOPLE ARE FILLING THEIR SHOPPINGCARTS. IT'S LIKE A MADHOUSE IN WESTERN SUPERMARKETS.

...HERE ARE SOME ACCOUNTS:

I LIVED THROUGH THE SECOND WORLD WAR! IT WAS HORRIBLE!

WE HAVE TWO BABIES! WE HAVE TO STOCK UP ON POWDERED MILK AND DIAPERS.

THERE ARE GOING TO BE ATTACKS! THEY'LL COUNTER-ATTACK! THEY'LL COME AFTER US ON OUR OWN TERRITORY!

HA! HA! HA! HA!HA!HA!

IT'S CRAZY, THE WAR IS HAPPENING 4,000 MILES AWAY AND THEY'RE SCARED! TO THINK THAT THEY HAVE SO LITTLE TO WORRY ABOUT THAT THEY ARE GETTING WORKED UP ABOUT NOTHING!

WHAT ARE YOU LAUGHING ABOUT?

WE SAW SOME EUROPEANS TERRIFIED BY THE GULF WAR ON TV AND DAD AND I WERE SAYING THAT THEY MUST NOT HAVE ENOUGH OF THEIR OWN PROBLEMS.

SINCE WHEN HAVE YOU TRUSTED OUR MEDIA? THEIR OBJECTIVE CONSISTS OF MAKING ANTI-WESTERN PROPAGANDA.

DON'T LET IT GET TO YOU, MOM! THE WESTERN MEDIA ALSO FIGHTS AGAINST US. THAT'S WHERE OUR REPUTATION AS FUNDAMENTALISTS AND TERRORISTS COMES FROM!

YOU'RE RIGHT. BETWEEN ONE'S FANATICISM AND THE OTHER'S DISDAIN, IT'S HARD TO KNOW WHICH SIDE TO CHOOSE.

PERSONALLY, I HATE SADDAM AND I HAVE NO SYMPATHY FOR THE KUWAITIS, BUT I HATE JUST AS MUCH THE CYNICISM OF THE ALLIES WHO CALL THEMSELVES "LIBERA-TORS" WHILE THEY'RE THERE FOR THE OIL.

EXACTLY. JUST LOOK AT AFGHANISTAN! THEY FOUGHT THERE FOR TEN YEARS. THERE WERE 900,000 DEAD AND TODAY THE COUNTRY IS STILL IN CHAOS.

NO ONE LIFTED A FINGER! BECAUSE AFGHANISTAN IS POOR!

THE WORST IS THAT THE INTERVENTION IN KUWAIT IS DONE IN THE NAME OF HUMAN RIGHTS!!!

WHICH RIGHTS? WHICH HUMANS?

AT THE TIME, THIS KIND OF ANALYSIS WASN'T COMMONPLACE. AFTER OUR OWN WAR, WE WERE HAPPY THAT IRAQ GOT ITSELF ATTACKED AND DELIGHTED THAT IT WASN'T HAPPENING IN OUR COUNTRY.

SADDAM STOLE MY LEG FROM ME. I HOPE THEY KILL HIM.

THERE'S NO MORE WAR IN IRAN. I DON'T CARE ABOUT THE REST.

NOW OUR ECONOMY WILL FINALLY PICK UP!

MY HUSBAND IS A WAR MARTYR. I HOPE SADDAM GOES TO HELL!

I'LL DO MY MILITARY SERVICE IN PEACETIME.

I HAVE A HEART CONDITION. HAPPILY, WE'RE THROUGH WITH BOMBS!!!

DOWN WITH SADDAM!

WE WERE FINALLY ABLE TO SLEEP PEACEFULLY WITHOUT FEAR OF MISSILES...

WE NO LONGER NEEDED TO LINE UP WITH OUR FOOD RATION COUPONS ...

DETERGENT

SUGAR

RICE

OIL

...THE REST MATTERED LITTLE.

AND THEN, THERE WASN'T ANY MORE OPPOSITION. THE PROTESTERS HAD BEEN EXECUTED.

OR HAD FLED THE COUNTRY ANY WAY POSSIBLE.

THE REGIME HAD ABSOLUTE POWER ...

... AND MOST PEOPLE, IN SEARCH OF A CLOUD OF HAPPINESS, HAD FORGOTTEN THEIR POLITICAL CONSCIENCE.

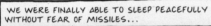

I WASN'T ANY DIFFERENT FROM THEM. ASIDE FROM THE TIME I SPENT WITH MY PARENTS, I LIVED FROM DAY TO DAY WITHOUT ASKING MYSELF ANY QUESTIONS. NEVERTHELESS, IN JANUARY 1992, A BIG EVENT OCCURRED:

THAT WAS FARIBORZ ON THE TELEPHONE. HE JUST INSTALLED A SATELLITE ANTENNA AT HIS HOUSE!

COME ON, HURRY UP! LET'S GO!!

THE SATELLITE ANTENNA WAS SYNONYMOUS WITH THE OPENING UP OF THE REST OF THE WORLD.

WE COULD FINALLY EXPERIENCE A VIEW DIFFERENT FROM THE ONE DICTATED BY OUR GOVERNMENT.

LOOK AT THIS ONE! HE'S SO IMPATIENT THAT HE DIDN'T EVEN SAY HELLO!

WHERE IS THIS ANTENNA?

HERE IT IS!

WE SPENT THE ENTIRE DAY AT FARIBORZ'S WATCHING MTV AND EUROSPORT.

BY THE END OF THE EVENING, OUR MINDS WERE MUCH BROADER!

SOON THIS DEVICE DECORATED THE ROOFS OF ALL THE BUILDINGS IN THE NORTH OF TEHRAN.*

THE REGIME BECAME AWARE THAT THIS NEW PHENOMENON WAS WORKING AGAINST THEIR INDOCTRINATION. IT THEREFORE DECREED A BAN, BUT IT WAS TOO LATE. PEOPLE WHO HAD TASTED IMAGES OTHER THAN THOSE OF BEARDED MEN RESISTED BY HIDING THEIR ANTENNAS DURING THE DAY.

NIGHT SATELLITE | DAY SATELLITE

*THE CHIC NEIGHBORHOODS

MY PARENTS PROCURED ONE FOR THEM-SELVES, TOO. FROM THEN ON I SPENT WHOLE DAYS AND NIGHTS AT THEIR HOUSE WATCHING TV.

THE PROGRAM DIDN'T MATTER. FROM THE MOMENT THERE WERE BEAUTIFUL PEOPLE, I WAS HAPPY. ONE NIGHT ...

HI! ARE YOU STILL HERE? WHERE'S YOUR MOTHER?

WITH HER FRIENDS.

THAT BASTARD! HE ESCAPED UNSCATHED AGAIN!

LISTEN, WE NEED TO TALK!

WAIT, WAIT, THEY'RE GOING TO ARREST HIM!

NO! WE'RE GOING TO TALK FIRST.

BUT ... WHAT'S GOT INTO YOU??

THIS MORNING WHEN I LEFT FOR WORK, YOU WERE ON THE SOFA. I COME HOME TWELVE HOURS LATER, AND YOU ARE STILL IN THE SAME PLACE.

WHAT'S GOING ON? IS IT YOUR MARRIAGE THAT'S MAKING YOU DEPRESSED? I DON'T RECOGNIZE YOU ANYMORE! YOU WERE ALWAYS CURIOUS, YOU READ, YOU WERE INTERESTED IN EVERYTHING! YOU WERE ALWAYS AHEAD OF YOUR YEARS ... NOW ...

... NOW I AM A MARRIED WOMAN. I'M TWENTY-TWO. I'M AN ADULT!

ANYONE CAN BE TWENTY-TWO AND BE MARRIED. IT DOESN'T REQUIRE AN EXCEPTIONAL INTELLECTUAL EFFORT!! ... YOU WOULD BE BETTER OFF THINKING ABOUT GET-TING YOUR DIPLOMA! IT'S IN LESS THAN A YEAR.

IF THAT'S HOW IT IS, I'M GETTING OUT OF HERE!

GOODBYE THEN.

MY FATHER WAS RIGHT. ANYONE COULD GET MARRIED. IN FACT, EVERYONE WAS GETTING MARRIED. THERE WERE THOSE WHO WERE MARRYING IRANIANS IN AMERICA IN THE HOPES OF ONE DAY BECOMING ACTRESSES IN HOLLYWOOD,

THOSE WHO WERE JOINING THEMSELVES TO RICH OLD MEN,

LUCKIER ONES WITH RICH YOUNG MEN,

THERE WERE ALSO SOME REAL LOVE STORIES, LIKE THAT OF NIYOOSHA AND ALI.

... AND THEN THERE WAS REZA AND ME.

AS FOR THE SINGLE ONES, THEY WERE WAITING THEIR TURN:

RIGHT NOW, I HAVE THREE CANDIDATES: ONE IS A DOCTOR BUT HE LIVES IN IRAN, THE OTHER LIVES IN LOS ANGELES BUT HE'S SUPER UGLY AND THE THIRD IS VERY HANDSOME BUT POOR.

IF I WERE YOU, I'D TAKE ALL THREE!

MY FATHER WAS SO RIGHT THAT THE NEXT DAY, I APOLOGIZED TO HIM.

DAD, DO YOU STILL WANT TO TALK TO ME?

WHAT DO YOU THINK?

I DIDN'T MEAN TO HURT YOU. I JUST WANTED TO SHAKE YOU A LITTLE.

I KNOW, DAD. I REACTED VIOLENTLY BECAUSE YOU HIT A NERVE.

THEN HE RUSHED INTO THE LIBRARY AND CAME BACK WITH THREE BOOKS.

HERE, READ THESE. THERE'S "THE SECRETS OF THE CIA," "FREEMASONRY IN IRAN" AND "THE MEMOIRS OF MOSSADEGH."*

OH GREAT! COOL!!

TO CATCH UP, I READ ALL OF THEM IN TEN DAYS. DESPITE MY ASSUMPTIONS, I FOUND THEM REALLY INTERESTING.

*IRANIAN PRIME MINISTER. HE NATIONALIZED THE OIL INDUSTRY IN 1951.

MY NEW SPHERES OF INTEREST BROUGHT ME INTO CONTACT WITH NEW PEOPLE, OFTEN MUCH OLDER THAN ME. AMONG THEM, A CERTAIN DR. M, AT WHOSE HOUSE ALL THE INTELLECTUALS GATHERED ON THE FIRST MONDAY OF EVERY MONTH.

IN A COUNTRY LIKE OURS, WITH AS MANY RESOURCES AS WE HAVE, IT'S NOT RIGHT THAT 70% OF THE POPULATION SHOULD LIVE BELOW THE POVERTY LINE!

IF MOSSADEGH HAD BEEN ABLE TO SEE OUT HIS PROJECT OF REFORM, IRAN WOULDN'T BE FINDING ITSELF IN THIS SITUATION TODAY.

IT'S THE ENGLISH AND THE AMERICANS' FAULT. THEY'RE THE ONES WHO DEPOSED HIM BY ORGANIZING THE COUP D'ETAT IN 1953!

MAYBE, BUT WHAT DID WE DO TO STOP THEM? OUTSIDERS WOULD NEVER HAVE BEEN ABLE TO ACHIEVE THEIR ENDS WITHOUT CERTAIN IRANIAN TRAITORS! IF WE WANT TO RECONSTRUCT THIS COUNTRY, WE HAVE TO BEGIN BY ADMITTING OUR OWN MISDEEDS!!

PUSHED BY MY PARENTS, ENCOURAGED BY DR. M AND HIS FRIENDS, AND ALSO A LITTLE THANKS TO MYSELF, I CHANGED MY LIFE.

ONCE AGAIN, I ARRIVED AT MY USUAL CONCLUSION: ONE MUST EDUCATE ONESELF.

THE END

IN JUNE 1993, AT THE END OF OUR FOURTH YEAR OF STUDY, REZA AND I WERE CALLED IN BY THE PROFESSOR WHO WAS HEAD OF THE VISUAL COMMUNICATIONS DEPARTMENT.

YOU ARE MY TWO BEST STUDENTS. I THEREFORE HAVE A FINAL PROJECT TO PROPOSE TO YOU. IT INVOLVES CREATING A THEME PARK BASED ON OUR MYTHOLOGICAL HEROES.

THE SUBJECT WAS SO EXTRAORDINARY THAT WE FORGOT OUR CONFLICTS AND AGREED TO WORK TOGETHER.

WE SPENT THE WHOLE SUMMER IN LIBRARIES, ...

MUSEUMS, ...

WITH SCHOLARS, RESEARCHERS AND DOCTORS IN THE HUMAN SCIENCES.

IN GREEK MYTHO- LOGY, HEROES ARE PREDESTINED, WHILE OUR MYTHOLOGY IS LACKING IN THE NOTION OF DESTINY!

FROM JUNE 1993 TO JANUARY 1994, WE WERE SO BUSY THAT WE DIDN'T EVEN FIGHT ONCE.

WE WANTED TO CREATE THE EQUIVALENT OF DISNEYLAND IN TEHRAN. WE HAD THOUGHT OF ALL THE DETAILS: DINING, LODGING, ATTRACTIONS...

HOTEL

RESTAURANT

...IT WAS EXCITING.

WE WORKED NIGHT AND DAY FOR SEVEN MONTHS.

FINALLY CAME THE DAY OF GRADUATION.

BEFORE THE JURY ARRIVED, OUR FRIENDS AND FAMILIES WERE GIVEN A CHANCE TO APPRECIATE OUR WORK UP CLOSE.

DR. M, THANK YOU FOR BEING HERE. I'M TRULY HONORED.

THE HONOR IS MINE.

SINCE I WAS A LOT MORE TALKATIVE THAN REZA, WE HAD DECIDED THAT I WOULD DEFEND OUR DISSERTATION.

OUR MYTHOLOGY IS ONE OF THE MOST COMPLEX MYTHOLOGIES ON EARTH, BUT WE HAVE NEVER KNOWN HOW TO MINE IT, FOR FEAR OF MAKING IT VULGAR. MANY THINGS, LIKE THE HOLY GRAIL, THE KNIGHTS OF THE ROUND TABLE, ETC., ETC., COME FROM IRAN. IN OUR COUNTRY, WE HAVE THEME PARKS, BUT THE MOTIFS ARE AMERICAN. WHICH IS THE REASON BEHIND OUR INITIATIVE.

WE GOT A TWENTY OUT OF TWENTY. AFTER THE DELIBERATION ...

BRAVO, MY CHILDREN! IT WAS PERFECT! THANKS TO YOUNG PEOPLE LIKE YOU, I STILL HAVE HOPE FOR THE FUTURE OF IRAN. YOU SHOULD PROPOSE YOUR PROJECT TO THE MAYOR OF TEHRAN. I PERSONALLY KNOW THE MAYOR'S DEPUTY. YOU CAN USE MY NAME.

ONE WEEK LATER.

I HAVE AN APPOINTMENT WITH THE MAYOR'S DEPUTY.

YOU CANNOT ENTER WITH JUST A SCARF, YOU MUST BE WEARING A HOODED HEAD-SCARF.

THE NEXT DAY.

I HAVE AN APPOINTMENT WITH THE MAYOR'S DEPUTY.

YOU CANNOT ENTER. YOU'RE WEARING MAKEUP.

THE DAY AFTER.

I HAVE AN APPOINTMENT WITH THE MAYOR'S DEPUTY.

IT'S ON THE THIRD FLOOR, OFFICE 314.

... THIS IS GORD AFARID, AN AMAZING WARRIOR. WITH THE TIP OF HER SWORD, SHE POINTS THE WAY TO THE HIPPODROME.

SHOW ME.

MMM ...

HALF OF YOUR CHARACTERS ARE WOMEN WITHOUT VEILS, SEATED ON THE BACKS OF ALL SORTS OF REAL OR MYTHIC ANIMALS. WE CAN SEE THEIR SHAPES AND THEIR HAIR!

WE'LL COVER THEM!

A GORD AFARID IN A CHADOR IS NO LONGER A GORD AFARID. YOU KNOW THAT AS WELL AS I DO!

I'M GOING TO BE FRANK WITH YOU: THE GOVERNMENT COULDN'T CARE LESS ABOUT MYTHOLOGY. WHAT THEY WANT ARE RELIGIOUS SYMBOLS. YOUR PROJECT IS CERTAINLY INTERESTING, BUT IT'S UNACHIEVABLE!!

... I UNDERSTAND ...

AFTER CITY HALL, I HAD A RENDEZVOUS WITH A CHILDHOOD FRIEND, FARNAZ.

THE ONLY THING THAT COULD HAVE SAVED MY RELATIONSHIP WAS THIS PROJECT. NOW THAT IT'S A LOST CAUSE, I THINK WE'LL SEPARATE.

I DON'T SEE THE CONNECTION BETWEEN YOUR THEME PARK AND YOUR RELATIONSHIP!

SINCE WE BEGAN OUR SHARED LIFE, IT'S THE FIRST TIME THAT WE REALLY INVESTED IN SOMETHING TOGETHER. IT BROUGHT US CLOSER.

DO YOU STILL LOVE HIM?

I DON'T KNOW.

THEN LISTEN TO ME. A YEAR AGO, MY SISTER LEFT HER HUSBAND ...

...FROM THE MINUTE SHE HAD THE TITLE OF DIVORCED WOMAN, THE BUTCHER,

THE PASTRY CHEF,

THE BAKER,

THE FRUIT AND VEGETABLE SELLER,

THE ITINERANT CIGARETTE SELLER,

EVEN BEGGARS IN THE STREET, ALL MADE IT CLEAR THEY'D LIKE TO SLEEP WITH HER.

FROM MEN'S POINT OF VIEW, FOR ONE THING, THEIR DICKS ARE IRRESISTIBLE, AND FOR ANOTHER THING, SINCE YOU ARE DIVORCED, YOU'RE NO LONGER A VIRGIN AND YOU HAVE NO REASON TO REFUSE THEM. THEY HAVE COMPLETE CONFIDENCE!!! LISTEN, THERE'S NOTHING SURPRISING ABOUT IT! EVER SINCE THEIR BIRTH, THEIR MOTHERS HAVE CALLED THEM "DOUDOUL TALA."*

SO, AS LONG AS YOUR LIFE ISN'T HELL, STAY WITH YOUR HUSBAND! I KNOW YOUR FAMILY IS OPEN-MINDED, BUT EVERYONE ELSE WILL JUDGE YOU!

*GOLDEN PENIS

THIS CONVERSATION WITH FARNAZ SHOOK ME, BUT I DIDN'T AGREE WITH HER SUGGESTIONS. I REALIZED SUDDENLY THAT I NO LONGER REALLY LOVED REZA. I HAD TO GET DIVORCED! I RUSHED HOME TO TELL HIM.

SO, CITY HALL?

THEY DON'T WANT OUR PROJECT.

DON'T LET IT GET TO YOU! AFTER ALL, IT'S ONLY ONE PROJECT. WE'LL HAVE OTHERS!

I KNOW ... I HAVE TO GO SEE GRANDMA.

GOOD IDEA! SHE'LL KNOW HOW TO COMFORT YOU.

TWENTY MINUTES LATER.

GRANDMA, ...

WHAT IS IT, WHAT'S WRONG??

DON'T YOU WANT TO TAKE OFF THAT PAIN-IN-THE-ASS OF A HOOD?? IT MAKES ME CLAUSTROPHOBIC!

GRANDMA, IT'S HORRIBLE!

WHAT IS IT THAT'S SO HORRIBLE?

I THINK I NO LONGER LOVE REZA, I THINK WE SHOULD SEPARATE.

THAT'S YOUR "HORRIBLE" THING? OH MY! YOU SCARED ME! I THOUGHT THAT SOMEONE HAD DIED!

YOU KNOW I HAVE A HEART CONDITION! ALL THESE TEARS FOR A DIVORCE?

LISTEN TO ME! I GOT ONE, FIFTY-FIVE YEARS AGO, AND LET ME TELL YOU THAT AT THE TIME, NO ONE ENDED THEIR MARRIAGE. BUT I ALWAYS TOLD MYSELF THAT I WOULD BE HAPPIER ALONE THAN WITH A SHITMAKER!!

YES, BUT ...

NO BUTS ABOUT IT! A FIRST MARRIAGE IS A DRY RUN FOR THE SECOND. YOU'LL BE MORE SATISFIED THE NEXT TIME. IN THE MEANTIME, IF YOU'RE CRYING SO MUCH, MAYBE IT MEANS THAT YOU STILL LOVE HIM! THERE'S NO REASON YOU HAVE TO TELL HIM EVERYTHING RIGHT AWAY. TAKE YOUR TIME, THINK ABOUT IT, AND THE DAY YOU DON'T WANT IT ANYMORE, YOU LEAVE HIM! WHEN A TOOTH IS ROTTEN, YOU HAVE TO PULL IT OUT!

I FOLLOWED MY GRANDMOTHER'S ADVICE. I WAITED. I FOUND A JOB AS AN ILLUSTRATOR AT AN ECONOMICS MAGAZINE.

I WAS BORED AT HOME, I CAME TO DRAW HERE. I'M NOT DISTURBING YOU?

NOT AT ALL!

MAKE YOUR-SELF AT HOME!

EVERYTHING WAS GOING WELL. THE RAPPORT WITH MY COLLEAGUES MADE ME FORGET THE REST.

BUT TWO MONTHS LATER, IN MARCH 1994, AN ILLUSTRATOR MADE THE FOLLOWING DRAWING FOR AN ARTICLE ON IRANIAN SOCCER:

* ASSASSIN

THE GOVERNMENT COULDN'T TOLERATE A MULLAH BEING CALLED AN ASSASSIN. THEY THEREFORE ARRESTED THE ILLUSTRATOR IN QUESTION.

NO ONE KNEW WHAT HAD HAPPENED TO HIM, BUT EVERYONE HAD HIS OWN THEORY.

THEY MUST HAVE HANGED HIM!!

THEY CUT OFF HIS HANDS SO HE CAN'T DRAW ANYMORE!

THEY SHOT HIM!

THEY TOR-TURED HIM!

HE'S ALIVE BUT HE IS BLIND!

WHATEVER THE CASE, FROM THAT MOMENT ON, ALL THE PRESS WAS EXAMINED WITH A MAGNIFYING GLASS.

A FEW DAYS LATER, WHEN I GOT TO WORK.

MARJANE! THEY ARRESTED BEHZAD!

OUR BEHZAD? BEHZAD RADI?

YES.

THE MAGAZINE CAME OUT YESTERDAY AND THEY WENT TO COLLECT HIM AT HIS HOUSE TODAY, AT FIVE O'CLOCK IN THE MORNING!

...ALL BECAUSE OF THIS!!...

HIS DRAWING ILLUSTRATED AN AR-TICLE ABOUT ALARM SYSTEMS TO PROTECT THE VILLAS IN THE NORTH OF TEHRAN AGAINST BURGLARIES.

BEHZAD HAD MADE THE MISTAKE OF DRAWING A BEARDED MAN.

BUT A FEW HAIRS NOT BEING ENOUGH TO CONDEMN HIM, HE WAS SET FREE AFTER TWO WEEKS. GILA, THE MAGAZINE'S GRAPHIC DESIGNER, AND I WENT TO VISIT HIM.

HELLO!

HELLO, COME IN!

SO, WHAT HAPPENED? TELL US!

NOTHING! I EXPLAINED TO THEM THAT MY DESIGN CAME FROM A FAIRY TALE IN WHICH A PRINCESS' LOVER CLIMBS INTO HER ROOM BY USING THE LONG HAIR OF HIS LOVED ONE AND, NOT BEING ABLE TO DRAW A WOMAN WITHOUT A VEIL, I HAD DRAWN A BEARDED MAN.

AT THAT, THEY STARTED TO YELL, SAYING THAT I WAS INSINUATING THAT BEARDED MEN WERE SISSIES. I SWORE THAT THAT WASN'T IN ANY WAY MY INTENTION.

AND THEY BEAT ME UP... I HAD BRUISES ALL OVER MY BODY. FINALLY, WELL... YOU PAY DEARLY FOR FREEDOM OF EXPRESSION THESE DAYS.

DING! DONG!

I'M GOING TO GET THE DOOR. IT MUST BE MY WIFE. I'LL BE RIGHT BACK.

HELLO, I'M MANDANA.

MARJANE, I'M VERY HAPPY TO MEET YOU.

AND THIS IS NIMA.

MANDANA, CAN'T YOU SEE WE HAVE GUESTS? GO MAKE US SOME TEA. ACTUALLY, THEY BROUGHT SOME CAKES, BRING THOSE IN, TOO!

THANKS SO MUCH.

YOU'RE WELCOME.

POOR MANDANA SUFFERED A LOT DURING MY TWO WEEKS OF INCARCERATION.

SO, WHAT DO YOU DO?

WELL, I ...

SHE STUDIED PHARMACOLOGY, BUT WE HAD NIMA VERY QUICKLY AFTER GETTING MARRIED. SO NOW SHE'S A HOUSEWIFE.

AND HOW OLD IS NIMA?

HE'S ...

EIGHT AND A HALF!

IN JULY, HE'LL BE NINE!!!

DO YOU HAVE CHILDREN?

NO!

UHH ... NO!

MARJANE'S NOT EVEN TWENTY-FIVE, AS FOR GILA, SHE DOESN'T HAVE A HUSBAND YET!

N OUR WAY BACK.

TO THINK THAT HE WAS MY HERO FOR TWENTY DAYS!! HIS WHOLE SPIEL ABOUT FREEDOM OF EXPRESSION, WHILE HE DIDN'T EVEN LET HIS WIFE SAY ONE WORD! AH, IRANIAN MEN!

DON'T SAY THAT! IT'S NOT IRANIAN MEN, BUT MEN, PERIOD. TWO YEARS AGO, I WAS GOING OUT WITH A SPANISH DIPLOMAT. ON THE SURFACE, HE BEHAVED BETTER, BUT DEEP DOWN, IT WAS THE SAME THING.

EXCEPT HERE, ALL THE LAWS ARE ON THEIR SIDE!

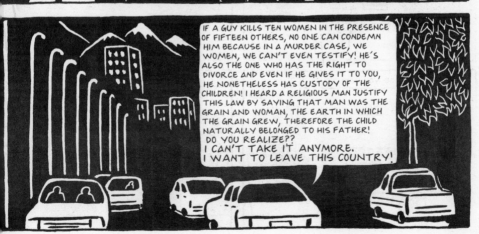

IF A GUY KILLS TEN WOMEN IN THE PRESENCE OF FIFTEEN OTHERS, NO ONE CAN CONDEMN HIM BECAUSE IN A MURDER CASE, WE WOMEN, WE CAN'T EVEN TESTIFY! HE'S ALSO THE ONE WHO HAS THE RIGHT TO DIVORCE AND EVEN IF HE GIVES IT TO YOU, HE NONETHELESS HAS CUSTODY OF THE CHILDREN! I HEARD A RELIGIOUS MAN JUSTIFY THIS LAW BY SAYING THAT MAN WAS THE GRAIN AND WOMAN, THE EARTH IN WHICH THE GRAIN GREW, THEREFORE THE CHILD NATURALLY BELONGED TO HIS FATHER! DO YOU REALIZE??
I CAN'T TAKE IT ANYMORE.
I WANT TO LEAVE THIS COUNTRY!

GILA DROPPED ME OFF AT HOME. MY SISTER-IN-LAW WAS THERE.

HELLO KATAYONE, HOW ARE YOU FEELING?

LIKE A WOMAN WHO'S EIGHT MONTHS PREGNANT! I FEEL HEAVY, BUT AT LEAST I ONLY HAVE TO BEAR IT FOR A FEW MORE WEEKS.

WELL, I'LL LEAVE YOU TWO. DON'T FORGET THAT MY SON NEEDS A COUSIN. WHAT ARE YOU WAITING FOR?

WE NEED TO TALK.

WE'VE BEEN MARRIED FOR THREE YEARS, AND FOR THREE YEARS WE'VE HAD OUR OWN ROOMS. WE'RE NOT A REAL COUPLE...

WE'RE NOT A COUPLE AT ALL.

WE'VE STAYED TOGETHER OUT OF AFFECTION, CERTAINLY, BUT MOSTLY OUT OF HABIT. WE WEREN'T ABLE TO ADMIT THAT WE AREN'T MADE FOR EACH OTHER, BECAUSE THAT WOULD MEAN THAT WE RECOGNIZED OUR FAILURE.

YES, BUT I'M STILL IN LOVE WITH YOU.

WHEN I WAS IN LOVE WITH YOU, YOU DIDN'T LET ME IN. NOW IT'S TOO LATE, REZA. I DON'T LOVE YOU ANYMORE.

LET'S GO TO FRANCE TOGETHER. I'M SURE IT'S THE SOCIAL PRESSURE THAT'S AFFECTING US.

BUT IT'S FOR THIS SAME REASON THAT WE GOT MARRIED, TO GET AROUND THE SOCIAL PRESSURE. OUR LOVE HAS BEEN DEAD FOR A LONG TIME! THERE'S NO POINT IN TRYING AGAIN. IT'S A WASTE OF TIME.

I DON'T KNOW HOW I MANAGED TO TELL HIM ALL THAT SO SUDDENLY. MY GRANDMA WAS RIGHT: I HAD TAKEN MY TIME, AND I NEVER REGRETTED WHAT I SAID.

A FEW DAYS LATER, I WENT OVER TO MY PARENTS' HOUSE.

I WANT TO GO TO FRANCE!

THAT'S GREAT. YOU'LL BOTH NEED VISAS, HAVE THE TWO OF YOU THOUGHT OF ...

DAD, IT'S NOT US, IT'S ME. REZA WILL GO IF HE WANTS TO, BUT WE'RE GOING TO GET DIVORCED!

I KNEW IT ALL ALONG!

YOU KNEW IT ALL ALONG AND YET YOU TALKED MY EAR OFF FOR A WEEK SO THAT I WOULD APPROVE OF THIS MARRIAGE?

YES, BUT IF SHE HADN'T GOTTEN MARRIED, SHE WOULD NEVER HAVE KNOWN THAT IT WOULDN'T WORK BETWEEN THE TWO OF THEM—EVERYONE HAS TO HAVE HER OWN EXPERIENCE.

MANIPULATOR!

WHAT MANIPULATION?

I'M NOT TALKING TO YOU ANYMORE.

WELL, WE'RE VERY HAPPY WITH YOUR DECISION. YOU WEREN'T MADE TO LIVE HERE. WE IRANIANS, WE'RE CRUSHED NOT ONLY BY THE GOVERNMENT BUT BY THE WEIGHT OF OUR TRADITIONS!

OUR REVOLUTION SET US BACK FIFTY YEARS. IT WILL TAKE GENERATIONS FOR ALL THIS TO EVOLVE. YOU ONLY HAVE ONE LIFE. IT'S YOUR DUTY TO LIVE IT WELL. AND NOW THAT YOU ARE TWENTY-FOUR, IT'S NOT LIKE WHEN YOU WENT TO AUSTRIA. YOU DON'T NEED US ANYMORE.

WHAT DID I TELL YOU: "DON'T WORRY ABOUT HER, OUR DAUGHTER HAS ALWAYS KNOWN HOW TO TAKE CARE OF HERSELF."

IT'S TRUE.

WERE YOU WORRYING ABOUT ME?

I WAS SCARED THAT YOU'D RUIN YOUR LIFE.

ME TOO.

...NOT HAVING BEEN ABLE TO BUILD ANYTHING IN MY OWN COUNTRY, I PREPARED TO LEAVE IT ONCE AGAIN. I WENT TO FRANCE FOR THE FIRST TIME IN JUNE 1994 TO TAKE A TEST TO ENTER THE SCHOOL OF DECORATIVE ARTS IN STRASBOURG. I WAS ACCEPTED. THEN I HAD TO GO BACK TO IRAN TO EXCHANGE MY TOURIST VISA FOR A STUDENT VISA.

BETWEEN JUNE AND SEPTEMBER '94, THE DATE OF MY DEFINITIVE DEPARTURE, I SPENT EVERY MORNING WANDERING IN THE MOUNTAINS OF TEHRAN, WHERE I MEMORIZED EVERY CORNER.

I WENT ON A TRIP WITH MY GRANDMA TO THE SHORE OF THE CASPIAN SEA, WHERE I FILLED MY LUNGS WITH THAT VERY SPECIAL AIR. THAT AIR THAT DOESN'T EXIST ANYWHERE ELSE.

I WENT TO MY GRANDFATHER'S TOMB, WHERE I PROMISED HIM THAT HE WOULD BE PROUD OF ME.

I ALSO WENT BEHIND THE EVINE PRISON WHERE THE BODY OF MY UNCLE ANOOSH LAY IN AN UNMARKED GRAVE, NEXT TO THOUSANDS OF OTHER CADAVERS. I GAVE HIM MY WORD TO TRY TO REMAIN AS HONEST AS POSSIBLE.

I ALSO SPENT SOME WONDERFUL MOMENTS WITH MY PARENTS ...

... UNTIL SEPTEMBER 9, 1994, WHEN, ALONG WITH MY GRANDMA, THEY ACCOMPANIED ME TO MEHRABAD AIRPORT.

I HAD CHOSEN THIS DEPARTURE BUT DESPITE EVERYTHING, I FELT VERY SAD.

MY FATHER CRIED AS USUAL,

AND MY MOTHER KEPT HER HEAD.

THIS TIME, YOU'RE LEAVING FOR GOOD. YOU ARE A FREE WOMAN. THE IRAN OF TODAY IS NOT FOR YOU. I FORBID YOU TO COME BACK!

YES, MOM.

THE GOODBYES WERE MUCH LESS PAINFUL THAN TEN YEARS BEFORE WHEN I EMBARKED FOR AUSTRIA: THERE WAS NO LONGER A WAR, I WAS NO LONGER A CHILD, MY MOTHER DIDN'T FAINT AND MY GRANDMA WAS THERE, HAPPILY...

...HAPPILY, BECAUSE SINCE THE NIGHT OF SEPTEMBER 9, 1994, I ONLY SAW HER AGAIN ONCE, DURING THE IRANIAN NEW YEAR IN MARCH 1995. SHE DIED JANUARY 4, 1996... FREEDOM HAD A PRICE...

CREDIT
Lettering: Céline Merrien

THANKS TO
Emile Bravo
Amber Hoover
Jean-Christophe Menu
Céline Merrien
Anjali Singh